STUDIES IN CHRISTIAN HISTORY AND THOUGHT

Baptism, Church and Society in Modern Britain

From the Evangelical Revival to *Baptism, Eucharist and Ministry*

STUDIES IN CHRISTIAN HISTORY AND THOUGHT

A full listing of all titles in this series
appears at the close of this book

STUDIES IN CHRISTIAN HISTORY AND THOUGHT

Baptism, Church and Society in Modern Britain

From the Evangelical Revival to *Baptism, Eucharist and Ministry*

David M. Thompson

Wipf & Stock
PUBLISHERS
Eugene, Oregon

Wipf and Stock Publishers
199 W 8th Ave, Suite 3
Eugene, OR 97401

Baptism, Church and Society in Modern Britain
From the Evangelical Revival to Baptism, Eucharist and Ministry
By Thompson, David M.
Copyright©2005 Paternoster
ISBN: 1-59752-795-5
Publication date 6/23/2006
Previously published by Paternoster, 2005

This Edition Published by Wipf and Stock Publishers
by arrangement with Paternoster

Paternoster
9 Holdom Avenue
Bletchley
Milton Keyes, MK1 1QR
Great Britain

STUDIES IN CHRISTIAN HISTORY AND THOUGHT

Series Preface

This series complements the specialist series of *Studies in Evangelical History and Thought* and *Studies in Baptist History and Thought* for which Paternoster is becoming increasingly well known by offering works that cover the wider field of Christian history and thought. It encompasses accounts of Christian witness at various periods, studies of individual Christians and movements, and works which concern the relations of church and society through history, and the history of Christian thought.

The series includes monographs, revised dissertations and theses, and collections of papers by individuals and groups. As well as 'free standing' volumes, works on particular running themes are being commissioned; authors will be engaged for these from around the world and from a variety of Christian traditions.

A high academic standard combined with lively writing will commend the volumes in this series both to scholars and to a wider readership.

Series Editors

Alan P.F. Sell, Visiting Professor at Acadia University Divinity College, Nova Scotia, Canada

David Bebbington, Professor of History, University of Stirling, Stirling, Scotland, UK

Clyde Binfield, Professor Associate in History, University of Sheffield, UK

Gerald Bray, Anglican Professor of Divinity, Beeson Divinity School, Samford University, Birmingham, Alabama, USA

Grayson Carter, Associate Professor of Church History, Fuller Theological Seminary SW, Phoenix, Arizona, USA

*This book is dedicated to
Henry Chadwick
an encouraging friend,
who once threatened to take the manuscript
by night and ensure that it was published!*

Contents

Introduction xi

Chapter 1
Baptismal Practice in the Eighteenth Century 1

Chapter 2
A New Birth? 25

Chapter 3
Baptists and the Evangelical Revival 46

Chapter 4
The Oxford Movement and After 67

Chapter 5
'A Spiritual and Universal Kingdom' 92

Chapter 6
The Twentieth-Century Debate 114

Chapter 7
Popular Belief and Practice 138

Chapter 8
The Sacrament of Unity 165

Bibliography 189

General Index 201

Introduction

This book is based on the Hulsean Lectures delivered in Cambridge during the Lent Term, 1984. I have taken advantage of the opportunity to expand on some points that were only briefly treated in the original lectures, and to add some material which it was not possible then to discuss at all.

Anyone who is elected to one of the endowed Lectureships of the University of Cambridge is likely to be humbled, if not unnerved, by the thought of those who have gone before. The oldest book that I instinctively associate with the Hulsean Lectureship is F.J.A. Hort's *The Way, the Truth, and the Life* of 1871. Indeed reading some of the letters Hort wrote while working on his Hulseans, I felt that someone had trodden the same path before me.[1] The terms of the Lectureship were changed under the new University Statutes of 1926 and in the years following men like Charles Raven, H.G. Wood, J.M. Creed and John Burnaby were Hulsean Lecturers. Hendrik Kraemer's influential book, *A Theology of the Laity*, began as a series of Hulseans: more recently John Robinson's *Human Face of God* and Maurice Wiles's *The Remaking of Christian Doctrine* found their first audience in the Divinity School, whilst Owen Chadwick, David Edwards and Peter Hinchliff have been among the historians honoured in this way.

My confidence was not increased by the knowledge that John Hulse's concern in his various benefactions was to ensure that the errors of popery and Methodism would be confuted by the exposition of Christian doctrine. Although I am not a Methodist I do not think that his opinion of dissenters would have been much higher, but I took some comfort from the fact that the then Norris-Hulse Professor (and indeed his successor) were papists. I venture to hope that the topic, if not necessarily the manner of treating it, would have satisfied the original benefactor. I am grateful to the Hulsean electors for the honour of election, and for the opportunity of developing a topic which has claimed my interest for many years.

The original lectures are contained in the latter part of chapter 2 and chapters 3 to 8. I was aware when I gave the lectures that I had omitted one important topic—the Methodist view of baptism, particularly as represented in the attitude of John Wesley himself, which left an ambiguous legacy to his successors. This material has been incorporated in chapters 2 and 4. But I am grateful to an anonymous reader of the Lectures when they were considered for publication at an earlier stage,

---

1 A.F. Hort, *Life and Letters of Fenton John Anthony Hort* (London 1896), ii, 148, 160-1, 163-4.

who suggested that the chapter on 'Popular Belief and Practice' added nothing to the argument. This made me realise that I had completely failed to convey my conviction that the history of theology cannot effectively be considered in detachment from its context; furthermore, that in sacramental theology in particular popular perceptions are part of the story, regardless of whether they are 'right' or 'wrong'. Hence, in reworking this material now I have written a new chapter 1 on baptismal practice in the eighteenth century before the Evangelical Revival introduced new emphases. In this I have been dependent on the large amount of work on the seventeenth and eighteenth centuries which has been done in recent years. This has also necessitated a rewriting of parts of what is now chapter 7, and a reworking of the original analysis. Finally, although a complete analysis of the responses of the churches to *Baptism, Eucharist and Ministry* (which was still very new when the original lectures were given) falls outside the scope of this book, it is now possible to offer a more considered discussion in the light of developments in the last twenty years.

My colleagues and family have been impatient to see the publication of these lectures for many years—some may indeed have given up hope. However, shortly after the Lectures were completed I became deeply involved in College and Faculty administration, which led in time to ten years service on the central bodies of the University of Cambridge. Only since 2000 has it been possible to return to research and the reconsideration of the original material. This book is the result.

One of the most striking differences in the life of the British Churches between the last quarter of the eighteenth century, when Hulse was in his prime, and the last quarter of the twentieth must surely be the changed attitude to the sacraments. It is a commonplace to speak of a sacramental revival in the Church of England in the modern period, but the Church of Scotland and nonconformity have been no less affected. Sacramental theology has not figured largely in past series of Hulsean Lectures, but even when sacraments are being discussed the tendency is to speak of Holy Communion rather than Holy Baptism. In the 1980s the Churches of the world made their responses to the Statement from the Faith and Order Commission of the World Council of Churches, *Baptism, Eucharist and Ministry*. Baptism is clearly the Cinderella of that trio. The history of the theology of baptism is similarly neglected. Most of those who have any interest in the history of the modern Church at all have heard of the Gorham Judgement of 1850; but for many this represents a brief explosion of baptismal controversy on to the nineteenth-century scene. In any case the significance of Gorham is usually seen as the establishing of theological comprehensiveness in the Church of England, rather than as a turning point in baptismal theology. Yet the Gorham case is but the tip of an iceberg of baptismal controversy.

What was the controversy about? At one level the answer is simple. For Anglicans the main issue was whether or in what sense the Thirty-Nine Articles and the Book of Common Prayer permitted or required a belief in baptismal regeneration. Among nonconformists the traditional division between baptists and paedobaptists was more prominent, with the associated questions of covenantal theology and the mode of baptism—immersion, pouring or sprinkling. At another level, however, the answer is not so simple. Why were these issues important to these people at this time? This is the historian's question, and as always it is easier to ask the question than to answer it.

When William Hale White was examined by the Council of New College, London, prior to his expulsion for heterodox opinions in 1852, he was asked this question, 'Do you believe something because it is in the Bible, or merely because it is true?'[2] In our understandable indignation at the use of the word 'merely' in that question we are apt to overlook the fact that truth is a necessary, but not always a sufficient, condition of believing something. In particular, the strength of certain beliefs or the urgency with which they are propagated cannot easily be explained by reference to the question of truth alone. So often the theological history of this period, as of others, is written as though theology is some kind of free-floating activity that is only loosely related to time. The dates of books are mentioned, of course, if only to remind us of the order in which they were written, but one is given only the dimmest impression of what else was happening at the time. Authors appear as the instruments through which particular ideas are expressed rather than as people with particular convictions and prejudices, banners to carry and axes to grind. Yet if the historical context of these discussions is emphasized, there is always the danger of reductionism, of making the theological content of the discussion epiphenomenal. We become so interested in why people believed something that we too easily assume that people believe what they like rather than what is true. In the case of baptism, however, I believe that such a discussion helps us to relate beliefs about baptism to other beliefs—especially beliefs about the nature of the Church, the family, society and the nation. One aim of this book is to make good this claim.

The doctrine of baptism concerns our relationship to God, to the Church and to one another in family and society. Challenges to the doctrine have often seemed to imply not only heresy but social revolution. Thus both Luther and Calvin, who did not hesitate to be

---

2 W. Hale White, *The Early Life of Mark Rutherford* (London 1913), 65; cf W. Stone, *The Religion and Art of W. Hale White* (Stanford 1954), 33-9.

critical of the Roman Catholic Church, adopted a particularly sharp tone towards more radical reformers who either wished to limit baptism to believers or to question its place altogether. Both give the impression that the whole social fabric is at stake if baptismal doctrine is questioned. In seventeenth-century England toleration was eventually secured both for Baptists and Quakers, though lingering suspicions remained.

The Evangelical Revival posed a slightly different problem. The emphasis placed on individual conversion or regeneration (the use of the terms was not always consistent) and the claim that this was the work of the Holy Spirit seemed to introduce a new subjectivism into the answer to the question of whether one was a Christian. Indeed, it might almost be said that the question itself would not have occurred to anyone as a relevant question to ask in a Christian country a century or two before. The emphasis on conversion was often regarded as a sign of 'enthusiasm', and as such contrasted with the objective claim to membership of the Church set out in baptism. For the evangelical, however, the claim that baptism secured all that was necessary did not do justice to the significance of saving faith. The conflict simmered during John Wesley's lifetime, but by the time of his death in 1791 the French Revolution had reawakened the fears of the established authorities in Church and State about the possibility of social revolution. Religious enthusiasm became suspect, the more so because dissenters of all kinds grew rapidly during the years of the Revolutionary and Napoleonic Wars. It seems hardly a coincidence that the politically troubled decade after 1815 should also have been one in which baptism was hotly debated in several ways.

The Oxford Movement marked a new stage in the debate. High churchmen had defended baptismal regeneration before 1833, and indeed it may well be that in the first instance the Oxford Movement's concern on this issue was taken by evangelicals as a sign of continuity rather than novelty. The evangelical *Christian Observer* in 1837 described baptismal regeneration as 'the very foundation of the Oxford Tracts'[3] and Newman certainly saw regeneration as a central issue. Nevertheless the consequences of the Movement and the new polarisation in the Church of England which it produced meant that a new kind of defensiveness emerged about the use of language in relation to baptism which would not have been apparent in an earlier generation. If evangelicals feared popery within, tractarians feared anti-sacramentalism within. An extreme illustration of that fear was W.H.B. Proby's *Annals of the 'Low-Church' Party in England*, published in 1888. Its argument, sustained over two volumes and covering the period since the Reformation (though the second volume covers the period 1850-88), was

---

3 *Christian Observer*, xxxvi (1837), 179.

Introduction

that Low Churchmen have no moral right to be regarded as part of the Church of England. Proby confessed that his publisher had wished him to moderate some of his language: the *Church Quarterly Review* thought that his case was weakened rather than strengthened by his violent language, and that the suggestion that Low Churchmen should be turned out of the Church was outrageous.[4] His book cannot, therefore, be regarded as a major source, by comparison with those of other writers on the eighteenth- and nineteenth-century Church in his generation. Proby was an ordained Anglican clergyman, but seems not to have held pastoral charge after 1871 and presumably lived on a private income until his death in 1915. The *Church Quarterly Review* agreed with him that the chief weakness of evangelical theology was that 'it utterly ignored the new resurrection life of Christ, the germ of which is planted in the Christian at holy baptism, and supported by the other great sacrament of the Gospel'.[5] Proby's earlier little book, *Letters on Christian Religion* (1884) was largely concerned with the benefits of baptism, being written in the form of letters to an emigrant to Canada, who was unbaptized.[6] Thus although Proby himself may have been extreme, the position he represented was not.

Nevertheless, in these circumstances it is perhaps not surprising that an increasing number of Christians, both Anglican and nonconformist, were attracted by F.D. Maurice's understanding of baptism as a declaratory act. Maurice's theology is notoriously slippery, and he saw himself as correcting the extremes of Quaker, Evangelical and High Churchman alike. It also won support among Congregationalists (notwithstanding R.W. Dale) and Methodists (notwithstanding J.H. Rigg). There is a sense in which the 'decline of hell', or the movement away from belief in eternal punishment, robbed many of the traditional arguments for the efficacy of baptism of their force. In fact, the question of how baptism was understood by ordinary people and what part it played in their lives is an extraordinarily difficult one. Although the evidence is both sketchy and patchy, it seems worth attempting some kind of summary, not least because it relates to wider questions of secularization which have been raised for the whole period since the Industrial Revolution.

The twentieth century saw significant shifts in liturgical emphasis as well as a lively theological debate; and baptism achieved new prominence in the ecumenical movement as the bond of unity among Christians. The closing chapters are therefore concerned with the way in which perspectives on baptism have changed by comparison with the

---

4 *Church Quarterly Review*, xxix (1889-90), 312, 316.

5 Ibid, 310; cf W.H.B. Proby, *Annals of the 'Low-Church' Party in England* (London 1888), i, v.

6 W.H.B. Proby, *Letters on Christian Religion* (London 1884), 4-7, 8, 11, 19, 20, 25, 41-2.

nineteenth century. On the one hand, sacramental understandings are much more readily received; on the other hand, the question of whether baptism has assumed a sectarian significance is much more starkly posed—especially as the boundary lines between the Church and the wider society in which it is set have been more sharply drawn . How far has the wish to recover some of the significance attached to baptism in the patristic period, with its greater sense of the Church as a separated society, necessarily made it more difficult for the Church to seem to welcome everyone who comes? If so, does that matter? These are the questions which make this survey of more than historical interest: they raise issues of direct contemporary pastoral relevance.

Chapter 1

Baptismal Practice in the Eighteenth Century

In the late seventeenth century, the Revd Isaac Archer at Freckenham in Suffolk lost eight of his nine children in infancy. In August 1675 he delayed the baptism of his newly born son because his elder son, Will, had worms and his wife was also ill; then the baby died unbaptized in the night, because the wet nurse had failed to tell him that the boy was ill. He tried to comfort himself in his diary,

> I know God is a God of the faithfull, and their seed, and baptisme is a signe of it; and I no more question the child's happiness (what ever St Austin thought) than that of the Jewish children who died before the 8th day. I take God to witnes I doe not, did not despise the sacrament; but now 'tis fallen out so, not through the fault of the infant, or our wilfull neglect, but through an unavoidable necessity, because of God's hand in Will's sickness; and my not knowing 'twas ill etc. I comfort my selfe with hopes that God, who is not tied to meanes, hath washed it's soule in Christ's blood![1]

He buried the boy in the chancel 'neer my seat' and near his baptized brothers and sisters. Archer had the advantage of being able to take the decision; for those who were not clergy the situation was often very different. This moving story is an apt introduction to the discussion of baptism in the post-Reformation period.

Although the Reformation is usually remembered for the controversies over Holy Communion, there was an equally important discussion over baptism.[2] The principal issues concerned the invariable necessity of baptism and who could perform it. The argument over the invariability of baptism was related in particular to the problem of infants dying unbaptized. If baptism was essential for salvation, and also for Christian burial, then there was an urgent necessity for baptism as quickly as possible in an age of high infant mortality. This led inexorably to the practice of private or household baptism, and permission for lay people,

---

1 M. Storey, *Two East Anglian Diaries, 1641-1729* (Suffolk Records Society vol xxxvi: Woodbridge 1994), 150-1; cf. D. Cressy, *Birth, Marriage and Death: Ritual, Religion, and the Life-Cycle in Tudor and Stuart England* (Oxford 1997), 116-7.

2 See G.W. Bromiley, *Baptism and the Anglican Reformers* (London 1953).

particularly midwives, to baptize. On the other hand, if baptism was not invariably essential, the particular problem of high infant mortality need not dominate the other issues: it would be possible to give unbaptized infants Christian burial on the ground that they had not committed mortal sin; and it would be possible to insist on baptism in church by the priest or minister, thereby discouraging private (and, by implication, lay) baptism. These issues were debated as early as the fourteenth century, even before the appearance of Wycliffe and Lollardy on the English religious scene, though the official teaching of the Church remained that baptism was essential.[3]

In the Reformation period the argument for the invariable practice of baptism came under attack on a number of grounds. In part this was simply a continuation of the medieval controversy. However, some new issues were raised: positively there was an emphasis on the importance of faith; negatively Catholic practice was attacked, either as superstition, or as something liable to lead to superstition with an undue emphasis on the form rather than the content of the rite. In terms of practice the effect of Reformation teaching is shown by the increasing delay in the time of baptism: whereas in the middle ages baptism took place as soon as possible after birth, by the end of the seventeenth century 'it was common for half the baptisms in a parish to have been postponed for a week or more after birth, although there were big variations in practice from one parish to another'.[4]

David Cressy has shown how technical theological points interacted with a host of apparently minor issues of practice which were quite capable of 'polarizing a parish or dividing a church'.[5] His comprehensive discussion of the communal context of baptism makes a detailed account of popular attitudes and practice in the immediate post-Reformation period unnecessary here. He has also drawn attention to some aspects of the baptismal ritual which have tended to be ignored, for example, the role of godparents. John Bossy has noted the way in which medieval practice in relation to godparents was changed by both Catholics and Protestants after the Refomation, but their role as 'spiritual kin' remained important, even though the restriction on the possibility of marriage was removed: only the followers of Calvin and the more extreme sectarians abolished godparents altogether.[6] George Herbert

---

3 See B.L. Manning, *The People's Faith in the Time of Wyclif* (Cambridge 1919).

4 R.A. Houlbrooke, *The English Family, 1450-1700* (London 1984), 130-1; R.A. Houlbrooke (ed), *English Family Life, 1576-1716* (Oxford 1988), 102-3.

5 Cressy, *Birth, Marriage and Death*, 3.

6 J. Bossy, 'Blood and Baptism: Kinship, Community and Christianity in Western Europe from the Fourteenth to the Seventeenth Centuries', D. Baker (ed), *Sanctity and Secularity; Studies in Church History* x (Oxford 1973), 129-43; J. Bossy, 'Godparenthood: the Fortunes of a Social Institution in Early Modern Christianity', K.

emphasised that it was no light thing to be a godparent but a great honour.[7]

Puritans in the Elizabethan Church pressed for a more disciplined approach to baptism, and particularly an end to private baptism. The Millenary Petition presented by the puritans in 1603 began by demanding an end to 'the cross in baptism' and to baptism administered by women.[8] A year later, the reforms agreed at the Hampton Court conference in 1604 included 'That the private baptism shall be called the private baptism by the ministers and curates only, and all these questions that insinuate women or private persons, be altered accordingly' and 'That the cross in baptism was never counted any part in baptism, nor sign effective, but only significative'.[9] However, the main result of the Conference was an extended defence of 'the lawful use of the cross in baptism' in Canon 30 of the Canons of 1604 — the longest canon in the collection.[10] No action was taken to restrict baptism to ministers. Indeed the fact that some episcopal Visitation Articles of the Jacobean Church of England, despite changes in the rubrics limiting baptism to 'lawful ministers', specifically asked about baptism implied that traditional practices continued.[11] In his discussion of the canons Cressy goes to some trouble to rebut older hostile views of midwives, noting that most were 'respectable married women or widows, almost all church goers, with years of practical experience'.[12] From Henry VIII's reign they were expected to take oaths in church before practising, and these survived into the seventeenth century; some early Stuart bishops' visitation queries enquired about them.[13] Visitations also enquired whether ministers used the sign of the cross, the font rather than a basin or refused to baptize infants in cases of necessity, and whether any parishioners had refused to

---

von Greyerz (ed), *Religion and Society in Early Modern Europe, 1500-1800* (London 1984), 194-201; Houlbrooke, *The English Family*, 39-40.

7 G. Herbert, *The Country Parson*, ch xxii, in J.N. Wall Jr (ed), *George Herbert, The Country Parson, The Temple* (London 1981), 85.

8 G.R. Bray, *The Anglican Canons 1529-1947* (Church of England Record Society, Woodbridge 1998), 817.

9 Ibid, 820-21.

10 Ibid, 302-9.

11 E.g. those at Norwich in 1619 and Gloucester in 1622: K. Fincham, *Visitation Articles and Injunctions of the Early Stuart Church* i (Church of England Record Society, Woodbridge 1994), 159, 208. Whether this constituted 'semi-official blessing' as suggested by Cressy (*Birth, Marriage and Death*, 122) is less clear, since the relevant question included lay persons, popish priests and other ministers as well as midwives.

12 Cressy, *Birth, Marriage and Death*, 60.

13 E.g. Archbishop Abbott, Canterbury and Gloucester in 1612: Fincham, *Visitation Articles* i, 107.

have their children baptized or had taken them to other parishes.[14] These questions became more detailed in the reign of Charles I, regardless of the churchmanship of the bishop.[15] On the whole the Church of Scotland was more successful in insisting that baptism only be conducted by ministers in the parish church, though some kirk sessions still made exceptions for midwives if the child was weak and for private baptism if the couple had special reasons. The fact that the Five Articles of Perth in 1618 permitted private baptisms meant that the issue was linked to the mounting resistance to episcopacy, which led eventually to the signing of the National Covenant in 1638.[16]

Cressy argues that, although baptism was still a disputed topic in the 1630s, the real point at which everything fell apart was the period of the Civil War and the Commonwealth. In the early 1640s some parishioners challenged ministers to omit the sign of the cross in baptism, with varying degrees of success.[17] The puritan or presbyterian ascendancy meant a sharper attack on traditional practices. The *Directory for the Public Worship of God throughout the three Kingdoms*, produced by the Westminster Assembly in 1644-5, did away with the sign of the cross and with god-parents, instead expecting the father to take responsibility for the child. Baptism should not be performed by a private person nor in a private place; indeed the minister's exhortation specifically stated that 'outward baptism is not so necessary, that through the want thereof the infant is in danger of damnation, or the parents guilty, if they do not contemn or neglect the ordinance of Christ, when and where it may be had'.[18] Thus the way was open for a movement away from the absolute necessity of baptism. Instead, the foundation became the idea of the church covenant, the free gathering of believers to walk in God's way; this also permitted freedom of opinion within congregations as to whether to baptize infants or not.[19]

---

14 E.g. Archbishop Bancroft in 1605, widely replicated: Fincham, *Visitation Articles* i, 8-9.

15 See e.g. those of Laud 1634, Wren 1635, and Juxon 1640: K. Fincham, *Visitation Articles and Injunctions of the Early Stuart Church* ii (Church of England Record Society, Woodbridge 1998), 87, 130, 230-1.

16 G. Donaldson, *The Scottish Reformation* (Cambridge 1960), 180-1, A.I. Dunlop, 'Baptism in Scotland after the Reformation' in D. Shaw (ed), *Reformation and Revolution* (St Andrew Press: Edinburgh 1967), 94-7.

17 A. Tindal Hart, *The Man in the Pew* (London 1966), 136.

18 P. Hall (ed), *Reliquiae Liturgicae*, iii (Bath 1847), 45-8. The quotation from p. 48 is cited in H. Davies, *The Worship of the English Puritans* (London 1948), 134.

19 G.F. Nuttall, *Visible Saints: the Congregational Way, 1640-1660* (Oxford 1957), 73-82, 115-27; J.M. Jones, 'The Church Covenant in Independency', *Transactions of the Congregational Historical Society*, xvi 2 (Dec 1949), 52-63, cf the comment on C. Burrage's *The Church Covenant Idea* (Philadelphia 1904) in 'Notes and Queries', *Transactions of the Congregational Historical Society*, ii 1 (1905), 72. The text of the

In 1651 the church at Altham, Lancashire, under the Revd Thomas Jolly (which included Presbyterians and Independents) agreed the following as part of its church discipline:

> 4th—Concerning admission by Baptism, we cannot understand that the children of such as are not members of the Church, and will not submit to the ordinances and ways of Christ, have any right to this ordinance, unless their predecessors that are worthy will covenant for them, and engage that they shall be educated in the nurture and admonition of the Lord...
>
> 10th—At the admission of any child by baptism, it is to be required that the parent, or who undertakes for the child as their own, shall not only promise the good education of the child, but covenant in behalf of it to do the things required at the admission of Members, and that the child when it comes at the years of discretion shall confirm this covenant or be refused.[20]

When the Church renewed its covenant in 1655, they once again took 'the Lord Jehovah in Jesus Christ to be our God, and Jesus Christ His Son to be our blessed King and Saviour, *according to our covenant in baptism*'.[21] The link between covenant and baptism was clear. However, English Independents were not drawn into the speculations of their New England cousins, who developed the idea of a 'half-way covenant' for families which did not feel assurance of salvation and therefore did not take part in the sacraments, but could nevertheless transmit their church membership and right to baptism to their children.[22]

In the early seventeenth century also the Baptists appeared as an organised movement. Although popularly they are often associated with an emphasis on baptism by immersion, their primary emphasis was on the importance of a personal confession of faith before church membership. In this perspective the act of baptism was secondary to faith and commitment. George Fox began to preach in 1646 and from his preaching the Society of Friends developed, which rejected the practice of both sacraments altogether. Thus more voices were heard against the whole practice of infant baptism.

Private baptism in the early seventeenth century was a way by which strong-minded puritans had ensured that their children were baptized in

---

covenant of Hugh Peters for the English congregation in Rotterdam in 1633 is given in C. Burrage, *The Early English Dissenters in the light of recent research (1550-1641)* (Cambridge 1912), i, 301-3.

20 H. Fishwick (ed), *Extracts from the Church Book of Altham and Wymondhouses, AD 1649-1725* (Chetham Society vol 33, Manchester 1894), 121-2, quoted in Cressy, *Birth, Marriage and Death*, 176-7.

21 Ibid, 127 (italics mine).

22 H. Davies, *The Worship of the American Puritans, 1629-1730* (New York 1990), 157-61.

the way they wanted. John Greene had his eldest son baptized at home by his uncle, who 'used the Common Prayer Book, but signed it not with the cross'.²³ Ironically it became during the Commonwealth a way by which traditional Anglicans secured the preservation of their own customs. A pluralism of baptismal practice was legitimated which the Restoration Church of England was unable completely to eliminate. Moreover, from the later seventeenth century a wider difference developed between the baptismal practice of the 'better and the lower sort' of people, and much of the older sense of baptism as an essentially communal rite was lost.²⁴

As Jeremy Gregory has noted, one of the main needs of the Restoration Church was to restore the Anglican baptismal service, which sometimes involved the restoration of fonts.²⁵ The 1662 Book of Common Prayer introduced a service for the baptism of 'those of riper years', in order to deal with the problem of those whose parents might have neglected their baptism in the Commonwealth period. Susanna Parr, a member of an Independent congregation in Exeter, wrote in 1659 that 'we were...in a bewildered condition, without either of the sacraments: some not having their children baptized in a long time, others did procure some congregational minister to do it'.²⁶ Bewilderment about the consequences of this period could even extend to bishops, as when the Bishop of Bristol sought Archbishop Sancroft's advice about a young woman baptized before the Restoration by a Presbyterian who thought she needed to be re-baptized by a priest in episcopal orders.²⁷ Although Baptists and Quakers were numerically smaller than the Presbyterians and Independents, the rejection of the possibility of a comprehensive Church of England in 1662 forced the Presbyterians out as well, and thus from 1662 groups of Protestant dissenters were to be found in many parishes.

The Church of England did make strenuous efforts to reimpose conformity with some considerable success, but this was never complete. For example, legislation to enforce baptism and catechizing was dropped in 1677-78.²⁸ In fact, it was William Wall's experience as a young curate

---

23 Houlbrooke, *English Family Life*, 110.

24 Cressy, *Birth, Marriage and Death*, 173-94. Bishop Trelawney of Bristol at his Primary Visitation in 1686 complained of 'the ill custom of private christenings, through the ministers' compliance with the richer sort of their parish'; J. Spurr, *The Restoration Church of England, 1646-1689* (New Haven 1991), 206.

25 J. Gregory, *Restoration, Reformation and Reform, 1660-1828: Archbishops of Canterbury and their Diocese* (Oxford 2000), 280.

26 *Susanna's Apology against the Elders* (1659) in E. Graham, H. Hinds, E. Hobby and H. Wilcox (eds), *Her Own Life* (London 1989), 106, quoted in Cressy, *Birth, Marriage and Death*, 177: the 'bewildered condition' described seems to refer to the early 1650s. See also Nuttall, *Visible Saints*, 124-30.

27 Spurr, *Restoration Church of England*, 159: Sancroft said the baptism was valid.

28 Ibid, 194.

of the number of people who were indifferent or inclined to adopt baptist views in this period that led him to write his classic *History of Infant Baptism*, eventually published in 1705.[29] In the Archdeaconry of Shropshire, citations for not sending children for baptism or catchism fell away immediately after James II's Declaration of Indulgence in 1687.[30] From 1689, when the possibility of a more comprehensive Church of England was rejected again, all these dissenting groups were officially tolerated; and the multiple Christian allegiances of modern Britain were established. Much recent work has argued that the late-seventeenth and early-eighteenth century Church of England was more successful at the parochial level than the Victorians suggested. But much depended on the attitudes of the local clergy. In 1663 Isaac Archer at Chippenham, Cambridgeshire, in baptizing according to the Prayer Book, did not 'signe with the crosse, because it gave offence', nor did his bishop (who had been a member of the Westminster Assembly) require it; he was also prepared to baptize on the parents' promise without god-parents.[31] But in Wiltshire the laity resented Anglican clerical inflexibility over matters of worship, which was either a direct legacy of the Commonwealth or something which went even further back, implying that Laudian policies on worship were deeply resented. Not only were there disputes in the church courts in which laity and clergy in turn accused one another of neglect; but there was particular resentment when clergy were not available for baptisms and funerals. The churchwardens of Horningsham in 1669 said that their minister 'being resident in another parish & many times not at home, the Neighbours are greatly troubled to get a ministr to baptize a weake nere-born babe'.[32]

Roger Schofield has noted interesting shifts in the preferred day for baptisms in the sample group of parishes used by the Cambridge Group for the History of Population and Social Structure.[33] The Protestant

---

29 W. Wall, *The History of Infant Baptism* (ed H. Cotton, Oxford 1836), i, vii.

30 W.M. Marshall, 'The Dioceses of Hereford and Oxford, 1660-1760' in J. Gregory and J.S. Chamberlain (eds), *The National Church in Local Perspective: The Church of England and the Regions, 1660-1800* (Woodbridge 2003), 203.

31 Storey, *Two East Anglian Diaries*, 88-9, 92. Archer was the son of a nonconformist, who succeeded a minister who left the Church of England on St Bartholomew's Day, and became the patron's private chaplain. By contrast, in Wiltshire a minister refused to baptize a child without god-parents: Spurr, *Restoration Church of England*, 206, 209.

32 D.A. Spaeth, *The Church in an Age of Danger: Parsons and Parishioners 1660-1740* (Cambridge 2000), 173-224; the quotation is from Churchwardens' Presentments to the Dean of Salisbury, 197.

33 R. Schofield, '"Monday's child is fair of face": favoured days for baptism, marriage and burial in pre-industrial England', *Continuity and Change*, xx (2005), 93-109, especially 100-2 and 107: I owe this reference to Mr S.J. Thompson.

preference for baptisms on Sundays changed a more or less even spread among the days of the week in the early Reformation period into 60% on Sundays by 1640. Then this pattern collapsed and was not re-established until after 1737. Schofield's article is descriptive and offers no explanation for the changes, though he also notes variations between parishes. Since, however, the data are inevitably based on parish registers, it would be interesting to know what the practice was in relation to the entry of private baptisms, and in particular whether the baptism would be entered in the register on the day it happened or on the Sunday when (and if) the baby was presented in church and signed with the cross.

How then was baptism viewed at a popular level in the early eighteenth century? The evidence for this is not easy to obtain. Cressy's work is based mainly on surviving diaries and the records of episcopal visitations and cases presented in the church courts. Diaries do suggest an awareness of the theological significance of baptism. Mrs Alice Thornton, described by Ralph Houlbrooke as 'a staunchly loyal member of the Church of England', lost her sixth child ten days after he was born in 1657, but she wrote that she was 'blessed with the life and comfort of my dear child's baptism, with its enjoyment of the holy seal of regeneration'. Similarly the Countess of Bridgewater said of her daughter, Katy, who died of smallpox when nearly two in 1660, that she had always been good during the sermon or prayers: 'She had received the sacrament of baptism, which washed her from her original sin, and she lived holily'.[34] From 1689 there was a marked decline in the attempt to use church courts to enforce ecclesiastical discipline. By comparison with the early seventeenth century, episcopal visitation queries showed no interest in baptism, fonts, midwives, etc. William Wake, as Bishop of Lincoln, asked his clergy seven questions (compared with seventy a century earlier) at his Primary Visitation in 1706, and these were copied and expanded, both by his successors at Lincoln and by bishops in other dioceses. The only question relating to baptism was whether incumbents knew of any who came to church who were not baptized; whether there were those who were baptized and of a competent age who were not confirmed; and whether any adults had been baptized. Thomas Herring and Robert Drummond, as Archbishops of York later in the century, asked the same question: the Bishops of Winchester did not.

The returns for Bedfordshire (which was in the Lincoln diocese) for five visitations between 1706 and 1720 have been published. They are extremely useful—though perhaps not typical—because Bedfordshire had a high proportion of dissent, particularly Baptists and Quakers. They can be compared with the results of Thomas Herring's Primary Visitation of the Diocese of York in 1743, of Robert Drummond's Primary

---

34 Houlbrooke, *English Family Life*, 102, 121, 152.

Visitation of 1764 (though only the returns for Yorkshire have been published), and of the Bishops of Winchester in Hampshire and Surrey between 1725 and 1788.[35]

Care has to be taken in assessing the answers to these returns. The deference which clergy showed to their bishop is often clearly apparent, and the answers given to the questions sometimes seem to be those which might be expected. Nevertheless, many clergy gave quite detailed answers, and even when they said, for example, that there was only one person unbaptized, and went on to offer an explanation, one feels that one is getting nearer to the actual situation on the ground. In addition, there are a number of related comments that open up fascinating insights into the wider picture.

The first point to be noted is the strength of dissent. In Bedfordshire in 1706 only eighteen parishes out of 124 reported no dissent, but another seventy-four reported dissenters in varying numbers but no meeting house. In 1720 out of 104 parishes reporting, there were only seven without any dissent and sixty-six where there were dissenters but no meeting house. 'Anabaptists', as they were usually called, were the most numerous dissenters, but there were also many Quakers, as well as Presbyterians and Independents. This is similar to the situation noted by Donald Spaeth in the diocese of Salisbury, where he suggests that dissenters were present in two-thirds of the parishes.[36] Obviously many of those in parishes without meeting houses went to worship elsewhere, but this evidence certainly suggests that an account of nonconformity which is primarily based upon the history of the meeting houses which survived the century is likely to under-estimate its extent.

In the diocese of York in 1743 there were dissenters in only about one third of the parishes. The largest group was the Quakers, and several incumbents mentioned Quakers as being those who were unbaptized; and there were only a few Baptist churches, though there seem to have been Baptist families in more communities than the number of churches would suggest. The Wesleyan Revival was only just beginning—the year of the first Methodist Conference was 1744—and at that stage relations between Methodists and Moravians were still very close. So despite the presence of Quakers and Baptists the majority practice in the diocese was Anglican.

---

35 P. Bell (ed), *Episcopal Visitations in Bedfordshire, 1706-1720* (Bedfordshire Historical Record Society, vol 81, 2002); S.P. Ollard and P.C. Walker, *Archbishop Herring's Visitation Returns 1743*, i-v (Yorkshire Archaeological Society Record Series, lxxxi 1928, lxxii, 1929, lxxv, 1929, lxxvii, 1930, lxxix 1931); W.R. Ward (ed), *Parson and Parish in Eighteenth-Century Surrey* (Surrey Record Society, vol 34, Guildford 1994); W.R. Ward (ed), *Parson and Parish in Eighteenth-Century Hampshire* (Hampshire Record Series, vol 13, Winchester 1995).

36 D. Spaeth, 'The Failure of Reform in the Diocese of Salisbury', in Gregory and Chamberlain, *National Church in Local Perspective*, 129.

Only in one parish—Allendale in Northumberland—was the presence of dissent cited as an obstacle to the Church of England: here the Curate, John Toppin, said that the Stewards of the Lead Mines were Quakers, who proselytised the parishioners for Quakerism, deriding the sacraments; and that, since they were dependant on them for bread, this was difficult to resist—though he also said that another Steward dispersed popish books among his workers.[37] There is some evidence to suggest that the strength of nonconformity in the north-east of England was systematically under-reported by clergy, just as the distinction between Presbyterians and Independents had already become blurred in the post-Restoration period.[38] By the time of Archbishop Drummond's Visitation in 1764 there was more dissent, though Professor Royle has noted that in Huddersfield the vicar, Henry Venn, clearly regarded the Methodist society 'only as evangelical parishioners with no separate existence from the Church', and hence did not refer to them in his return.[39] By contrast Professor Ward found relatively little dissent in Surrey and particularly Hampshire, apart from the towns. He also found clear evidence of decline by mid-century.[40] Clearly much depended on episcopal policy. Early in the century William Wake at Canterbury was prepared to go some way to make it easier for dissenters to conform, particularly when this involved baptism as adults; but later in the century 'as dissent became...more of a dynastic tradition' it became less easy to win them over.[41] Secker, also later at Canterbury, pursued a similarly tolerant policy while Bishop of Oxford, being prepared to let Baptists delay baptism of their children and still come to 'our sacraments'.[42]

The identity of dissenters was not always clear to incumbents, and sometimes apparently not even to themselves. Edward Hall, the rector of Aspley Guise (where there was no meeting house) said in 1717 that out of eighty families, five were Quakers and three Presbyterians, and then added, 'Divers who have come to Church (now, since the Toleration) goes no where, mere Libertines, two chief Farmers, besides the Prophane Rabble Goes no where!'[43] That, however, was quite a small proportion. At Blunham, where there was a similar number of families, the rector wrote in 1706, 'About one halfe of the parish are Dissenters. There are 3

---

[37] Ollard and Walker, *Herring's Visitation Returns*, iii, 245.

[38] F. Deconinck-Brossard, '"We live so far North": the Church in the North-East of England', in Gregory and Chamberlain, *National Church in Local Perspective*, 226-7.

[39] E. Royle, *Queen Street Chapel and Mission, Huddersfield* (Huddersfield Local History Society: Huddersfield 1994), 4.

[40] Ward, *Parson and Parish in Eighteenth-Century Hampshire*, xxv-xxvi.

[41] Gregory, *Restoration, Reformation and Reform*, 212-3.

[42] Marshall, 'The dioceses of Hereford and Oxford', in Gregory and Chamberlain, *National Church in Local Perspective*, 213.

[43] Bell, *Episcopal Visitations in Bedfordshire*, 106-7.

Quakers. The rest seem to be Antinomians. and most of them never Baptize in any manner, or at any Age. They are of different sects, yet meet together in the same Barn, within the parish, and are backward to own their principles.'[44] Similarly at Sandy in 1706, where there was no meeting house, the rector said that there were about twenty families (out of 150) who were dissenters 'whereof 3 are Quakers, the rest generally infected with Antinomian principles, and for the most part against Infant baptism, which is all that can certainly be said of them'.[45] The vicar of Portsea, John Ballard, described one group of dissenters in his parish as ' a meeting of no certain sect, David Orange teacher; first in Lady Huntingdon's Connections (*sic*), then Mr Westley's, next an Independent, then an Anabaptist, now approaching to the Church of England, about 100 members'.[46] At first sight this looks like a group which could not make up its mind, or alternatively went in which ever direction its minister for the time being was inclined; and this could have been the case. But it is also possible that this was a group where the primary emphasis was on preaching the gospel and being in a state of grace; in such a situation the sacraments became a secondary consideraticn, even in nominally paedobaptist groups like the Methodists and Independents. This point will be developed later in considering the impact of the Evangelical Revival. However, it illustrates the extent to which the Presbyterians remained the group closest to the establishment. At Ravensden, Bedfordshire, in 1706 the four Presbyterian families (out of forty) were said to 'all Baptize, Marry and Bury according to the Church of England', but these were evidently exceptional.[47] As the century progressed, however, many Presbyterians became effectively, and eventually formally, Independents and their attitudes to the establishment changed. The Revd Thomas Pease, vicar of Cottingham, reported in 1743 that the dissenters in his parish (who were presbyterians) gave thanks after childbirth in their meeting house, but nevertheless had paid a churching fee to the vicar since his predecessor's time. Now, however, they were not paying it very willingly, 'questioning the legality of the Demand'; and he asked for advice.[48] That such a custom should ever have developed perhaps indicated that the sense of community overcame the significance cf the difference between Church and dissent; but it is also a reminder of the continuing significance of churching as the last stage of the process of giving birth, discussed by Cressy.[49]

---

44 Ibid, 18.
45 Ibid, 76.
46 Ward, *Parson and Parish in Eighteenth-Century Hampshire*, 314.
47 Ibid, 72.
48 Ollard and Walker, *Herring's Visitation Returns*, i, 156.
49 Cressy, *Birth, Marriage and Death*, 197-229.

Clearly, therefore, it cannot be assumed that the practice of infant baptism was universal, even though it may have been the majority practice. In his study of eighteenth-century France, Professor McManners was able to begin his chapter, 'From Baptism to the *Requiescat in Pace*', with the words, 'The Laws of both Church and State made baptism obligatory. An exception was made for the children of Jews, Turks, and pagans; heretics, like the Calvinists, who baptized their own, could be compelled to resort to the ministrations of a Catholic priest, though only by special decree of the public authority'.[50] Such a statement illustrates how far England was different.

Nevertheless, the Bedfordshire incumbents generally affirmed that all who came to church were baptized. Some returns referred to the baptism of adults, but only in a few parishes was this any more than occasional, and in many no adults were baptized at all. However, there were several baptized in certain parishes, and in some cases they were explicitly said to be former Quakers. At Houghton Conquest—again a parish without a meeting house—it was said in 1709, 'One Un-baptized comes now and then to Church. He is newly brought off from Quakerism. Severall of the same kind, though long baptized, are not yet Confirmed.'[51] By 1720 the number of adults baptized seems to have tailed off, suggesting that at last things were settling down.

There were several curious situations. At Wilden in 1712 the rector noted that there was 'one Girle born deaf and dumb not Baptized', who was presumably the one reported as having been baptized in 1717.[52] At Toddington in 1717 the rector reported baptizing five people between the age of thirteen and twenty-two—but for no stated reason he said that he gave infant baptism to the thirteen-year old girl.[53] At Clifton in the same year, where the rector baptized two people, the second one was described as 'Ruth the Daughter of Widow Mouse, about 12 years old, a Clinic'—defined by the *Oxford English Dictionary* as 'a person who defers baptism until the deathbed'.[54]

The incumbents in the diocese of York in 1743, with only a few explained exceptions, said that all those who attended church were baptized. Only a few specifically alluded to the possibility of there being people who did not attend church, and may have been unbaptized—usually in towns. However, to argue that these answers implied that everyone in the parish attended church and was therefore baptized is to argue from silence. The unbaptized were usually

---

50 J. McManners, *Church and Society in Eighteenth-Century France, ii, The Religion of the People and the Politics of Religion* (Oxford 1998), 3.
51 Bell, *Episcopal Visitations in Bedfordshire*, 51.
52 Ibid, 97, 178.
53 Ibid, 174.
54 Ibid, 123.

specifically identified, as at Beswick (between Beverley and Driffield), where the curate, Thomas Mease, referred to 'one call'd Beswick, a Black, who is above twenty years of age; he was born in the East Indies, sold to Mr William Draper who gave hime to his Father William Draper Esqr: of this Town'. Although a youth of 'no Learning, and but of very slender capacity', he had been instructed for baptism if the Archbishop would permit it.[55] Jonathan Hardy, Curate of Kirkburton (near Huddersfield), said he had one man, formerly a Quaker, and a girl, who now wished for baptism, 'But being adult they cannot be baptized without the Arch:Bishop's Leave which I hope his Grace will grant.'[56] The last point seems to be a misunderstanding (albeit widespread), because the rubric in the service of the public baptism to such as are of riper years simply refers to 'timely notice' being given to the bishop.

By the time of Archbishop Drummond's Primary Visitation of 1764, at least in the Yorkshire parishes, only a handful of adults were recorded as having been baptised, most of them former Quakers (often prior to confirmation or marriage),[57] an occasional 'Anabaptist',[58] a few blacks[59] and several for whom no explanation was offered.[60] Most of these were in their late teens or early twenties. One woman at Langtoft was noted as unbaptized and a man at Luddenden.[61] In 1765 the incumbent of Newtown Burghclerc in Hampshire referred to 'William Hawkins gardener and his wife, Catherine, who have not brought their last 2 children to be baptized', but they were almost alone in the county in being singled out in this way.[62]

The fact that an overwhelming majority of people were probably baptized is not particularly surprising; but confirmation was a different matter. Many clergy in the diocese of York said that no-one was unconfirmed; many others said that the only ones not confirmed were those who were being presented for confirmation at the Visitation. But just over 100 (out of 800) incumbents acknowledged that there were several and sometimes many who were unconfirmed. There were a variety of reasons for this. For some it was lack of opportunity. The returns for

---

55 Ollard and Walker, *Herring's Visitation Returns*, i, 105.
56 Ollard and Walker, *Herring's Visitation Returns*, ii, 116.
57 C. Annesley and P. Hoskin, *Archbishop Drummond's Visitation Returns 1764*, i-iii (Borthwick Texts and Calendars, York 1997, 1998, 2001): Batley i, 47, Bradford i, 77, Danby in Cleveland i, 131, Patrington ii, 170, Ripponder ii, 186, Thornton in Craven iii, 79, Topcliffe iii, 92, Whitby iii, 121, York St Margaret iii, 159.
58 Ibid: Barnoldswick i, 43.
59 Ibid: Darfield i, 132, Hutton Rudby ii, 67, Pontefract ii, 174, Wakefield iii, 97.
60 Ibid: Doncaster i, 138, Easington, Cleveland i, 141, Guiseley i, 191, Hull, Holy Trinity ii, 57, Normanton ii, 155, Skipsea iii, 35, Sowerby Bridge iii, 47.
61 Ibid, ii, 106, 123.
62 Ward, *Parson and Parish in Eighteenth-Century Hampshire*, 205.

Hexhamshire, an isolated part of the diocese in Northumberland, suggested that there had not been a confirmation there within 'the memory of man'; nor is there any evidence that Archbishop Herring held one, though in 1760 the Bishop of Durham confirmed there on behalf of Archbishop Gilbert.[63] There were also isolated places within the main part of the diocese of York: James Borwick, Curate of Whitby, said that many of those who were qualified for confirmation could not attend at present 'by Reason of their great Distance'.[64] A similar comment was made in Walkeringham (the other side of the River Trent from Gainsborough), where it was said that 'the Parents objected to the great Distance of the Place & the Expence it wou'd be attended with'.[65] Two rather different reasons were offered in Nottinghamshire: at Kirkton (now Kirton, near Ollerton) the confirmation coincided with the town feast, and the candidates opted for the latter, while at Staunton (presumably Staunton-in-the Vale [of Belvoir]) although thirty-six were confirmed at the Primary Visitation, two were not because 'they could not break through the press'![66] In many more, however, the suggestion is that people, either after some attempt at persuasion or not, simply were not interested, for example at Scamuden (now Deanhead, west of Huddersfield).[67] Class was also relevant: Thomas Wakefield, Rector of Rowley near Hull, said there were some servants who couldn't be brought to say their Catechism and whom he supposed 'dont Intend to be Confirm'd'. Servants were also mentioned as being unconfirmed at Darlton and Rempston in Nottinghamshire.[68] Two unusual reasons for lack of confirmation were given: one was at Hunslet where some were said to be above the age 'limited by your Grace's injunction'; the other because their parents or masters were busy with the harvest and Welwick was a long way from Hull.[69]

All this suggests that baptism was more highly regarded than confirmation, probably because confirmation was essentially a religious event, since it had no particular significance in the life-cycle. It would be wrong to detach religion from the life-cycle in an artificial way at this time; but baptism clearly had a wider significance than the purely theological, whereas confirmation was not seen as marking the end of childhood and the beginning of adulthood. Nevertheless, it would appear

---

63 Ollard and Walker, *Herring's Visitation Returns*, i, xv.
64 Ollard and Walker, *Herring's Visitation Returns*, iii, 208.
65 Ollard and Walker, *Herring's Visitation Returns*, iv, 170.
66 Ibid, 137. This provoked a footnote from the Editors about 'the scandalous conditions under which Confirmation was sometimes given, when it was administered only at the Episcopal Visitations'.
67 Ollard and Walker, *Herring's Visitation Returns*, iii, 51.
68 Ibid, 31; Ollard and Walker, *Herring's Visitation Returns*, iv, 43, 118.
69 Annesley and Hoskin, *Drummond's Visitation Returns*, ii, 61; iii, 111.

that confirmation was more widely practised in eighteenth-century England than France, but this was because First Communion was the significant point in France.[70]

Baptism had a legal and financial significance too, as the story of West Stockwith in Nottinghamshire illustrates. The chapel at West Stockwith had no cure of souls, since it was the chapel of the hospital there. But the minister, Robert Pindar, pointed out that the inhabitants brought their children to be baptized at the chapel since the mother church at Misterton was two miles away. In his predecessor's time a copy of the children baptized was entered in the parish register and the vicar received his usual fees; but recently he had refused to do this 'to the great Discontent of the Inhabitants who's Children must either want the Benefit of a Register or be carried in Winter Time Two Miles in Roads almost impassable to be baptised'.[71] It must have been particularly galling that the Vicar of Misterton lived at Beckingham, which was three or four miles further away still. This illustrates both that legal registration was important to people, and also that fees to the clergy for baptisms was a sore in the background.

The Visitation Returns also showed some evidence of the theological issues which had vexed people since the thirteenth century. In 1720 the vicar of St Paul's, Bedford, asked, 'In the case where Adult persons depart this life without baptism, or without Regular baptism, and desire to be laid by their Baptised Relations in the Church or Church yard, what does the Church appoint in this case?'[72] Many dissenting meeting houses had their own graveyards, even in towns, but this was obviously a slightly different problem, because of the reference to 'baptised relations'. There is no hint of an answer.

More significant was the traditional problem of unbaptized infants. Benjamin Wainman, curate of Kildwick near Skipton (whose father and brother were dissenting ministers, and who had himself been trained by Philip Doddridge), asked Archbishop Herring in 1743 whether he did not think that the words at the end of the service for the public baptism of infants, 'It is certain by God's Word, that Children which are baptized, dying before they commit actual sin, are undoubtedly saved', were 'directly contrary to what the church of England has taught in her 9th article of religion'. In any case, he thought the words were an article of faith and therefore improper as a rubric; and suggested that they should be omitted in new editions of the prayer book. He also asked whether the 39th Canon was defective in asserting that children ought not to be communicants, without mentioning the age or qualifications of

---

70 McManners, *Church and Society in Eighteenth-Century France*, ii, 6-9.
71 Ollard and Walker, *Herring's Visitation Returns*, iv, 150.
72 Bell, *Episcopal Visitations in Bedfordshire*, 191-2.

children.[73] The Revd Peter Dubourdieu (a French refugee), Rector of Kirkby Misperton (just south of Pickering), commented that 'the great severity of our rubrick towards children who dye unbaptiz'd, in not allowing the burial office to be read over them, is probably the reason, why hardly one in twenty is baptized in the church, their parents usually sending for me to give them private baptism, soon after they are born, for pretended reasons of weakness which I cannot contradict'.[74]

Private baptism in cases of genuine illness was generally uncontroversial. Donald Spaeth found little evidence of private baptism in Wiltshire in the later seventeenth century; and cited the case of William Gale, the vicar of Downton, who refused to christen a child at home in the 1680s, 'saying if the Child be ill I'le goe to them, but otherwise lett them bring it to Church'. He was irritated to find that the vicar of a neighbouring parish was prepared to perform the ceremony.[75] The Revd William Cole of Bletchley noted two occasions when he was called upon to baptize children at home because they had 'fits' and their parents feared they would die.[76] In 1768 James Woodforde baptized the child of a poor man in Castle Cary 'very dangerously ill in convulsions', and added in his diary, 'Never did I any ecclesiastical duty with more pleasure as it gave such great satisfaction to its Parents'; but it died the following day.[77] Again in 1784 a poor woman from Witchingham brought a child to him for private baptism, since it had been 'very bad ever since it was born—which I did directly'.[78] At the opposite end of the social scale Woodforde 'publicly christned' Mr Custance's son in April 1779, noting that 'it had been privately named before'; 'there were Coaches at Church', and he received four guineas. (Mr Custance was the local squire.) Eighteen months later he privately named another of Mr Custance's sons—though he died two months later.[79] He privately baptized most of Mr Custance's children, though in the case of the last, Charlotte, in 1792, it is clear that the public presentation was delayed almost six months, until Mrs Custance recovered: when she was churched

---

73 Ollard and Walker, *Herring's Visitation Returns*, ii, 109-10. The second query is a puzzle, because Canon 39 (Bray, *Anglican Canons*, 322-3) does not refer to children not communicating, and I have been unable to find either a canon or rubric that does.

74 Ibid, 123-4.

75 Spaeth, *The Church in Danger*, 198.

76 F.G. Stokes (ed), *The Blecheley Diary of the Rev. William Cole* (London 1931), 44-5 (27 April 1766), 232 (21 June 1767).

77 J. Beresford (ed), *Woodforde: Passages from the Five Volumes of the Diary of a Country Parson 1758-18* (London 1935), 41 (14 April 1768).

78 R.L. Winstanley (ed), *The Diary of James Woodforde*, vol x 1782-84 (The Parson Woodforde Society, 1998), 225 (27 March 1784).

79 Beresford, *Woodforde*, 125 (11 April 1779), 135 (22 September 1780), 136 (12 November 1780).

a week or so before, it was the first time she had attended church since before the birth.[80]

But there were other reasons for the growth of private baptism. Cressy suggests that this was a way of avoiding disputed practices, such as the sign of the cross. 'Taking the sacrament indoors, from public to private space, was an easy way to achieve liturgical simplification while maintaining the sanctity of the ordinance. This seems to have been the strategy of post-Restoration dissenters, even more than of pre-Civil War puritans.'[81] But private baptism also became a social occasion, detached from the crowd, for the better off as well. The later Stuart bishops campaigned to restore public baptism, but it is not clear how successful they were. Cressy says that the primary evidence for its growth comes from complaints by the clergy and entries in various diaries. However, 'its significance lies in the withdrawal of élite groups from the common parish assembly, the accommodation of religious ritual to social convenience, and the remaking of a major life-cycle event as a domestic, rather than an ecclesiastical occasion'.[82] Sometimes it could result in a battle of wills. John Johnson, one of the leaders of the high church party in Convocation, wrote of one of his gentleman parishioners in 1715, 'My only crime is ecclesiastical pride. I would not baptize his child at home while he was in perfect health, nor church his wife, till the child was baptized.'[83] But Johnson was swimming against the tide; and it did mean that it was more difficult for clergy to resist private baptism for the lower orders as well. By 1717 the curate at Burstow in Surrey said in the Visitation Return,

> The parishes are extremely large in this neighbourhood and a custom has prevailed (but not of very long standing) to baptize everybodies' children at home, and the ministers hereabouts use the form of publick baptism upon such occasions. Nay the women desire to be churched at home, and I have been used a little rudely sometimes for not complying with them in that particular, as some of my neighbours do.[84]

In the hill-country areas of Herefordshire the clergy in icy weather were prepared to perform 'so-called "public" baptisms in houses sometimes as far as two miles from the church', though they did ensure public reception in church at a later date.[85]

---

80 Ibid, 334 (3 January 1792), 339-40 (30 May and 17 June 1792), 340 (26 June 1792): the day of the presentation was a Tuesday, and it was not a Holy day.

81 Cressy, *Birth, Marriage and Death*, 189.

82 Ibid, 194.

83 Gregory, *Restoration, Reformation and Reform*, 241.

84 Ward, *Parson and Parish in Eighteenth-Century Surrey*, 153. Burstow was part of the Diocese of Canterbury and both the questions and replies were fuller than in the Diocese of Winchester.

85 Marshall, 'The dioceses of Hereford and Oxford', 213.

Private baptism also raised other problems. The Vicar of Blidworth, Robert Stanley, said that before he came to the parish it was customary to have children privately baptized and never bring them afterwards to be received in the church; but he had persuaded all but two to comply with the directions in the rubric.[86] Granville Wheeler, Rector of East Leake also had difficulties getting one or two people to bring their children to the church after private baptism.[87] Thomas Beaumont, Rector of Bulwell, Nottinghamshire, spelt this out: 'There are nine Children which have had private Baptism, and not yet brought to the Church to be received into the Number of Christ's Flock and to be sign'd with the sign of the Cross. I have used what means I can to prevail with 'em; They promise, but do not perform.'[88] This suggests that the issue of the sign of the cross may still have had some force. But it also suggests that the ecclesiastical part of the ceremony was seen as less important. Jeremiah Milles, vicar of Merstham in Surrey, reported in 1758 that 'one John Richardson whose child had private baptism about 3 years ago, after repeated friendly admonitions, obstinately defers bringing it to church'.[89] James Woodforde said in a Visitation Return to the Bishop of Norwich in 1784 that he wished 'that parents could be prevailed to bring these children to be publicly presented into Church', and many other incumbents said the same.[90] Generally, Woodforde seems to have treated private baptisms on their merits, never hesitating to baptize if the child was ill. But he was uncomfortable if there did not seem to be an adequate reason. For example, on a visit to Mr Micklethwaite on 22 September 1784 he seems to have been asked to perform a baptism before dinner. He wrote 'before Dinner I publickly baptised their little Boy at home, which I did not much like, but could not tell how to refuse—he was privately named before at Norwich I believe'; and the godparents were listed.[91] William Cole, however, notes an occasion, when he baptized a boy 'or rather received him into the Congregation' when four people 'stood Gossips [i.e. godparents] for other People'.[92] This was on 6 August 1767, a Thursday, so it is doubtful whether there were any more people present than would have been there for the private baptism, even though it was the Feast of the Transfiguration and therefore satisfied the Prayer Book rubric that it

---

86 Ollard and Walker, *Herring's Visitation Returns*, iv, 26.
87 Ibid, 87.
88 Ibid, 15.
89 Ward, *Parson and Parish in Eighteenth-Century Surrey*, 165. Merstham was also part of the Diocese of Canterbury.
90 W.M. Jacob, *Lay People and Religion in the Early Eighteenth Century* (Cambridge 1996), 73; there are few indications of this view in Woodforde's Diary on the various occasions when he conducted private baptisms.
91 Winstanley, *Diary of James Woodforde*, x, 278-9.
92 Stokes, *Blecheley Diary of Cole*, 246.

should be a Sunday or Holy Day. (He made no reference to holding any other kind of service.)

Another reason for private baptism was to avoid publicity in situations when the child had been conceived out of wedlock. In January 1766 William Cole was asked to marry a couple on the following day so that he could baptize their child which had been born some time ago. The matter was urgent because the two fathers had now consented to their children's marriage. Hence on Thursday 16 January:

> I married John Hinchley to Elizabeth Crane in the Church, but desired them to come into the Parlour to sign the Book & for me to write the Entry into it, as it was so cold. When I was got there, they had got the Child there to be baptised: & when that was done, the Mother begged that I would also church her. As it was absurd to do it in a Parlour; yet as I had just baptised the Child there & as the Woman was pressing to have it done, being ashamed to appear publicly: & as the Discipline of our Church, thro' the Practices of the Dissenters, is now so relaxed as to come to nothing, there is no parlying with your Parishioners on any Point of Doctrine or Discipline: for if you are rigid, they will either abstain from all Ordinances, or go over to the Dissenters: so I complied with her Request.[93]

Cole was, if anything, a high churchman, but he was also a realist in his pastoral care for his parish. The practice of requiring mothers of illegitimate children to do public penance gradually died out in the eighteenth century, and Michael Snape found that the parish registers of Whalley in Lancashire recorded the baptism of dozens of illegitimate children all the way through the century.[94]

By the mid-eighteenth century private baptism was also becoming more common in the nonconformist churches which practised infant baptism. Philip Doddridge gave his lectures on preaching and pastoral care in the last year of the course at his Academy in Northampton from 1730. He advised his students not to insist on their members bringing their children to meeting to be baptized. His reasons were interesting:

> If you have a mixture of baptists it may perhaps give offence, and private baptisms will give you greater freedom in your address to the parents: And for this reason do not baptise many children together, nor grudge an hour or two to any family on such an occasion.[95]

He also urged them to show moderation in the entertainment 'that generally follows': 'Allow yourself intervals of moderate cheerfulness, but rather err on the grave extreme; and always retire as early as you

---

93 Ibid, 8-9.
94 M.F. Snape, 'The Church in a Lancashire Parish: Whalley, 1689-1800', in Gregory and Chamberlain, *National Church in Local Perspective*, 259.
95 *The Works of the Rev. P. Doddridge, D.D.*, v (Leeds 1804), 483.

conveniently and decently can'.[96] Horton Davies commented that 'a household of believers was a fitting background for the family ordinance of Baptism';[97] but that comment itself, in describing baptism as a 'family ordinance', illustrates the shift away from a church understanding. Davies may be right in saying that this provided a better opportunity for the serious instruction of the parents than the Anglican service 'which often degenerated into a social occasion at which godparents were invited to take part, not as the Christian custodians of the child, but only as friends of the family who would be expected to provide financially for the child'.[98] However, it has already been noted that Doddridge recognised the social nature of the occasion, so the difference may be more apparent than real. Another consequence of the transfer of infant baptism to the home, however, was a greater chance that baptism might not happen at all.

The importance attached to baptism, however, is illustrated by an interesting comment in the return to Archbishop Drummond's visitation in 1764 from Ilkley. The vicar, Edmund Beeston, reported that Peter Oddy, whose wife was still living, cohabited with Anne Atkinson and had had several children by her; both were at present under sentence of excommunication. However, 'when he has a child his method is to get it privately baptized under pretence of indisposition and he never afterwards sends it to church to have full baptism'. Beeston wanted to know whether a minister was obliged to give private baptism 'under any pretence to a child when 2 or 3 months old or more'.[99] Thus an unmarried couple under excommunication still regarded baptism as sufficiently important to seek it even by this subterfuge.

The issues surrounding baptism could be raised in some surprising places. It was the only theological topic to be discussed in the *Gentleman's Magazine* in the first twenty years of its history from 1731. There was a brief exchange on the question of sprinkling or dipping as a mode of baptism in March 1737, April 1738 and June 1738 which was concluded by appeal to the fact that dipping was prescribed in the First Prayer Book of Edward VI.[100] In April 1739 there was a letter from 'Cleomenes' which began, 'It may be a Question, both of natural and revealed Religion, What becomes of Infants after Death?' In suggesting that it was not without difficulty, he went on to argue that if happiness in another world was a reward for virtue, it was difficult to see how this might apply to those incapable of such qualities; but he clearly did not like the argument that it was the result of God's absolute and arbitrary decree, and was concerned that if baptism was the cause, this left the

---

96 Ibid, 484.
97 Davies, *Worship of the English Puritans*, 220.
98 Ibid, 221.
99 Annesley and Hoskin, *Drummond's Visitation Returns*, ii, 71.
100 *Gentleman's Magazine*, viii (April 1738), 182-4, (June 1739) 285-6.

position of those who died without it doubtful. Hence he suggested that 'without some plain Reason or Scripture to the contrary, this, I think, proves itself, That all Infants, baptized or not; the Children of regenerate Parents, or of wicked Christians, and ignorant Heathens; are all in the same Relation to God. For Baptism is not a Charm to put a Difference between the Condition of one Infant and another with respect to God, where there is no Concurrence of the Will to make an Obedience to the Command acceptable or rewardable; neither to convey saving Grace to such a Being, if saving Grace be any thing that requires Reason and Understanding to operate upon.' Since he felt that baptism made no difference, and also that infants never became moral subjects of God's government, to suppose that God did dispose his favour upon them was to suppose that God acted 'without Reasons and Motives, and without Regard to the Natures of Things'—in other words 'without Regard to any Thing besides *mere Will*'. Hence he proposed that the souls of infants, if they had them, either transmigrated into other bodies or were annihilated; and concluded by saying that he would be 'glad to hear Reason on this Subject, and am ready to be convinced of an Error'.[101] The repeated references to reason suggest that this was in effect a rationalist response to the issues involved.[102]

It was some time before any reply to 'Cleomenes' was published, but then in February, May, July, August and September 1740 letters appeared in response. One argument was that God did not make souls merely 'to be born and to die and be damned', another that God could make distinctions between the fate of baptized and unbaptized infants without condemning all, and yet another that such distinctions were impossible and the matter was inconclusive. In August 1740 it was suggested that there was no evidence for God's authority for infant baptism, which produced a sharp response that the whole debate was shifted if infant baptism was challenged.[103] And then the correspondence stopped. It is almost as though raising the question of infant baptism as such was a step too far, even for a discussion of the rational basis for mainstream beliefs. The only other issue which came up was a passing reference in July 1748 to the question of whether the children in the Foundling Hospital could be baptized, since their parents were unknown; but it was not taken up.

---

101 Ibid, ix (April 1739) 177-9.

102 Ralph Houlbrooke suggests that 'a public discussion of this sort could not have taken place in any century before the eighteenth': R.A. Houlbrooke, *Death, Religion and the Family in England, 1480-1750* (Oxford 1998), 52-3. This might imply (wrongly) that the issues had never been raised before; but an exchange of correspondence in a monthly magazine seems different from the pamphlet exchanges of the sixteenth and seventeenth centuries.

103 *Gentleman's Magazine*, x, (May 1740) 245-6, (July 1740) 341-2, (August 1740) 396, (September 1740) 441-3.

The other challenge to the traditional cluster of beliefs about infant baptism came, of course, from the Evangelical Revival. The Revd John Berridge, rector of Everton, near Sandy in Bedfordshire, from 1755 to 1793, is an example of the most negative Anglican evangelical attitude towards baptism. The epitaph he composed for himself asks the characteristic question

> Reader art thou born again?
> No Salvation without a new Birth.

It also explains his hesitation over the catechism.

> I do not much prize our Church catechism [he wrote to John Thornton in 1787], it begins so very ill, calling baptism our new birth, and making us thereby members of Christ, children of God, and heirs of the kingdom of heaven.... The acting as sponsors is now become a mere farce, and a gossipping business; and the promising for infants, what they cannot engage for themselves, may suit a covenant of works but not a covenant of grace.[104]

By 'a gossipping business' Berridge was presumably referring to the importance attached to godparents (the gossips) and the entertainment associated with a christening, which he presumably felt detracted from its primary significance.[105]

Berridge had been a Fellow of Clare College, Cambridge, and was presented to the college living of Everton in Bedfordshire in 1755. Around Christmas 1757 he underwent an evangelical conversion, which he subsequently described as a change to a belief in faith rather than works. His preaching resulted in his church becoming crowded, and from 14 May 1759 he began to preach out of doors. This attracted the attention of John Wesley in the summer of 1759.[106] Dyer in his *History of the University* compared Berridge to Francis Holcroft, the ejected puritan of the previous century, because of his preaching in Cambridgeshire, Huntingdonshire and Bedfordshire: '[Berridge] soon sent forth lay preachers. Many dissenting churches now in those counties were

---

104 Berridge to John Thornton, 27 October 1787, R. Whittingham (ed), *Works of the Rev John Berridge* (London 1838), 457, quoted by C. Smyth, *Simeon and Church Order* (Cambridge 1940), 258, but Smyth misquotes the date. It is not clear whether his use of the word 'gossipping' was intended to be deliberately ambiguous in view of the common description of those involved in childbirth and baptism as 'gossips': Cressy, *Birth, Marriage and Death*, 84-7.

105 Woodforde referred to 'the Gossips' without further explanation at the public baptism of Mr Custance's son, Hambleton Thomas, on 11 April 1779: Beresford, *Woodforde*, 125; as did Cole (see note 76).

106 Berridge, *Works*, 9-14, 45-58; N. Curnock, *The Journal of John Wesley* (London 1909-16), iv, 317-22, 333-43, 344-8, 349-50.

originally formed of his disciples.'[107] He was a friend of both Wesley and Whitefield, and moved from Arminianism to Calvinism and back again, though in the latter years of his life he used to preach at Whitefield's Tabernacle in London between January and Easter. Nevertheless the churches which owe their origin to his preaching were usually Independent rather than Methodist, such as the Congregational churches (now United Reformed) at Fowlmere, Bassingbourn and Duxford.[108]

Berridge's preaching produced effects which have often been regarded as characteristic of revivals—people falling down in faints, crying for mercy, and eventually finding release, with confessions of having experienced Christ's forgiveness. In Scotland revivalist preaching was often associated with the communion seasons, especially in the summer and this was found in America also. This could be linked with admission to first communion, as with William McCulloch at Cambuslang in the 1740s. The usual age was the mid-teens, though it could be any time between twelve and twenty. In fact, in some cases the opportunity was taken to use the communion season as an occasion for baptisms as well, usually on the Monday preceding the celebration of communion on Sunday.[109] The accounts of Catherine Cameron's experience as she attended three communion services in 1742, culminating in that at Cambuslang, contain very similar phrases about sorrow for Christ's suffering and experience of his forgiveness of her sins as are found in the descriptions of Berridge's preaching, but set in a sacramental context.[110] Perhaps surprisingly Scottish revivalism seems to have been inspired by the sacraments, whereas that in an Anglican context was not. Even more intriguing is the fact that the rise of the evangelical party in the Church of Scotland later in the eighteenth century put a stop to the old communion seasons and confined reception of communion to those in the parish to impose some kind of order on what had become significant occasions of popular religion.[111]

The most significant feature of the Evangelical Revival in Britain in relation to baptismal practice is that (apart from the various Baptist groups) it did not attempt to make the experience of baptism central. This is in striking contrast to the contemporary Roman Catholic missions in mainland Europe. The missions organised by Jesuits and others of the new religious orders from the Catholic Reformation made the renewal of

---

107 G. Dyer, *History of the University and colleges of Cambridge* (London 1814), i, 122-4.

108 C. Stell, *An Inventory of Nonconformist Chapels and Meeting-Houses in Eastern England* (English Heritage, Swindon 2002), 26, 27, 32.

109 L.E. Schmidt, *Holy Fairs: Scotland and the Making of American Revivalism* (2 ed, Grand Rapids 2001), 83-7.

110 Ibid, 118-22.

111 Schmidt, *Holy Fairs*, 192-205.

baptismal commitments central to the programme of bringing the laity back into the churches, beginning in Italy and extending into France and Germany. 'The mission is for those who return to God as in a new baptism', wrote Louis-Marie Grignion de Montfort, one of the leading missioners in the early eighteenth century.[112] Fr Francois-Xavier Duplessis described the procession around the church to the font after a sermon on the baptismal promises:

> The deacon sings the Gospel of the Feast of the Most Holy Trinity, which tells of the power which Jesus Christ conferred on his Church, to baptise all nations in the name of the Father, the Son and the Holy Spirit. After which he places the Gospels, open, upon the baptismal fonts, below the Holy Sacrament. Then, with everyone kneeling, the preacher pronounces the acts of renewal of the commitments at baptism, and when they are finished the celebrant intones the Credo, so as to remind those present that it is by baptism that we have received the precious gift of the Faith. And during the singing the clergy and all who were in the Procession go, one after another, to the middle of the Altar to kiss the Gospel, or the baptismal fonts, so as to express the gratitude and affection with which everyone is disposed to observe the promises he has made to God.[113]

What is striking about this, as indeed in the Scottish examples related to Holy Communion, is the determined attempt on the part of the missioners to bring home the theological significance of the sacrament of baptism. There is a decisive movement from the world of popular piety to that of sacramental theology. That discussion forms the subject matter of the next three chapters.

---

112 Grignion de Montfort, *Cantiques des Missions* (Poitiers 1759), 269, quoted in L. Châtellier, *The Religion of the Poor* (ET Cambridge 1997), 180; cf McManners, *Church and Society in Eighteenth-Century France*, ii, 90.

113 *Avis et pratiques*, 158-9, quoted in ibid, 180.

Chapter 2

A New Birth?

The pattern of baptismal practice described in the previous chapter presumed that for most people baptism was the 'religious consequence' of belonging to the local community. The puritan attempt to distinguish between the committed Christian congregation and the local community was, for the most part, a failure. It had been based on the biblical concept of covenant which, when applied to baptism, also evoked parallels with God's covenants with the people of Israel. Peter's proclamation that 'the promise is to you and your children' in Acts 2:39 echoed similar promises to Noah (Genesis 6:9), Abraham (Genesis 17:7, 19), and Moses (Exodus 19:5-6, Deuteronomy 7:9), and was used by the puritans to justify the practice of infant baptism. The chosen people were thus defined by their faith rather than their nationality. This was where the notion of the elect, developed by Paul in his Letter to the Romans, came from. However, in England the emphasis on election and predestination, and certainly upon double predestination (the idea that some were predestined for damnation as well as those predestined for salvation), was never so prominent in the thought of Presbyterians and Independents as it was in Reformed churches elsewhere in Europe. On the other hand, the Church of England retained within its baptismal service, and the exposition of it in the catechism and canons, the understanding that baptism was the new birth.

The Evangelical Revival put a question mark against all this. The use of the word 'revival' is a reminder that originally what was understood to be happening was the bringing back to life of faith which already existed, rather than preaching the gospel to those who had never heard it (as the colloquial, and sometimes not so colloquial, later interpretations of the term implied). Nevertheless the kinds of experience of those affected made them want to describe these experiences, rather than a baptism which they could not remember, as 'a new birth'. This explains John Berridge's acid comment about the catechism to John Thornton, in which he specifically lamented the fact that baptism was called the new birth 'making us thereby members of Christ, children of God, and heirs of the kingdom of heaven'.[1] Similarly, despite the ambiguities of Wesley's own beliefs about baptism, Julia Wedgwood's observation about the significance of his conversion in 1738 makes the same point in a different way:

> The birthday of a Christian was shifted from his baptism to his conversion, and in that change the partition line of two great systems is crossed ... The witness that the direct influence of God upon the spirit of man was not confined to a remote past or a mysterious future, but was an actual fact in the lives of all who truly deserved the name of Christian, came home to Wesley and to many others of that day as the one force that was to bind a society together and to give new life to the individual soul.[2]

The emphasis on personal religious experience in the Evangelical Revival, which Berridge typified, brought out the tension between individual and social religion, placing the debate between infant and believer's baptism in a new light. The emphasis on the Bible brought a new interest in biblical patterns for church life and a re-examination of the biblical evidence for infant baptism. The contrast drawn between vital and formal religion brought a new questioning of sacramental theology. All these issues crystallized around the emphasis on conversion. If conversion was necessary to the Christian life, what was the significance and meaning of baptism? Did baptism, particularly the baptism of infants, effect anything?

The primary manifestation of the Evangelical Revival in eighteenth-century England was John Wesley's Methodism, though its legal and ecclesiastical status was ambiguous for as long as he lived, and for some time afterwards. Wesley himself claimed to live and die as a clergyman of the Church of England, but it proved ultimately impossible to contain his connexion of societies within the Church, notwithstanding the numerous proprietary chapels which sheltered others who did not fall strictly within the bounds of the parochial system. Wesley's attitude to baptism was to be a source of confusion to his friends and his enemies in the following century. It is further complicated by the fact that the interpretation of Wesley is itself part of the story of shifting Methodist attitudes to baptism since his death. The problem may be stated relatively simply as follows. Wesley preached the need for conversion to adults who had been baptized as infants. In stressing their need for conversion he said that they could

---

1 Berridge to John Thornton, 27 Oct 1787, Whittingham, *Berridge's Works*, 457: see Chapter 1.

2 J. Wedgwood, *John Wesley and the Evangelical Reaction of the Eighteenth Century* (London 1870), 157. These sentences are quoted in J.H. Rigg, *The Churchmanship of John Wesley* (London n.d. [1887]), 37, but the first is made to appear the conclusion; Rigg also quotes that sentence in context in *The Living Wesley* (2 ed London 1891), 119, but he italicises it without indicating that the author did not.

not put their trust in what had happened to them as children in baptism. This was interpreted by Anglican contemporaries such as Daniel Waterland, and later high churchmen such as van Mildert and the Tractarians, as proof that Wesley did not believe in baptismal regeneration. Yet Wesley was himself brought up in the high church tradition, and his writings can also be cited to show that he did not deny that infants were regenerated in baptism (though this was to prove embarrassing for nineteenth-century Wesleyans who were hostile to Tractarianism). Was Wesley confused? Did he change his mind? Did he believe in both the baptismal regeneration of infants and the regeneration of adults in conversion; in which case what did he mean by regeneration?

The most thorough study of this question is by Bernard Holland; and its significance is increased by the fact that Dr Holland himself changed his mind on the matter as a result of trying to make sense of Wesley's views in the context of those of his preachers and early Anglican evangelicals more generally. This problem needs to be explained, because the position of Methodists as the largest beneficiaries of the Evangelical Revival was so important.

The basis for affirming Wesley's belief in baptismal regeneration for infants is his *Treatise on Baptism* of 1756. Although this is largely based on the *Discourse on Baptism* written by his father, Samuel Wesley, in 1700, there is no reason to suppose that it contains views with which John disagreed, particularly as it was modified in certain respects.[3] From the *Treatise* it is clear that John believed that 'infant regeneration is the invariable and unconditional accompaniment of infant baptism'—not on *ex opere operato* grounds, which he regarded as Roman and superstitious—but because 'it is God's free and gracious will to give regeneration to infants when they are baptised'.[4] A careful distinction between the sign and the thing signified was therefore preserved.

On the other hand, the reason for thinking that Wesley changed his mind on the matter is that in the 1786 edition of *The Sunday Service*, prepared for American Methodists, the explicit references to baptismal regeneration in the service for the baptism of infants in the Book of Common Prayer are for the most part removed.[5] Moreover, it is generally agreed that Wesley did not regard the baptism of adults as

---

3 B.J.N. Galliers, 'Baptism in the Writings of John Wesley', *Proceedings of the Wesley Historical Society*, xxxii, 6 (June 1960), 123-4.

4 B.G. Holland, *Baptism in Early Methodism* (London 1970), 59-60.

5 W.F. Swift, 'The Sunday Service of the Methodists', *Proceedings of the Wesley Historical Society*, xxix, 1 (March 1953), 16-19; cf. J.H. Barton and W.F. Swift 'The Sunday Service of the Methodists', *Proceedings of the Wesley Historical Society*, xxxii, 5 (March 1960), 97-101; A.R. George, 'The Means of Grace', in R.E. Davies and G. Rupp (eds), *A History of the Methodist Church in Great Britain*, i (London 1965), 268-9.

unconditionally linked to regeneration.⁶ Thus it is probably not surprising that many nineteenth-century Wesleyans regarded Wesley as having abandoned his earlier belief in baptismal regeneration.

In other words his primary concern was to leave room for preaching the need for a new birth (regeneration) to adults, which he identified not with baptism but with justification. Wesley believed that the grace given in infant baptism could be 'sinned away' (and indeed reckoned that until he was about ten years old he had not done this).⁷ This explains his criticism of certain clergy of the Church of England who, he claimed, departed from the doctrines of the Church in various respects, one of which was that 'they speak of the new birth as an outward thing—as if it were no more than baptism; or, at most, a change from outward wickedness to outward goodness'. He, by contrast, believed the new birth was an inward thing—'a change from inward wickedness to inward goodness; an entire change of our inmost nature from the image of the devil (wherein we were born) to the image of God'.⁸ Perhaps it is significant that on the day following that entry (14 September 1739) he preached in the garden of a house in Islington (the house being too small) and told the assembled company 'how vainly they trusted in baptism for salvation unless they were holy of heart, without which their circumcision was actually become uncircumcision'.⁹

Consequently, however much importance John Wesley attached to baptism, he did not believe it to be essential for salvation: 'if it were (he wrote to the Baptist, Gilbert Boyce), every Quaker must be damned, which I can in no wise believe'.¹⁰ Nevertheless he actually baptized several Quakers himself, and certainly defended baptism against them.¹¹ Baptism marked admission to the covenant—here the older Puritan influence on Wesley was strong; and strictly speaking nothing was necessary to salvation but the mind which was in Christ. On the other hand, the new birth, seen as the consequence of the individual's personal response to God's act of justification, was the necessary precursor of sanctification. This indeed gives the clue to Wesley's main concern, for he saw sanctification as the work of the Spirit. He used the distinction in the New Testament between baptism and the gift of the Spirit to support his

---

6 Holland, *Baptism in Early Methodism*, 45-52; R.E. Davies, 'Our Doctrines', in Davies and Rupp, *History of the Methodist Church*, i, 161.

7 Curnock, *Journal of Wesley*, i, 465. This begins the account of his conversion in May 1738.

8 Ibid, ii, 275.

9 Ibid, ii, 276.

10 J. Telford (ed), *The Letters of the Rev. John Wesley* (London 1931), iii, 36; H. Rack, *Reasonable Enthusiast* (London 1989), 395.

11 For a previously unpublished essay which seems to be addressed to Quakers, see Holland, *Baptism in Early Methodism*, 157-62.

position. It is not surprising, therefore, that his critics—and critics of evangelicals generally—fastened particularly on the claim to a gift of the Spirit distinct from baptism as the identifying mark of enthusiasm.

Daniel Waterland published an essay on regeneration in 1739, apparently to contradict the errors of the Methodists, though he nowhere refers by name to those whose views he is attacking. At the outset he defined regeneration as another word for the new birth of a Christian which, he said, 'means a spiritual change wrought upon any person, by the Holy Spirit, in the use of baptism; whereby he is translated from his natural state in Adam, to a spiritual state in Christ'.[12] In the nature of the case, like baptism, it was unrepeatable, whereas renovation, or the renewal of heart and mind, not only was repeatable but needed to be repeated constantly. If people fell away by desertion and disobedience, their baptismal consecration and consequent covenant state stood, but without their saving effect. Such persons needed not to be born anew but to be reformed; if this were done their regeneration 'before decayed, and as to any saving effect, for the time being well-nigh ruinated, but never totally lost, becomes again whole and entire'.[13] Consequently Waterland regarded it as at the least an improper use of language to call upon those who had been regenerated in infancy by baptism to expect a new birth; they should rather be called upon to repent and reform. It was also mischievous, not only because it confused terms, but more seriously because it might encourage people not to self-examination but to a quest for what they called 'impulses, or inward feelings of the Spirit; which commonly are nothing more than warm fancies, towering imaginations, and self-flattering presumptions'.[14] Worst of all, it led people to claim their own inventions or imaginations as the work of the Spirit. Those who caused most concern were those who were sincere, rather than obvious hypocrites.

Waterland was critical of the way in which some had spoken of the marks of regeneration. They did not, he felt, take sufficient account of the different circumstances in which different people were placed. Must good Christians, who had never experienced any decay of the spiritual life, 'be called upon, to recollect the day, week, month, or year of their conversion, or regeneration, who from their Christian infancy have never been in an unconverted or unregenerate state at all?'[15] He was particularly critical of trusting to inward feelings or secret impulses, unless they were tested by scripture; and significantly he mentioned

---

12 D. Waterland, *Regeneration Stated and Explained according to Scripture and Antiquity* (1739), in W. van Mildert (ed), *The Works of the Revd Daniel Waterland* (Oxford 1823), vi, 343.
13 Ibid, 358-9.
14 Ibid, 366.
15 Ibid, 370.

disobedience to lawful superiors, the breaking of comely order and regularity, and the invasion of other men's provinces as things which would count as evidence of the influence of the god of this world not the God of heaven. So he concluded with a warning against the dangers of passionate religion and a reiteration of the emphasis on the need to preserve, repair or improve the regeneration wrought in infancy by a daily renewing of the inner man and obedience to God's commandments.[16]

The tract was clearly directed against the Methodists, as van Mildert suggested in his 'Introductory Memoir' to Waterland's *Works* nearly a century later. From that moment Methodists have leaped to Wesley's defence. Tyerman in his *Life of Wesley* criticized Waterland's tract as 'immensely learned, but far from luminous; full of talent, but likewise full of error'.[17] It is more likely, however, that Whitefield rather than Wesley was the chief target of Waterland's attack. Waterland's criticisms follow closely those made by Edmund Gibson, Bishop of London, in his pastoral letter of 1 August 1739 of caution against lukewarmness and enthusiasm, which contained ninety quotations from Whitefield's *Journals*.[18] Moreover, Whitefield's first published sermon had been on 'The Nature and Necessity of our New Birth in Christ Jesus', which went through three editions in 1737 and his sermon on 'The Marks of the New Birth' had been widely distributed early in 1739.[19] His readiness to speak of 'baptized heathens'—a phrase which appeared in his *Journal* for 12 April 1739 as well as in his sermon, 'Spiritual Baptism'—was not likely

---

16 Ibid, 372-9.

17 L. Tyerman, *The Life and Times of the Rev. John Wesley* (London 1870), i, 330.

18 This letter was included in John Randolph's *Enchiridion Theologicum* of 1792, and Richard Mant, a keen critic of Methodism, was an admirer of Randolph.

19 L. Tyerman, *The Life of the Rev. George Whitefield* (London 1876), i, 79-83, 275-306; N. Sykes, *Edmund Gibson, Bishop of London* (Oxford 1926), 307-11. The text of these sermons in Whitefield's *Collected Works* was revised from that in the first editions, though the revisions vary in significance. Sermon XLIX, 'On Regeneration', in G. Whitefield, *Sermons on Inportant Subjects* (London 1832), is the 1737 sermon 'The nature and necessity of our new birth in Christ Jesus in order to salvation', first preached at St Mary Redcliff in Bristol, and published in G. Whitefield, *Sermons on Various Subjects* (London 1739), 5-30; and Sermon XLII, 'Marks of having received the Holy Ghost', is essentially the same as 'The Marks of the New Birth' of 1739, first preached at St Mary's Whitechapel, and published in G. Whitefield, *Sermons on Various Subjects* (London 1739), ii, 28-46 (confusingly a different collection from the previous one) and also in G. Whitefield, *The Christian's Companion* (London 1739), 37-55. (The British Library Catalogue gives the text for the separately printed version as Acts 19:5, which is repeated in the 1739 collections, even though it is in fact a misprint for Acts 19:2 which is given in the 1832 collection.)

A New Birth?

to endear him to those of more orthodox disposition.[20] Whitefield's disappearance to Georgia in August 1739 for nearly two years left Wesley as the main target at home. (Nevertheless, Whitefield's suggestion in 1740, when defending himself against critics who resented his statement that Archbishop Tillotson knew no more about true Christianity than Mahomet, that Wesley uttered this sentiment first, ensured that the controversy continued. Tillotson also preached on regeneration, but what made him suspect, apart from the popularity of his sermons, was the suggestion that he preached a gospel of good works.[21]) Wesley, however, seems to have made no reference in his *Journal* or letters to Waterland's tract at all. Although he also preached sermons on 'The Marks of the New Birth' and 'The New Birth' in 1743, they came much later than Whitefield's—though he had preached from John 3:8 as early as 10 June 1739.[22] Gordon Rupp remarked that 'perhaps this doctrine is the least coherent of his doctrines'.[23]

The fact that Wesley failed to make any response to Waterland's criticisms means that we do not know whether he would have found the use of a term such as 'renovation' to describe the process of 'improving one's baptism' as an adult satisfactory or not. It is clear that he attached little importance to confirmation in this context, and despite his voluminous letters and journals it is not known for certain when he was himself confirmed.[24] He did use the terms 'renewal' and 'conversion'—the latter perhaps not as much as an uncritical modern approach might suppose—but in the end was not convinced that alternative terminology was important. In fact, his language was trenchant:

> Lean no more on the staff of that broken reed, that ye *were* born again in baptism. Who denies that ye were then made 'Children of God, and heirs of the kingdom of heaven'? But notwithstanding this, ye are now children of the devil; therefore ye must be born again. And let not Satan put it into your heart to cavil at a word, when the thing is clear. Ye have heard what are the marks of the children of God; all ye

---

20 I. Murray (ed), *George Whitefield's Journals* (London 1960), 249; Whitefield, *Sermons on Important Subjects*, 738.

21 Tyerman, *Life of Whitefield*, i, 360.

22 A.C. Outler (ed), *The Works of John Wesley*, i (Nashville 1984), 415-30; ii (Nashville 1985), 186-201. E.H. Sugden suggested that 'The Marks of the New Birth' was first preached on 2 January 1743 and 'The New Birth' on 29 May 1743; the former was printed in the edition of 1748, but was then overtaken in popularity with the preacher by the latter, which was not published until 1760: E.H. Sugden (ed), *Wesley's Standard Sermons* (London 1921), i, 280; ii, 226. See also Curnock, *Wesley's Journal*, i, 215; iii, 61, 78-9.

23 E.G. Rupp, *Religion in England, 1688-1791* (Oxford 1986), 421.

24 Holland, *Baptism in Early Methodism*, 21, 100-1.

who have them not on your souls, baptized or unbaptized, must needs receive them, or without doubt ye will perish everlastingly.[25]

Hence Wesley, while affirming that infant baptism marked a genuinely new spiritual beginning which could be described as regeneration, nevertheless wished to argue that everyone, whether baptized or not, needed a new spiritual beginning in adulthood, which he also wished to describe as regeneration. Consequently, as Dr Holland remarked, 'in order to lay full stress upon the second re-birth, he stated dogmatically that there is always a lapse into total unregeneracy between the two'.[26] In the final analysis the reason for Wesley's apparent inconsistency, apart from his wish to do justice both to the Thirty-Nine Articles and Homilies of the Church of England, and to Scripture, was an emphasis on the distinction between the inward and outward parts of the sacrament, which was commonplace, and also the unargued assumption that baptism as a word referred to the outward part only. 'Nothing, therefore, is plainer, than that, according to the Church of England, baptism is not the new birth.'[27] Nevertheless he recognized the controversial nature of this claim, for later in the same sermon on 'The New Birth' (1760) he suggests an answer to the sinner who has been taught to say 'I defy your *new doctrine*; I need not be born again. I was born again when I was baptized (emphasis added).'[28] Wesley not only went further than most contemporary Anglicans were prepared to go, but also left a legacy of confusion in sacramental theology which produced the bitter charges and counter-charges of the nineteenth century.

Wesley was not, of course, alone. Dr Holland has shown that other mid-eighteenth century evangelicals affirmed a real benefit in infant baptism whilst at the same time urging that '*past* baptism does not mean a *present* state of salvation'.[29] John Berridge, in *The Christian World Unmasked* (1773), began his discussion of regeneration by contrasting it with morality. Like Whitefield earlier he criticized the anonymous *Whole Duty of Man* (1657), notwithstanding its good intentions, on the ground that morality could only thrive when grounded wholly upon grace.[30] (Nevertheless this was one of the books circulated by the Holy Club, Wesley eventually included it in his *Christian Library*, and the reading of

---

25 Outler, *Wesley's Works*, i, 430.
26 Holland, *Baptism in Early Methodism*, 80.
27 Outler, *Wesley's Works*, ii, 196-7.
28 Ibid, 199.
29 Holland, *Baptism in Early Methodism*, 120.
30 Berridge, *Works*, 335. For an account of *The Whole Duty of Man*, see Spurr, *Restoration Church of England*, 281-96.

it convinced Charles Simeon of his sins.[31]) After pointing out that a century of preaching a gospel of morality had not filled the churches or made the country a safer place to live in, Berridge argued that the doctrine of original sin proved the need of regeneration as well as outward reformation. Thus, although the new birth could be conveyed with baptismal water, 'yet the generality of Christians are not born of the Spirit when baptized with water, because no proof is given of it in their childhood, youth, or manhood'. Like Wesley he invoked the Quakers, but in a rather different way, for he suggested that the nature of the baptized child of a churchman was as 'forward and evil' as that of an unbaptized child belonging to a Quaker. So he concluded that

> The Spirit's birth brings a *meetness* for heaven; it teaches men to offer spiritual sacrifices, but gives no right to pardon, nor any claim to eternal life. These blessings are wholly treasured up in Christ, and *only* are obtained through faith in him.[32]

Regeneration was therefore only a beginning, which had to be completed by the atonement and justification by faith. So Berridge argued that infant baptism had the same blessing as infant circumcision did for the Jews: it brought children within the covenant (i.e. the covenant of grace with Abraham, not the covenant of the Law with Moses), hence it should not be neglected.

In the second decade of the nineteenth century a storm blew up in the Church over the question of baptismal regeneration, and it was slow to blow itself out. At the centre of the storm was Richard Mant, who eventually became Bishop of Killaloe in 1820 and Bishop of Down and Connor in 1824. He was a strong high churchman who in 1810 became rector of Great Coggeshall in Essex at the suggestion of Norris of Hackney, one of the leaders in the early nineteenth-century high church movement. In Coggeshall he found many signs of evangelical activity: he was invited to go to 'extemporaneous prayer-meetings', which he declined to do, offering instead weekday prayers according to the Liturgy—an offer which does not seem to have been taken up.[33] He also found many parishioners who, whilst professing to be members of the Church of England, had never been baptized; and many others who were

---

31 Curnock, *Wesley's Journal*, i, 94-7, ii, 369n, W. Carus, *Memoirs of the Life of the Rev. Charles Simeon, M.A.* (London 1847), 6-10, H.E. Hopkins, *Charles Simeon of Cambridge* (London 1977), 27-8. Simeon's conversion was brought about by reading Bishop Thomas Wilson's *Instruction for the Lord's Supper* (1734).

32 Berridge, *Works*, 343.

33 E. Berens, *A Memoir of the Life of Bishop Mant* (London 1849), 70; J.H. Overton, *The English Church in the Nineteenth Century* (London 1894), 143.

Baptists. His response was to write two short tracts in dialogue form—one on the necessity of baptism, and the other in defence of infant baptism.[34]

In 1812 Mant gave the Bampton Lectures at Oxford under the title, *An Appeal to the Gospel; or, an Inquiry into the Charge that the Gospel is not preached by the National Clergy*. Although they concentrated upon Methodist criticisms of the lack of evangelical preaching in the Church of England, they also explicitly criticized 'some of our own brethren in the ministry, who are attached to certain peculiar tenets, and who in consequence claim the appellation of Evangelical or Gospel preachers'.[35] His lectures take their place in a series of works critical of Anglican Evangelicals, though in his preface Mant said that his work had been completed before the publication of Bishop Tomline's *Refutation of Calvinism* in 1811.[36] They also followed hard on the heels of Viscount Sidmouth's unsuccessful bill to restrict Methodist preachers, and thus came at a time when anxiety in the Church of England about the spread of dissent was reaching a new peak. His opening chapter presumably reflected his experience in Coggeshall. It was concerned with the right interpretation of scripture, and the examples he cited of wrong interpretation were as much concerned with Baptists and Calvinists as Methodists. Indeed, as was to be expected of a high churchman of that date, he did not hesitate to criticize the Church of Rome for misinterpreting and adding to scripture.

In view of the fuss provoked by the later re-publication of two of the lectures as tracts, it is interesting that there were not many reviews of the work. The *Eclectic Review*, however, did not mince its words when after recounting Mant's low view of the intellectual and moral character of the Methodists it commented, 'It is difficult which to admire most, the fatuity or impudence of a preacher, who could venture on such a description as this, in a public lecture, before the University of Oxford'.[37] John Stoughton drily remarked that 'a much more useful work, though bearing signs of strong Church predilections and of dislike to Romanists and sectaries, is Mant's history of the Church of Ireland'.[38] Nevertheless, Mant's defence of the articles and formularies of the Church of England was highly regarded in influential quarters. The Archbishop of Canterbury, Manners Sutton, made him one of his chaplains and he was also given the rectory of St Botolph's, Bishopsgate.

In 1814, on the recommendation of the Shropshire District Committee, the Society for Promoting Christian Knowledge decided to publish the

---

34 Berens, *Memoir of Mant*, 64; R. Mant, *Two Dialogues on Baptism between a Minister of the Church of England and one of his Parishioners* (London 1810).

35 R. Mant, *An Appeal to the Gospel* (5 ed, Oxford 1813), 6.

36 Ibid, vi-vii; Overton, *English Church in the Nineteenth Century*, 185-90.

37 *Eclectic Review*, viii (1812), 1038.

38 J. Stoughton, *History of Religion in England* (2 ed, London 1901), vii, 89.

sixth and seventh lectures on regeneration and conversion as tracts, and circulated them with the annual report for the year. The coincidence that Bishop Samuel Bradford's tract on baptismal and spiritual regeneration went out of print at the same time led many evangelicals to suspect a plot, and a hue and cry developed. The republication of part of Mant's Bampton Lectures as tracts gave them a different significance. Whilst the University of Oxford's election of Mant as Bampton Lecturer was doubtless influenced by his known high churchmanship, the choice of subject was his own. Though probably prompted by his experience of dissent in Coggeshall, he had been contemplating the topic since 1808.[39] The SPCK's decision to publish represents a much more self-conscious attempt to publicise certain views: as the *British Critic* said, the tracts were 'recommended to the Board as a work calculated in the highest degree to promote the objects and views of the Society'.[40] Whether the Shropshire District Committee was particularly high church in outlook is difficult to say, though a county on the Welsh border could not but be aware of the strength of Calvinistic Methodism in north and central Wales. Mant dedicated his tracts to the Revd Hugh Owen, the secretary, and the other members of the Committee, presumably in response to their request for publication. The introduction of district committees into the SPCK in 1810 had been part of the high church coup whereby Joshua Watson's 'Hackney phalanx' gained control of the Society.[41]

Taking John 3:5 as his text for the tract on regeneration, Mant claimed that it was the doctrine of the Bible and of the Church of England that by baptism 'we are made Christians, and are born anew of water and of the Holy Spirit'. Yet, he said,

> this doctrine...is virtually at least, if not actually, denied *by some ministers of our Church*: and *it is* denied in terms which charge the maintainers of it with blindness and ignorance; with innovating on evangelical truth; with being opposers of the doctrine of the Gospel, and patrons of a heathenish superstition.[42]

There followed a detailed discussion of the Prayer Book offices and the Thirty Nine Articles, an examination of scripture and some concluding references to Justin Martyr, Augustine, Hooker, Jeremy Taylor and Waterland. He also criticised the subjectivism of evangelicals: if

---

39 Berens, *Memoir of Mant*, 58-66.

40 *British Critic*, v (1816), 541.

41 Overton, *English Church in the Nineteenth Century*, 190-92; A.B. Webster, *Joshua Watson* (London 1954), 115; H. Cnattingius, *Bishops and Societies* (London 1952), 69-70.

42 R. Mant, *Two Tracts intended to convey correct notions of Regeneration and Conversion according to the sense of Holy Scripture and of the Church of England* (London 1815), 6-7: (words in italics omitted in 1817 edition).

regeneration is not effected by baptism, he argued, it is impossible to say when and by what means it is effected, and

> we are thus left without any other guide, than the very questionable criterion of our own imaginations or our own feelings, to determine, whether we are in possession of that, which our Saviour has pronounced to be an indispensable requisite of salvation.[43]

The second tract on conversion, based on Matthew 18:2-3, criticized the claim 'that every Christian whatever must experience a conversion to be in a state of salvation'[44] and the emphasis placed by Whitefield and others on rapid or instantaneous conversions. In particular, he condemned Whitefield's assertion that

> in every Christian congregation there are two sorts of people, some that know Christ, and some that do not know him, some that are converted, and some that are strangers to conversion

as a conceit unwarranted by revelation, and disclaimed by reason and experience (the classic sources for Anglican theology).[45] Furthermore he cited Bishop Randolph's view that Scripture did not call clergy to divide their hearers into the classes of converted and unconverted:

> That among men baptized as Christians, (Randolph had said in a Charge of 1808), taught from their infancy to believe the doctrines and practise the duties of Christianity, a special conversion also at some period of their life is necessary to stamp them true Christians, is an unheard-of thing in the Gospel, and is plainly a novel institution of man.[46]

John Randolph was first Bishop of Oxford, and then Bishop of Bangor before becoming Bishop of London from 1809 to 1813. He had ordained Mant, and Mant's Bampton Lectures were dedicated to him.

Whilst Mant's Bamptons had passed with very little comment, very few religious periodicals failed to notice the two tracts. The centre of attention was what the *Eclectic Review* called 'this monstrous dogma, that we are made Christians by baptism'.[47] But the *Methodist Magazine* scored a double hit at Mant and the SPCK when picking up Mant's sentence

---

43 Ibid, 22-23.
44 Ibid, 60.
45 Ibid, 61, quoting Whitefield, *Works*, v, 338.
46 Ibid, 64, quoting J. Randolph, *Charge delivered to the Clergy of the Diocese of Bangor at his Primary Visitation* (Bangor 1808), 16.
47 *Eclectic Review*, viii (1815), 1046.

It was the supernatural earthquake, and the composure, little less supernatural, of Paul and Silas, which forced from the jailor at Thyateira his earnest enquiry, 'Sirs, what shall I do to be saved?'[48]

Passing over the fact that Mant declined to attribute the conversion to the operation of the Spirit of God, the reviewer went on, 'Here the poor Methodist will naturally ask, "Who was the Jailor of *Thyateira*?.... With the history of the Jailor of Philippi, I am well acquainted."' The explanation, he suggested, perhaps lay in the fact that in a Cambridge Stereotype edition of the New Testament distributed by the SPCK, the running title for Acts 16 was 'Paul and Silas imprisoned at Thyateira' and that Mr Mant, having only a superficial acquaintance with the Scriptures, looked no further than the top of the page.[49]

Evangelical Anglicans also joined in. Charles Simeon distinguished between the sacraments as means of grace and means of salvation. Douglas Webster has suggested that Simeon thought of baptism 'as something objective, but objective in a covenant sense and therefore not unconditional'.[50] In his series of University Sermons of 1811 on 'The Excellency of the Liturgy' he had defended evangelical love of the liturgy in general and the baptismal service in particular, defending the charitable and comprehensive language of the Prayer Book by reference to similar language in scripture.[51] His University Sermon at Cambridge on 19 November 1815 on the new birth was one in another series under the general title 'An Appeal to Men of Wisdom and Candour', and seems to have been specifically intended to correct the accusations made by Mant.

Thus he took care to deny that the new birth meant a sudden impulse of the Spirit such that the day and the hour could be specified (thereby meeting Waterland's criticism). He also denied that the Spirit's action was irresistible, 'for man is in all cases a free agent; he is never wrought upon as a mere machine'. Nevertheless, on the basis of John 3 he claimed that the new birth was necessary to salvation and that it could not be identified with baptism. Jesus, he felt, drew a clear distinction between being born of water and being born of the Spirit, and his comparison of the new birth with the wind of the Spirit in his conversation with Nicodemus did not make sense if it was identical with baptism. The issue in Simeon's view turned on what was meant by regeneration. He agreed that baptism

---

48 Mant, *Two Tracts*, 69-70.

49 *Methodist Magazine*, xxxix (1816), 275-6.

50 D. Webster, 'Simeon's Pastoral Theology', in A. Pollard and M. Hennell (eds), *Charles Simeon* (London 1959), 108.

51 W.J.C. Ervine, 'Doctrine and Diplomacy: Some Aspects of the Life and Thought of the Anglican Evangelical Clergy, 1797-1837', unpublished Cambridge Ph.D. thesis, 1979, 59.

introduced people to a new state, which gave them 'a right and title to all the blessings of salvation'; he agreed that all adults baptized into Christ in penitence and faith had the remission of their sins sealed to them and received the Holy Spirit in a more abundant measure; he agreed that 'infants dedicated to God in baptism *may* and sometimes *do* (though in a way not discoverable by us, except by the fruits) receive a new nature from the Spirit of God, *in*, and *with*, and *by* that ordinance'. But he regarded as 'a fundamental error' the view that '*all persons* do *necessarily* by a divine appointment receive the Holy Ghost in such manner and degree as really to be changed in the spirit of their minds into the very image of God in righteousness and true holiness, and so to partake of the divine nature that they never need afterwards to seek so great a change again'. In other words, baptism was a change of state, 'for by it we become entitled to all the blessings of the new covenant', but it is not a change of nature. A change of nature may be communicated at the same time, but the ordinance does not communicate it; and he saw the solution to the controversy in a proper distinction between the sign and the thing signified.[52]

Finally, he took the accusations of enthusiasm levelled at the evangelicals back to those who identified baptism with the new birth. Such a position, he suggested, made the new birth sudden, irresistible, without any co-operation on our part, arbitrary according to the will of man (*contra* John 1:13), so determinable in point of time that anyone could consult the baptismal register in order to find out, and carrying an assurance not only without evidence but in the face of all imaginable evidence to the contrary. Who, he asked, were the enthusiasts now? Simeon's primary concern, as Webster pointed out, was to preserve the morality of the sacraments. An emphasis on an entire change of heart and life was likely to stir people to righteousness and true holiness; the identification of baptism with the new birth was likely to lull people to sleep in their evil ways. He concluded with an appeal to experience: if his hearers recognized that the current of their affections still flowed according to the bias of their corrupt nature, then notwithstanding their baptism they were still unrenewed. Simeon was, therefore, prepared to talk about baptismal regeneration so long as regeneration was not identified with conversion.[53]

A rather different intervention from a moderate evangelical came from one of those who owed his faith to Simeon, J.B. Sumner, a schoolmaster at Eton who was later Bishop of Chester and Archbishop of Canterbury. His book, *Apostolical Preaching considered*, was a more general response

---

52 A. Pollard, *Let Wisdom Judge: University Addresses and Sermon Outlines by Charles Simeon* (London 1959), 51, 53-4, 55, 58.

53 Ibid, 59, 60, 62; Pollard and Hennell, *Charles Simeon*, 110-11; Proby, *Annals of the 'Low-Church' Party*, i, 215-8.

to the development of Calvinistic preaching in the Church of England, which in this context meant an emphasis on election as the way of understanding the availability of grace. He knew that his subject was controversial, but he did not write 'either to defend or confute', and reverenced no party. He was aware that he was discussing 'some questions, upon which it becomes us to inquire humbly, rather than to decide positively', but his object was 'practical utility'.[54] His chapter on grace led inevitably into a discussion of baptism: and it is important to note that the text underwent various changes in the nine editions of the book, which would make a study in itself. On the basis of various texts from St Paul, Sumner was clear that 'grace was given to all who are dedicated to Christ in baptism'.[55] Hence he rejected the idea that there was special grace which St Paul had failed to mention; and he also denied that there was another test of God's favour beyond and subsequent to the covenant of baptism. Sumner therefore affirmed that 'our Church identifies regeneration and baptism' on the basis of the language in the Prayer Book.[56] The first edition contained a long footnote at this point, noting that all depended here on the definition of 'regeneration'. If, as in Doddridge, regeneration meant 'so being born of God as to receive Christ, overcome the world and sin not', baptism was not Scripture regeneration; 'but if it be interpreted as signifying an exemption from the penalty of Adam's sin by admission into the covenant of Christ, it does take place at baptism', and that was the sense in which the Church of England used the word. 'Particularly it should be observed,' he added, 'that this latter is the only sense in which it can be said to take place *at a definite time.*'[57]

Sumner went on to say that there were problems of 'plain understanding or a timid conscience' if people were told that the sinfulness or innocency of their actions did not depend on whether they were permitted or forbidden by the divine law, but whether they were in a regenerate or unregenerate state at the time they were doing them. On the one hand the Church told them that they were regenerate, and on the other the preacher treated them as though they were not: but 'let not the salvation of a flock hang upon their rightly understanding a difficult

---

54 [J.B. Sumner], *Apostolical Preaching considered in an Examination of St Paul's Epistles* (London 1815), v-vi.

55 Ibid, 128-9. By the ninth edition (London 1850) this had become 'grace sufficient to salvation is denied to none, to whom the offer of salvation is made through faith in Christ Jesus, and who are united to him in baptism', 150.

56 Ibid, 137. In the ninth edition, this was 'our Church considers Baptism as conveying regeneration', 160.

57 Ibid, 137. This footnote was omitted in the ninth edition, and the argument on the same point moved to 167-71.

term, or seeing their way clearly through the unrevealed will of God'.[58] In the 9th edition he sharpened and clarified the intervening argument, saying that there might be a danger 'in addressing a congregation collectively as *regenerate*, since the term has neither been accurately defined in Scripture, nor restricted to one sense in the common language of divines'.[59] He also thought it wrong to call people to some renovation or transformation which had to take place 'at a definite time and in a sensible or memorable manner'.[60] The mistake was to assume that there was a uniform pattern applicable to everyone, which he thought was necessarily implied if the phrase 'new birth' was used. He acknowledged that some of those baptized as infants revolted from the obedience which they owed to God, but many did not; indeed many more might be saved 'if parents and sponsors universally made the baptism of infants a spiritual service, and accompanied it with that prayer of faith which is expected and taken for granted by the Church'.[61] Nevertheless the conclusion was the same: the problem with the doctrine of special grace was that

> it absolutely nullifies the sacrament of baptism. It reduces it to an empty rite, an external mark of admission into the visible church, atttended with no real grace, and therefore conveying no real benefit, nor advancing a person one step towards salvation.[62]

Moreover Sumner believed that there was a human role in co-operating with divine grace, and he firmly backed the Remonstrants at the Synod of Dort in this respect, saying that they had St Paul on their side. Indeed, if human beings were entirely passive in the work of salvation they could never fall away. Hence he denied the doctrines of final perseverance and assurance, noting in a footnote that 'Both this point, and final perseverance and regeneration, have been recently treated by Mr Mant, in a manner which leaves little to be added'.[63] It is noteworthy that the emphasis in the first edition was very much on the appeal to common sense philosophy, although the classic Anglican divines, from Hooker, through Butler to Paley, were mentioned. By the ninth edition the emphasis had shifted much more firmly to the Anglican divines. Sumner's book is credited with persuading both Newman and Gladstone

---

58 Ibid, 139-40; cf 9 ed, 162-3 amended.
59 Sumner, *Apostolical Preaching* (9 ed), 166.
60 Ibid, 167.
61 Ibid, 171.
62 Sumner, *Apostolical Preaching* (1 ed), 146. The phrase 'absolutely nullifies the sacrament of baptism' was omitted in the ninth ed, 176.
63 Ibid, 163. This footnote disappeared in subsequent editions.

A New Birth? 41

of baptismal regeneration.[64] The ninth edition was much more nuanced in its language—in some cases modifying the directness of identification of baptism and regeneration in an evangelical direction, in others implying that a sacramental understanding of baptism did not depend on a high church approach.

It is perhaps not surprising that the evangelical *Christian Observer* was not completely persuaded by all his interpretations, though its overall verdict was positive.[65] Other evangelicals were more hostile to Mant, with John Scott and T.T. Biddulph leading the way.[66] One point which was made again and again was that Mant's doctrine came perilously close to the kind of *ex opere operato* view of the sacraments which was regarded as Popish and superstitious. Thomas Biddulph, like others, emphasized that the Catechism taught that the sacraments were *generally* necessary for salvation, and argued that the benefits of baptism were conditional upon repentance and faith.[67] When a second edition of Mant's tracts was published in 1817 a number of alterations were made.[68] One of them touched this point. In the first edition Mant had written that not only are all real Christians regenerate by the Holy Spirit

> but that those also are so regenerated, to whom baptism is rightly administered, notwithstanding by their future conduct that they may forfeit the privileges of their new birth.[69]

This was amended in the second edition to read

> those also are so regenerated, who receive baptism rightly, or, what in the case of infants at least in a Christian country, amounts to the same thing, to whom baptism is rightly administered...

Although the controversy rumbled on, for most evangelical Anglicans these concessions were satisfactory. A small group of six or so Anglican

---

64 N. Scotland, *John Bird Sumner, Evangelical Archbishop* (Leominster 1995), 16. For Newman, see T.L. Sheridan, *Newman on Justification* (Staten Island, NY 1967), 82-8, 97-108, 117-34; for Gladstone, see D.W. Bebbington, *William Ewart Gladstone: Faith and Politics in Victorian Britain* (Grand Rapids 1993), 34-5 and M.R.D. Foot (ed), *The Gladstone Diaries*, i, 1825-1832 (Oxford 1968), 228-30: he copied out several extracts on baptism between 22 February and 2 March 1829.

65 *Christian Observer* (1815), 327.

66 For some account of this, see Ervine, 'Doctrine and Diplomacy', 60-74.

67 T. Biddulph, *Baptism: a seal of the Christian Covenant* (London 1816), cf L.P. Fox, 'The Work of the Revd Thomas Tregenna Biddulph, with special reference to his influence on the evangelical movement in the West of England', unpublished Cambridge Ph.D. thesis 1953, 100-8.

68 Listed in *Christian Observer*, xvi (1817), 429-30 by J.S. (John Scott?)

69 Mant, *Two Tracts*, 7.

clergymen in the west of England, including Biddulph's curate at Durston, seceded because they could not longer accept infant baptism. They were the first of a steady trickle of men who left the Church of England to establish what they felt to be a more scriptural Church, of whom the leaders of the Brethren are the best known.[70] But it left lasting marks. Mant's biographer remarked that the controversy gave occasion

> for the publication of that learned, able, and most satisfactory book, a 'General View of the Doctrine of Regeneration in Baptism' by Dr Bethell, a book calculated to do as much towards setting at rest the controversy on Baptism, as had been effected with respect to the other Sacrament by Waterland's 'View of the Doctrine of the Eucharist'.[71]

Ironically that was written a year before the Gorham Judgement!

Despite the vigorous evangelical response to Mant, the accusations against the Methodists persisted. When William van Mildert, Bishop of Llandaff (and later of Durham), published his edition of the *Collected Works of Daniel Waterland* in 1823, he did not mince his words in explaining the origin of Waterland's tract on regeneration. At that time, he said, Wesley and Whitefield had drawn multitudes after them 'by their fanatical views of the gospel system'. Their understanding of regeneration was the groundwork of a 'delusive scheme of spiritual experiences, or inward perceptible motions of the Spirit'. Their separation of spiritual regeneration from baptismal regeneration rendered baptism 'in effect, a nugatory and unavailing ordinance', and led believers to seek for some other proof of actual regeneration:

> This proof their disciples were taught to expect in the perception of certain divine impulses, or impressions immediately proceeding from the Spirit of God, and the influence of which it would be impossible for them to resist... Their harmony of opinion on this point seems to be still the main bond of union between the two great parties of Wesley's and Whitfield's (sic) followers; and when such a persuasion has once got possession of the mind, it sets reasoning at defiance. It opens an inlet to every wild imagination; and by making the whole of vital religion to depend only upon internal feelings, renders it amenable to no higher authority than that of the individual himself.[72]

It is significant that van Mildert's concern was not only with subversion of reason or 'reasoning', but also with the undermining of (ecclesiastical)

---

70 See Fox, 'T.T. Biddulph', 108-21; C. Hole, *A Manual of English Church History* (London 1910), 391-92; H.H. Rowdon, 'Secession from the Established Church in the early nineteenth century', *Vox Evangelica*, iii (1964), 78-80; *Christian Observer*, xviii (1819), 31-55.

71 Berens, *Memoir of Mant*, 70.

72 Van Mildert, *Waterland's Works*, i, pt I, 180-1.

authority in religion. He specifically referred to the 'recent controversies', suggesting that these made reference to the tract timely. Nothing was more conformable with the Scriptures, the Articles and Formularies of the Church of England than this tract; nor had anyone ever attempted to controvert it, either when it was first published or more recently. This kind of attack on Methodists was not new: Shute Barrington, in his inaugural charge to the clergy of Salisbury in 1783, said that the evangelicals' lack of restraint threatened to undermine the basis of government and society itself.[73]

The Revd Thomas Jackson, one of the leading Wesleyan ministers of the second generation, attacked van Mildert's characterisation of Wesley's doctrine in the *Wesleyan Methodist Magazine* for 1824. His attack was twofold. First, he denied that Wesley's (and Whitefield's) view of regeneration was novel; indeed he cited Archbishop Leighton, Bishop Hopkins and Bishop Pearson in its support. Secondly, he enumerated the scriptural marks of regeneration and said that, if the connection between baptism and regeneration was a necessary one, the issue became a simple question of fact: did the actual conduct of the millions of baptized persons in 'the christian world' demonstrate that they all showed the marks of regeneration? Since the answer was obviously No, there was 'no necessary and inseparable connexion between the administration of baptism, and that renewal of human nature which our blessed Lord describes as a "birth from above"'.[74] He went on to cite Paul's words in 1 Corinthians 1:17 that Christ sent him not to baptize but to preach the gospel as evidence of the proper priority of the latter over the former, and like most evangelical critics of baptismal regeneration he referred to the story of Simon Magus in Acts 8 as showing that baptism in the name of Christ had not delivered him from the gall of bitterness and the bond of iniquity.

Jackson then turned to the question of whether Wesley and Whitefield had really made baptism a 'nugatory and unavailing ordinance'. His defence was twofold: first, that Wesley had affirmed baptismal regeneration in the case of infants, though not invariably in the case of adults, citing the sermons which have already been quoted; and secondly, that whether or not baptismal regeneration was denied, baptism served many important purposes 'without being an infallible means of conveying a new nature to the minds of those who are its subjects'. Similarly, he argued that the opposite position flew in the face of various scriptural texts about the dire consequences of sin and even threatened to become essentially antinomian in its consequences; for it could be argued

---

73 D. Spaeth, 'The enemy within', in Gregory and Chamberlain, *National Church in Local Perspective*, 142-3.

74 T. Jackson, 'A defence of Mr Wesley and of his doctrines', *Wesleyan Methodist Magazine*, xlvii (1824), 445.

that someone who lived a life of piety but happened not to have been baptized would have no share in the birth from above, whereas someone who had been baptized and had yet lived 'in the daily practice of the most atrocious crimes' was a child of God and an heir of glory. 'But, in the mean time', he asked, 'what becomes of the moral government of God?'[75]

Jackson's second letter a month later was concerned to differentiate between Wesley and Whitefield, particularly over the latter's Calvinism, and to rebut van Mildert's charges about the way in which the two understood the operation of the Holy Spirit. Wesley was certainly concerned to inculcate the religion of the heart, but that did not depend upon feelings or the imagination, but upon scripture and conscience. He showed that Wesley's doctrine was derived from the formularies and homilies of the Church of England, and concluded that van Mildert had never studied Wesley's writings carefully:

> Had he ever perused those admirable works, even in a slight and desultory manner, he would never have represented Mr Wesley as holding the Calvinistic doctrine of election, of irresistible grace, and of the unconditional perseverance of the saints. He found the charge of enthusiasm preferred against him by such men as Warburton and Lavington, and repeated in more modern times, even to satiety, but without explanation, and therefore without proof, by the Poet Laureate; and appears passively to have acquiesced the general voice, without exercising that manly independence of thought, for which his Lordship is so admirably qualified.[76]

In censuring Wesley's doctrine of spiritual experiences van Mildert was condemning the Church of England of which he was himself a member; like all blessings they were liable to abuse, but the abuse of something was no argument against the thing itself or its legitimate use.

Canon Overton claimed that this controversy over baptismal regeneration was 'really part of the Calvinistic controversy'[77] in the sense that the 'Calvinists', such as R. Hawker, held that a conscious sense of pardon and peace with God was necessary to the justified state whereas the 'orthodox' held that there was no such thing as a second birth which took place after the one in baptism. If the issue had simply been one in which all those on one side were Calvinists, then such a judgement might be valid. But Overton, like those about whom he wrote, tended to assume that anyone who denied baptismal regeneration was a Calvinist. This reflected the general ignorance of the continental Reformation in the Church of England at this period. However, Robert Wilberforce in the

---

75 Ibid, 445-50.
76 Ibid, 527.
77 Overton, *English Church*, 190. This view is echoed, without amplification, in P. Nockles, *The Oxford Movement in Context* (Cambridge 1994), 229.

next generation said that John Scott was an unanswerable witness when he asserted that Calvin's theory and the doctrine of baptismal grace were not irreconcilable.[78] In any case, the linkage with the Calvinistic controversy ignores the fact that the primary target of Mant's criticism (and indeed van Mildert in his introduction to Waterland's *Works*) was Wesley's Methodism, which was definitely not Calvinistic! What actually made these controversies more than academic was the fact that they related directly to the contemporary religious experience of the time—in this case the need of the Church of England to respond to the Evangelical Revival.

---

78 R. Wilberforce, *The Doctrine of Holy Baptism* (2 ed, London 1849), 2.

CHAPTER 3

Baptists and the Evangelical Revival

The discussion outlined in the previous chapter was among people who all shared a belief in the rightness of infant baptism. But, as the first chapter showed, infant baptism, whilst remaining the majority practice, had ceased to be universal in post-Reformation Britain. The Radical Reformation made a sharper distinction between the local community and the gathered Christian community than the other churches. For them Christian life depended upon a personal commitment of faith which could not be made by anyone else on an individual's behalf. It followed that if this personal commitment was to represented symbolically by the act of baptism then this must be by believer's baptism. But many radical Reformers—including many Baptists—did not regard baptism as necessary to the life of faith at all. Quakers represented the extreme here, rejecting all sacramental acts as unnecessary for the Christian life.

In the early eighteenth century, however, this radical upsurge seemed to have become a spent force. Baptists and Quakers had become more defensive and introspective: the threat to religious orthodoxy seemed to come from elsewhere, socinianism and unitarianism within, and deism and scepticism without. The Evangelical Revival brought the question of baptism back into theological debate in a new way, which particularly affected the dissenting churches with a Calvinist theology. There was also a sharpening of the division between Independents and Baptists on the right form of baptism, which meant that those congregations in which it remained an open question gradually became a small minority.

The division between baptists and paedobaptists went back to the early seventeenth century. However, the difference between those who retained a Calvinist theology and those who did not (and there were baptists on both sides of this divide) was more important for much of the eighteenth century. Those with an Arminian theology who had reacted against the harsh views of predestination, and especially double predestination, tended to move in a Socinian direction and away from an orthodox belief in the divinity of Christ. The fact that the Wesleys were self-professed Arminians therefore made them suspect to many Calvinists. Nevertheless, the Wesleys' commitment to itinerant evangelism was new—at least on the organised scale with which it was practised, and there seems to have been a more general shift among late eighteenth-century dissenters in favour of such a policy.

Traditionally, the explanation of this has been found in theological change, and particularly the moderate Calvinism represented by the publication of Andrew Fuller's book, *The Gospel Worthy of All Acceptation*, in 1785. Fuller was a Particular Baptist minister in Kettering who was very much involved in the Northamptonshire Association and the foundation of the Baptist Missionary Society. Deryck Lovegrove has argued that more pragmatic considerations may have been at work, pointing both to the fact that Congregationalists underwent a similar change without any obvious book to hang it upon, and that there were seventeenth-century precedents for itinerant activity among Baptists and Congregationalists anyway.[1] Whilst Fuller's role may have been exaggerated, it remains true that he and those of like mind had to work hard to convince high-Calvinists, especially among the Baptists of London and East Anglia; and Fuller did draw significantly upon Jonathan Edwards's *Enquiry into the Freedom of the Will* (1754), which specifically argued that Arminian criticisms that Calvinism destroyed personal moral responsibility were wrong.[2] The work of Edwards in New England and also of Isaac Watts at home had therefore inhibited the development of high-Calvinism among English Congregationalists.

But the Revival also produced new kinds of Baptist. On the one hand, there were the General Baptists of the New Connexion. Beginning in north-west Leicestershire and spreading from there in all directions in the midlands and north of England, this grouping was a characteristic product of the Revival in its social composition, evangelical theology and itinerant spirit. It was perhaps the nearest thing in Britain to the revivalist baptist congregations formed on the American Frontier as the Great Awakening moved west across the Appalachians. Their founder, Dan Taylor, was ordained by a General Baptist minister because Taylor was an Arminian in theology. But although he retained links with the old General Baptists for a number of years, he gradually separated from them because of their tendency towards unitarianism. Hence the New Connexion drew into its fellowship in the early nineteenth century a number of old General Baptist churches that had not been tempted by unitarianism. On the other hand, in Scotland and Ireland, which previously had had little experience of independency, there were various secessions and disruptions which led to the formation of independent congregations, some of which became Baptist. Presbyterian church order was criticised because the New Testament evidence for its binding nature

---

1 D.W. Lovegrove, *Established Church, Sectarian People: Itinerancy and the Transformation of English Dissent, 1780-1830* (Cambridge 1988), 17-31.

2 B. Stanley, *The History of the Baptist Missionary Society* (Edinburgh 1992), 3-5; cf. J. Edwards, *Freedom of the Will* (ed P. Ramsay: New Haven 1957), 432-5.

was regarded as insufficient, and those independents who moved in a baptist direction did so because of similar doubts about the New Testament basis for infant baptism by sprinkling.

How widespread was this concern about baptism? Was it a private debate among a few ministers or did it extend more widely? Obviously the debate in the sense of published material is confined to a very small number of people. The ground for regarding it as significant lies in the fact that books, pamphlets and tracts were being written on baptism in the early nineteenth century, whereas thirty years before they were not. Publication was a response to the fact that the issues were being debated among Christians; and some indication of this is seen in the growth of the Baptists during the period, and also in the divisions that produced new Baptist congregations. As far as the growth of Baptists in general is concerned it is fair to point out (from the rather scrappy statistical information available) that the Baptists seem to have grown as fast as, but no faster than, the Independents. This may suggest that the question of baptism was irrelevant for their growth: but it also means that it was no obstacle to it.

Moreover, although the Evangelical Revival is often regarded as essentially undenominational, it is clear that baptism was always a sensitive point.[3] In the area of foreign missions, the fact that the Baptist Missionary Society was the first modern missionary society to be founded in 1792, meant that the (London) Missionary Society founded in 1795 did not have to face the question of baptism—though Anglican doubts about churchmanship led to the foundation of the Church Missionary Society in 1799. In the area of evangelical work at home, baptism could be a sensitive issue when Baptists and Independents wanted to work together in itinerant evangelism: a resolution of the London Itinerant Society in 1798 said that it was better for baptists and paedobaptists to work together in societies of their own persuasion.[4] It is not plausible therefore to suppose that people became Baptists without knowing what they were doing.

In the period 1800-1830 both non-Anglicans and Anglicans were involved in controversies in which baptism came to the fore, and in each case the Evangelical Revival significantly affected the way in which they were articulated and discussed. For Scottish and Irish Presbyterians and English nonconformists the controversy primarily concerned the old question of whether baptism should be confined to believers or extended to infants. It had a new force (and sometimes bitterness) because the authority of seventeenth-century confessions of faith was now set against scripture, whereas they had been formulated on the assumption that they

---

3 See D.M. Thompson, *Denominationalism and Dissent, 1795-1835: a question of identity* (Dr Williams's Library: London 1985), 10-17.

4 Lovegrove, *Established Church, Sectarian People*, 32-37.

summarised scriptural doctrine. Alongside this question went a second, concerned with what was called 'mixed' or 'open' communion, i.e. whether admission to communion should be confined to those baptized as believers. This question was debated among the English Particular Baptists, but it did raise the related question of whether baptism was necessary for communion, or indeed church membership, at all, and that question also involved Congregationalists and Presbyterians. For Anglicans the focus of attention was rather different, namely the relation of baptismal regeneration to conversion or new birth, as discussed in the previous chapter. It was largely the result of a high church reaction against the growth of nonconformity outside the Church and evangelicalism within it. But it was able to exploit the ambiguity of John Wesley's teaching, and as such had particular implications for Methodists.

English Baptists emerged from the separatist movement in the late Elizabethan Church, insisting that a 'gathered' church (rather than an all-inclusive parish) was the New Testament model of the church. From there it was but a short step to insisting that baptism was for believers only, though most Independents remained paedobaptist. John Smyth and Thomas Helwys rejected Calvinism in their *Declaration of Faith* of 1611 by asserting that 'God would have all men saved'. Thus the earliest English Baptists were called General Baptists, because they believed that Christ died for all.[5] The Particular Baptists first came to public attention with the publication of their *Confession* of 1644, with its clear affirmation of the points of Calvinist orthodoxy established at the Synod of Dort (1618). Their origins lay in rigorist movements within Independent congregations in London, which began with protests against members having their children baptized in parish churches and led to a conviction that only believer's baptism could be justified from scripture.[6] Rather later they came to the view that the proper mode of baptism was by immersion. It needs to be remembered that, although the use of the name 'Baptist' to describe the group implies a special emphasis on baptism, in fact for both groups of Baptists commitment to believer's baptism by immersion was only one of a cluster of beliefs which made them a distinct group. Others included beliefs about the nature of the church, the role of the ministry, and the relation of church and state.

For both groups the belief about baptism depended essentially on the view that this was what a right interpretation of scripture required. That unanimity existed alongside a diversity of view as to whether baptism was necessary for church membership or admission to communion. General Baptists tended to insist on 'closed communion' and 'closed

---

5 B.R. White, *The English Baptists of the Seventeenth Century* (London 1983), 21-27.

6 Ibid, 58-62.

membership' (i.e. baptism by immersion was a prerequisite for participation), whereas some Particular Baptists moved from that position in the later seventeenth century to practise 'open communion' and 'open membership' (i.e. baptism by immersion was not a prerequisite for participation).[7] This was not so paradoxical as it might seem, for the Calvinist belief in election was compatible with laying less emphasis on the outward rite, whereas the greater emphasis on personal response in the Arminian tradition of the General Baptists made the act of baptism more important.

For English Baptists, therefore, there was no necessary link between baptism and the understanding of conversion or regeneration; and the relationship between baptism and communion and church membership was also an open question. In effect the Evangelical Revival did not so much reopen these questions as give them a new urgency in the wider context of outward looking evangelism.

The situation was different north of the border in Scotland, and over the water in Ireland. Apart from a brief period of activity while Cromwell's army was in Scotland during the Commonwealth, there is no evidence of Baptist activity before the eighteenth century. Indeed, in 1672 a Scottish law made it compulsory for every child to be baptized within thirty days of birth.[8] The Scotch Baptists began through the work of Robert Carmichael and Archibald M'Lean. Carmichael was an Anti-Burgher Seceder Presbyterian minister who left that church and became a pastor of the Glasite church in Glasgow in 1762, and M'Lean was a Glasgow printer who had joined the same church after leaving the Church of Scotland. (John Glas believed that Christ's Kingdom was purely spiritual and that a national church could not therefore be justified on New Testament grounds: the only appropriate form of church polity was local independence.) In 1763 both men left the Glasites after a disciplinary dispute and by 1764 they had come to believe that believer's baptism by immersion was alone scriptural. The first Scotch Baptist church was formed in Edinburgh in November 1765 with Carmichael as pastor. The movement grew and spread into England and North Wales in the 1790s.[9] From the first the emphasis of these churches was on a restoration of New Testament Christianity, and this led to some rather acrimonious disputes on what the New Testament did and did not oblige Christians to follow.

---

7 Ibid, 7-12.

8 D.W. Bebbington (ed), *The Baptists in Scotland* (Glasgow 1988), 10-12; G. Yuille (ed), *History of the Baptists in Scotland* (Glasgow 1926), 24-37.

9 Yuille, *Baptists in Scotland*, 44-50; W. Jones (ed), *The Works of Mr Archibald M'Lean with a Memoir of his Life and Writings*, vi (London 1823), xx-xxii, liv, lxxvii-viii.

As in England, however, the development of itinerant evangelism brought matters to a head. The impetus here did not come from the Scotch Baptists, but rather from various sections of opinion in the Church of Scotland and the Secession Church. Two brothers, Robert and James Haldane, were the leading figures. Both had served at sea, Robert in the Navy and James with the East India Company. In the mid-1790s each of them independently was aroused to a sense of the urgency of evangelistic work. Between 1795 and 1799 Robert pursued an ultimately abortive campaign to establish a mission in Bengal, while during the same period James first engaged in the distribution of tracts when he accompanied Charles Simeon on his tour of the highlands in July 1796 and then became involved in itinerant lay preaching from May 1797.[10]

Following a successful preaching tour in the north of Scotland during the summer of 1797, James Haldane and his friends formed a Society for Propagating the Gospel at Home at a meeting in Edinburgh on 20 December 1797, with an inaugural general meeting on 11 January 1798. The Church of Scotland was as unenthusiastic about field preaching as its sister establishment in England; but there was considerable support for the idea nevertheless. The Edinburgh Missionary Society, founded in 1796, supported Robert Haldane's scheme for Bengal and tried to persuade the General Assembly to take an initiative. Greville Ewing, minister of Lady Glenorchy's Chapel in Edinburgh, became editor of the Society's *Missionary Magazine* in 1796; in 1797-98 he reported on the itinerant preaching which had begun in Scotland and gave it his support.[11] The result of all this was a significant evangelical revival in Scotland, but the Church of Scotland condemned those involved in 1799; and this led to the emergence of Scottish Congregationalism. Ewing had withdrawn from the Church of Scotland before the condemnation of itinerant preaching, and became minister of the church founded in Glasgow in 1800, where he also became involved in the training of new preachers.[12] At about the same time Ralph Wardlaw, who had been in training for the ministry of the Secession Church, became a Congregationalist and, after serving as an itinerant preacher for three years, became minister of a new church formed as a daughter congregation of Ewing's in Glasgow.[13]

---

10 A. Haldane, *The Lives of Robert Haldane and James Alexander Haldane* (5 ed., Edinburgh 1855), 25-35, 42-59, 70-73, 83-87, 90-114, 126-42.

11 Ibid, 143-79; J.J. Matheson, *Memoir of Greville Ewing* (London 1843), 71-166; A.L. Drummond and J. Bulloch, *The Scottish Church, 1688-1843* (Edinburgh 1973), 151-3.

12 Matheson, *Memoir of Ewing*, 177-251; H. Escott, *A History of Scottish Congregationalism* (Glasgow 1960), 61-77.

13 W.L. Alexander, *Memoirs of the Life and Writings of Ralph Wardlaw, D.D.* (Edinburgh 1856), 45-69.

Ewing, who has been called 'the architect and builder of modern Scottish Congregationalism',[14] and Wardlaw were to be the leaders of the churches which did not follow the Haldane brothers when they changed their convictions about baptism in 1808, although the division was not on that matter alone. The primary concern of the Haldane brothers was evangelism, and they had no strong views on church polity.[15] Ewing, however, in justifying his new position argued the case for independency from the New Testament, and this opened up the question of how far New Testament practice and apostolic example should be followed. The continuing influence of the ideas of John Glas, who had argued that the scriptural pattern of church order should be followed to the letter, and of Archibald M'Lean, the founder of the Scotch Baptists, was significant here. Alexander Haldane maintained that the Haldane brothers were always critical of Glas and M'Lean because of their narrowness, and suggested that Ewing was attracted by certain Glasite ideas: Ewing alleged the opposite. Significantly, the first problem arose over what was called social worship, i.e. the practice of mutual exhortation whereby any member could stand and exhort the congregation during public worship. Ewing supported the idea of mutual testimony during meetings for fellowship on weekdays, but when James Haldane in 1805 published a book advocating this practice on the Lord's Day during public worship, and argued at the same time for a plurality of ministers in each church, even if some were involved in secular employment, Ewing (who, of course, had been trained as a minister) felt that the understanding of the ministry and of public worship was being undermined.[16] This was the context in which baptist views were also spreading—in 1805 Andrew Fuller, who did so much to broaden the Calvinism of Particular Baptists in England, remarked after his visit to Scotland that nine or ten of the Haldanes' students had adopted baptist views.[17]

The free way in which these various matters were discussed was very worrying for Ewing and Wardlaw. Wardlaw's biographer writes of this in highly-coloured, but revealing, tones:

---

14 Escott, *Scottish Congregationalism*, 86.

15 Haldane, *Lives of Robert and James Haldane*, 334: nevertheless it is possible that Alexander Haldane in retrospect actually exaggerated the Haldanes' lack of concern in this area.

16 Ibid, 330-34; Escott, *Scottish Congregationalism*, 82-83; Matheson, *Memoir of Ewing*, 325-31.

17 Yuille, *Baptists in Scotland*, 52-53.

In a short time everything became matter of discussion, and a restless cupidity of novelty raged in the bosoms of many of the most influential members of the Congregational churches, and infected even some of the pastors.[18]

The baptismal question acted as a kind of lightning conductor for all these issues. As early as 1806 about half a dozen of the members of Wardlaw's congregation in Albion Street, Glasgow, had been rebaptized, which caused him a good deal of soul-searching on the boundaries of Christian forbearance on such a matter. He based his own argument for infant baptism very much on the continuity between the Old and New Testaments, and in particular on the way in which Peter's declaration in Acts 2:38-39 that the promise is 'to you and your children' was an echo of God's promise to Abraham in Genesis 17:7. In 1807, Wardlaw published three lectures on Romans 4:9-25, which illustrated the link between the Abrahamic covenant and infant baptism. After expounding the nature and intention of circumcision in relation to the covenant with Abraham, he developed Paul's argument that the promise rested on grace through faith, rather than upon law, and therefore that it applied to all descendants of Abraham and not only the adherents of the law. Hence it was implausible to suppose that baptism under the new covenant would be more restricted in its extent than circumcision had been under the old. An appendix defended the mode of affusion or sprinkling in baptism.[19]

The Scotch Baptist leader, Archibald M'Lean, responded to Wardlaw's argument in a *Review of Mr Wardlaw's Lectures* published in 1808. M'Lean's biographer, William Jones, remembered him remarking '(with a smile) that Mr Haldane avowed himself a Baptist in about eight days after the publication of the *Review of Mr Wardlaw's Lectures*'.[20] In view of James Haldane's critical attitude towards both M'Lean and Jones, this remark seems to be essentially ironical: but subsequent historians have hastened to point out that Haldane's change of view was brought about by more than reading M'Lean.[21] In a letter written at the time, Haldane said that he had been examining the scriptural evidence on the question since the end of 1804, that he had at last come to the conclusion that he could not baptize children, and that then he had been baptized. Robert Haldane followed his brother's example soon afterwards.[22] The result of James Haldane's decision was a division in the Edinburgh Tabernacle where he was pastor, when two hundred followed him and more than a hundred others withdrew to form a Congregational church. The same kind of division was repeated in many places in Scotland, severely

---

18 Alexander, *Memoirs of Wardlaw*, 111.
19 Ibid, 92-102.
20 Jones, *Works of M'Lean*, vi, lxiii.
21 Yuille, *Baptists in Scotland*, 58; Escott, *Scottish Congregationalism*, 83.
22 Haldane, *Lives of Robert and James Haldane*, 334-35.

weakening the new movement and in the end (in Alexander Haldane's judgement) proving fatal to the progress of Congregationalism there. An alternative view is that, although the division was a shattering experience, it led to the foundation of the Glasgow Theological Academy in 1811 and the formation of the Congregational Union of Scotland in 1812 (essentially a continuation in a different form of the Society for Propagating the Gospel at Home which was wound up in 1808), thereby creating the main institutions of modern Congregationalism in Scotland.[23]

There was a similar movement in Ireland, which had a similar outcome. In October 1798, shortly after the abortive rebellion of that year, a group of ministers and laymen, drawn from the established Church of Ireland, Burgher and Anti-Burgher Seceder Presbyterians, and the Presbyterian Synod of Ulster, agreed to form the Evangelical Society of Ulster with the intention of supporting itinerant preachers supplied by the London Missionary Society. Both the Secession Synods in 1799 condemned the Society as being organised on principles which were inconsistent with the Secession Testimony. The result was that in the early 1800s several ministers became Independents and in 1805 Alexander Carson, one of the most distinguished of those involved, adopted a baptist position and withdrew from the Synod of Ulster.[24] Carson's *Reasons for Separating from the Synod of Ulster* were primarily concerned with matters of church polity, and in particular the reasons why independency was more in accordance with the divine model of church government found in the New Testament than presbyterianism. But certain characteristics were already present which indicate his sympathy with the kind of movement which the Haldanes had launched in Scotland. He supported the plurality of pastors, but not a non-pastoral ruling lay eldership; he noted that presbyterians had high fences around the Lord's Table, 'but in none of them...is *credible evidence of the new birth* the test of membership'.[25] Carson's conversion to baptist principles came as a result of a visit from a Scotch Baptist preacher, sent to his congregation by the Haldanes. Carson promised to write an article which would silence the Baptists, but after reading the scriptural evidence carefully he threw his manuscript into the

---

23 Yuille, *Baptists in Scotland*, 58-59; Haldane, *Lives of Robert and James Haldane*, 337; Matheson, *Memoir of Ewing*, 344; Escott, *Scottish Congregationalism*, 90-95.

24 J.S. Reid, *A History of the Presbyterian Church in Ireland* (Belfast 1867), iii, 415-8; T. Witherow, *Historical and Literary Memorials of Presbyterianism in Ireland, Second Series (1731-1800)* (London 1880), 310-2; D. Stewart, *The Seceders in Ireland* (Belfast 1950), 104-7; P. Brooke, 'Controversies in Ulster Presbyterianism, 1790-1836', unpublished Cambridge Ph.D. thesis 1980, 46-51.

25 A Carson, *Reasons for Separating from the General Synod of Ulster* in *Works*, iv (Dublin 1856), 87.

fire and announced his own conversion to a baptist position.[26] Nevertheless, as will be seen presently, Carson did not adopt a closed membership position. The main significance of Carson lies in the way he developed a doctrine of the plenary inspiration of scripture which in many respects was the basis for modern fundamentalism.

The Evangelical Revival made the crucial question for the churches whether they encouraged a ministry which gave priority to the preaching of the gospel. When churches responded negatively, the result was separation or division; and new churches were formed, often appealing to scripture as the model for their organisation, rather than more traditional confessional documents. Such an appeal, however, was apt to raise questions about the scriptural basis for infant baptism, and also the basis for fellowship within the church more widely, i.e. was a formal act such as baptism or the religious experience of conversion the test of fellowship? Whereas in England the Baptists were already well-established, so that personal changes of conviction were met by movement from one denomination to another, in Scotland and Ireland there were scarcely any Baptist groups to speak of before the Evangelical Revival, so that changes of conviction were usually associated with division. Thus arguments for infant baptism tended to be justifications of existing practice, whereas arguments against it tended to be based upon an emphasis on personal faith or conviction. There was also a tendency to mix or confuse arguments about the mode of baptism (immersion or sprinkling) with arguments about the appropriate subject of baptism (infants or believers). For these reasons there was relatively little meeting of minds.

This can be seen in the defences of infant baptism written by Greville Ewing and Ralph Wardlaw. Ewing argued on etymological grounds that the Greek word *baptizo* and its derivatives did not really mean to dip or to immerse. He first propounded this view in his *Greek Grammar and Greek and English Scripture Lexicon* in 1807 and then developed it in his *Essay on Baptism*, which he wrote in 1823 when preparing the third edition of his *Lexicon*.[27] Most of the *Essay* was concerned with the mode of baptism, because this was where antipaedobaptists thought they had the greatest advantage; but this did mean that the question of the appropriate subject tended to be a subordinate one. Moreover, his claim that the root of *baptizo* and *bapto* was 'pop' and hence that baptism meant being popped into water or having water popped upon something was a gift to those Baptist writers who wished to make fun of him. 'No one can deny after entertaining himself with this passage', wrote one critic (Francis

---

26 G.C. Moore, *Life of Dr Carson* (New York 1851), 22-23.
27 Matheson, *Memoir of Ewing*, 477-83.

Cox), 'that our author has *popped upon* a very amusing, if not a very convincing etymology.'[28]

Ewing was also concerned to justify family baptism, which, like Wardlaw, he traced to the Abrahamic covenant, extended to include Christians as well as Jews through the righteousness of faith.[29] In particular he emphasized the way in which family baptism was a sign of hope from one generation to the next:

> 'I will be a God to thee, and to thy seed after thee,' is an exceeding great and precious promise, of which many parents feel the value, while trembling at the thought of having been intrusted with the charge of immortal souls... It contains all that we can wish for ourselves and our children, in time and in eternity. Without it, one would think, that to be a parent would be one of the greatest trials which a serious mind could possibly experience.[30]

That passage is echoed in his daughter's *Memoir*:

> The Essay contains not the cold and barren speculations of a theorist, but the earnest convictions and fervent emotions of one who was writing of some of his dearest privileges and hopes. No believing parent, indeed, could ever have received the ordinance at his hands without being struck with the value which he evidently placed on it, as a confirmation of that promise, 'I will be a God to thee, and to thy seed after thee'.[31]

The rather odd reference to the parents' receiving the ordinance (rather than the children) is revealing. His daughter went on to say that while he was writing the essay he had felt as much for her little one as he formerly did for her. His love as a father was interwoven with his sense of 'the depravity of human nature, the preciousness of Christ and the absolute necessity of the Spirit's gracious influence. So that affection for his offspring was not only a strong, but a sacred principle.'[32] Behind all this once again lay the ever present awareness of infant and child mortality. Ewing wrote in the same year to his daughter about the illness of his eldest grandchild:

> What a call you must have felt his illness to be, to commit him, more earnestly than ever to the mercy of his heavenly Father, and of his kinsman Redeemer. I remember I used to feel very desirous, that the Lord would spare you, till you could read the Word of God, and hear the Gospel for yourself.[33]

---

28 F.A. Cox, *On Baptism* (London 1824), 17.
29 G. Ewing, *An Essay on Baptism* (2 ed, Glasgow 1824), 197-8.
30 Ewing, *Baptism*, 212.
31 Matheson, *Greville Ewing*, 483.
32 Ibid, 484.
33 Ibid.

Francis Augustus Cox of Hackney was a Baptist minister who replied to Ewing in 1824, and became one of the leading Baptists of the next generation.[34] With him we enter a very different world:

> It is, in the *personality* of religion, that we fix the very root of our argument. If there be one general consideration relating to the gospel of Jesus, more obvious, more essential...than another, it is this, that man is individually responsible to God for his actions, and as such an object of appeal, entreaty, warning, and promise, eligible to an immortal destiny of woe and delight, of condemnation or salvation. In this there can be no substitution... No one can profess faith, no one can put on Christ, no one can obey God, no one can perform a duty which is enjoined as a public expression and avowal of any Christian principle, for another.[35]

So Cox asked whether it was likely, given that all other Christian observances required personal religion, that baptism would be an exception to this. 'Are some to receive it because they *believe*, and others because they are *related* to those that believe?'[36] Cox also denied the analogy drawn between baptism and circumcision, and in particular criticised Wardlaw's view that circumcision represented the two great blessings of justification and sanctification. 'Each institution is of the nature of an independent law, a law of that economy under which it was appointed', he wrote,[37] and since neither circumcision nor baptism 'originated in the fitness of things, or in any consideration of a moral nature' the obligation to practise either rite depended on the will of the institutor and the revelation of that will. The practical effect of this was that the nature of the Abrahamic covenant depended on what was said in Genesis, and not on what Paul made of it in Galatians or Romans. Cox further distinguished between the covenant in Genesis 12 which contained the promise 'in thee shall all the families of the earth be blessed', which he regarded as a repetition of the covenant with Adam and Noah, and the covenant of circumcision in Genesis 17, which he took to apply to Abraham's descendants: and he argued that the righteousness of faith attributed to Abraham referred to the first rather than the second.[38] Cox's willingness to play down Paul's interpretation of the Abrahamic covenant

---

34 Stoughton, *History of Religion in England*, viii, 146-7; A.C. Underwood, *A History of the English Baptists* (London 1947), 234-5; E.A. Payne, *The Baptist Union: A Short History* (London 1959), 54-5. Cox was educated at Bristol Academy but completed his education at Edinburgh, and hence was familiar with the controversy provoked by the Haldanes' conversion to the principle of believer's baptism: J.H.Y. Briggs, *The English Baptists of the Nineteenth Century* (Baptist Historical Society: Didcot 1994), 43.
35 Cox, *Baptism*, 7.
36 Ibid, 10-11.
37 Ibid, 128.
38 Ibid, 128-51.

is interesting, though it is clear that Paul's concern in Romans 4–5 is more with faith than baptism. What is striking is the importance attached to covenant theology in this particular debate, which makes it quite different from the Anglican discussion considered in the previous chapter.

Not surprisingly Wardlaw responded with a *Dissertation on Infant Baptism* in 1825. His biographer, W.L. Alexander, denied that it was a reply to any particular person, and indeed it was concerned with more than the Abrahamic covenant. But it is quite clear that Cox's book was the occasion for Wardlaw's work. It is also interesting that Alexander regarded the first section on the Abrahamic covenant as the most important in Wardlaw's mind, and the least convincing:

> I question if any one ever tried to reproduce the argument in his own mind without feeling that there were some serious gaps in it, over which one had to take a flying leap in order to reach the conclusion.[39]

Alexander suggested that the weakness in Wardlaw's argument was that it assumed what had to be proved, namely that the children of Gentile believers were under the covenant in virtue of their parents' faith because Abraham's descendants were.[40] The second and third parts of Wardlaw's book, which are more valuable (as Alexander suggested), concerned the evidence for the baptism of children in the New Testament and the truths and duties shown by infant baptism. The particular truths he emphasized were the fact of original sin and the fact that children can be part of Christ's kingdom.[41]

It is significant that Wardlaw did not regard baptism as a church ordinance, in the sense that it introduced the person baptized to connection with a particular church. 'They were simply baptized into the faith of Christ, and the general fellowship of the gospel.'[42] This separation of baptism from church is a common feature of evangelical attitudes. Some signs of it may be seen in the statement on baptism in the 1833 *Declaration of Faith of the Congregational Union of England and Wales*. The *Declaration* was originally drawn up by the Revd George Redford, and presented by the Revd John Angell James of Carrs Lane church, Birmingham, to the 1832 meeting of the Union. Congregations and ministers were asked for their views and these were reviewed by a sub-committee at the 1833 meeting, which offered a revised version for approval. Wardlaw was in London at the time in order to give the

---

39 Alexander, *Ralph Wardlaw*, 237.
40 Ibid, 238.
41 R. Wardlaw, *A Dissertation on the Scriptural Authority, Nature and Uses of Infant Baptism* (2 ed, Glasgow 1826), 79-84.
42 Ibid, 184.

Congregational Lecture for that year and he was a member of the sub-committee. The article on the sacraments is brief, and simply descriptive:

> They believe in the perpetual obligation of Baptism and the Lord's Supper; the former to be administered to all converts to Christianity and their children, by the application of water to the subject, 'in the name of the Father, and of the Son, and of the Holy Ghost'; and the latter to be celebrated by Christian Churches as a token of faith in the Saviour, and of brotherly love.[43]

R.W. Dale, James's successor at Carrs Lane and a leading Congregational theologian of the later nineteenth century, commented that the 1833 statement on baptism makes no attempt to explain the meaning of the rite and marked a move away from the objective nature of baptism set out in the Savoy Declaration of 1658.[44] (Chapter 29 of the Savoy Declaration was substantially the same as Chapter 28 of the Westminster Confession, but omitting the phrase in the first clause of the Westminster statement that baptism was ordained 'for the solemn admission of the party baptized into the visible Church'.[45]) Wardlaw, like Ewing, believed that baptism should only be administered to a child if at least one of the parents was a believer, but he recognized that English opinion was already moving away from that position.[46] As the emphasis in church membership was increasingly placed on the profession of faith or testimony to spiritual experience, rather than baptism, the significance of baptism came to be neglected among Congregationalists, except as a rite for infants. Both Wardlaw and Ewing strove to distinguish their justification of infant baptism from that of the two national Churches which said that it should be administered to everyone; but the very force of the evangelical urge to preach the gospel to all was weakening the notions of covenant and election which still lay behind their theological defences.

The second issue concerned fellowship within and between churches. The division in the Haldanes' churches had spread after 1808 not only because of differences of view within congregations over baptism but also because of the necessity for congregations to decide with which part of a divided congregation they would remain in fellowship. When several members of Ralph Wardlaw's congregation adopted baptist sentiments in 1806, he worried over what were 'the boundaries of Christian

---

43 R.W. Dale, *History of English Congregationalism* (London 1907), 699-706; the quotation is from p 706.
44 Dale, *History of English Congregationalism*, 706-9.
45 D.M. Thompson (ed), *Stating the Gospel: Formulations and Declarations of Faith from the Heritage of the United Reformed Church* (Edinburgh 1990), 39, 108.
46 Wardlaw, *Infant Baptism*, 191-6, cf. Ewing, *Baptism*, 10-13.

forbearance'.[47] When James Haldane was baptized he wrote to his friend John Campbell that with regard to the church this question was to be a matter of forbearance, and added,

> If we are all acting on conviction, and both desiring to know the will of Jesus in this and in all other respects, I have no apprehension of discussion. Of one thing I am sure, that all who love the Lord Jesus, should, so far as they are agreed, walk by the same rule and mind the same things; and if it be improper for Baptists to be in fellowship in the same Church, it must be equally improper to have occasional fellowship in private.[48]

However, John Aikman, who had been James Haldane's colleague at the Tabernacle and since 1801 minister of the daughter church near Argyle Square, took a harder line. When Haldane became a Baptist, Aikman's church decided 'to decline the relation of a sister Church with a Church composed of Baptists and Paedobaptists under a Baptist pastor'.[49] It is significant here that Aikman declared that before he left the Church of Scotland 'mixed communion in the Lord's Supper—that is, communion with inconsistent or worldly professors—had been to him and others an "intolerable burden"'.[50] The contrast with the open character of several English Independent congregations of the mid-seventeenth century, noted in chapter 1, could not be more striking.

This issue of fellowship lay behind the controversy among Baptists in England on 'open' or 'mixed communion'—an interesting echo of Aikman's phrase though in a different context. From one point of view it could be argued that this debate was not really about baptism at all, since both sides were firm in saying that baptism was properly administered to believers by immersion. But it aptly illustrates the way in which the Evangelical Revival raised new questions, or reopened old ones, about the implications of certain beliefs.

The main protagonists were Robert Hall, formerly minister in Cambridge and in the early nineteenth century minister of Harvey Lane church, Leicester, and Joseph Kinghorn of Norwich.[51] They were perhaps the two most distinguished ministers who were not present at the meeting in June 1812 which decided to form a General Union of Baptist Churches.[52] Hall opened, or reopened, the debate in 1815 with the

---

47 Alexander, *Wardlaw*, 93-4.
48 Haldane, *Life of Robert and James Haldane*, 335.
49 Ibid, 336.
50 Ibid, 331.
51 The most thorough discussion of this controversy now is M.J. Walker, *Baptists at the Table* (Baptist Historical Society: Didcot 1992), 42-70; see also S.K. Fowler, *More Than a Symbol: The British Baptist Recovery of Baptismal Sacramentalism* (Carlisle 2002), 59-64.
52 Payne, *The Baptist Union*, 21.

publication of his book, *On Terms of Communion*. It is not clear why he chose this particular moment, since for three or four years before he had often advocated a revision of the existing policy, whereby only those baptized as believers could be admitted to communion.[53] In his preface he denied that he had intentionally published just after the death of Andrew Fuller, who was known to defend strict communion, and said that he had expected to encounter his opposition. Remarking that the defence of mixed communion by Robert Robinson, his predecessor at Cambridge, had relied on principles more lax and latitudinarian than he could conscientiously adopt, he said that the main author he professed to answer was Abraham Booth, whose *Apology for the Baptists* had first been published in 1778.[54] Hall had spoken to his church in 1812 on the disadvantages of the presence of non-communicants at the Lord's Supper, and the discomfort it caused him. For a while they ceased to attend. Later he tried to persuade the Harvey Lane congregation to adopt 'mixed communion' but when they refused he recommended the formation of a separate congregation which held a 'mixed communion' at the same time as the other held an exclusive one; it seems that this was adopted and the two groups continued in harmony so long as Hall was in Leicester. It seems, therefore, that Hall's intention was to remove one obstacle to fuller communion.[55]

Hall's argument began from the premise that unity is one of the essential characteristics of the Church of Christ in the New Testament, and that the schism in the members of Christ's mystical body is 'by far the greatest calamity that has befallen the Christian interest'. He then set out to ask 'how far we are justified in repelling from our communion those from whom we differ on matters confessedly not essential to salvation?' Since the word 'communion' in the New Testament is never used exclusively in relation to the Lord's Supper, why should there be more scruples about joining round the Lord's Table than about engaging in common prayer? Do not such scruples make the Lord's Supper 'a religious test, designed to ascertain and establish an agreement in points not fundamental'? If so,

> It is no longer a symbol of our common christianity, it is the badge and criterion of a party, a mark of discrimination applied to distinguish the nicer shades of difference among christians.[56]

---

53 O. Gregory, *A brief Memoir of the Rev. Robert Hall, A.M.*, in *The Works of Robert Hall, A.M.*, vi (London 1833), 90.
54 Hall, *Works*, ii (London 1831), 5, 7.
55 Hall, *Works*, vi, 93-4.
56 Hall, *Works*, ii, 9-10, 12, 13-14, 14-15.

Such an argument was bound to strike a sympathetic chord among dissenters who objected to precisely that use of Communion under the terms of the Test Act.

Hall considered and rejected various arguments for making baptism a qualification for participation in the Lord's Supper, but his main argument, presented in various ways, was to press the question whether paedobaptists were to be regarded as part of the Church of Christ, notwithstanding their erroneous beliefs about baptism. In practice, he suggested, Baptists did so recognise them: they did not hesitate to join with them in prayer and praise and would even welcome their participation in ordination services. This meant that strict communionists made a non-apostolic distinction between believers and communicants. No church, said Hall, had a right to establish terms of communion which were not terms of salvation. Joseph Kinghorn's response did not really meet Hall's basic argument, since he insisted on posing the issue as one between those who were baptized and those who were not. Hall's policy, he claimed, would 'promote the ruin and dissolution of the baptist denomination *as such*'.[57] Perhaps not surprisingly he rejected Hall's view that the fact that paedobaptists believed they had been baptized made a difference; but he did not touch the point, of which this was one part, that the division which existed was *within* the Church. Hence he was righteously indignant that Hall's terms for mixed and strict communion were 'Christian communion' and 'party communion'.

Hall's discussion of the effects of strict communion is particularly interesting. Only Baptists, said Hall, claimed the right of rejecting those whom Christ had received. Strict communion was the best way to render Baptist principles unpopular:

> Upon the system of strict communion, the moment a member of a paedobaptist church becomes convinced of the invalidity of his infant baptism, he must deem it obligatory upon him to...dissolve his connexion with the church... Viewed in such a connexion [the] prevalence [of our sentiments] is a blow at the very root of paedobaptist societies, since the moment we succeed in making a convert, we disqualify him for continuing a member. We deposit a seed of alienation and discord, which threatens their dissolution...[58]

Hall correctly perceived and clearly articulated the consequences of one particular way of setting out the implications of a believer baptist position, and this remains the most important problem in securing the coexistence of the two beliefs about baptism. The 'open communion' position was obviously gaining ground in the early nineteenth century,

---

57 J. Kinghorn, *Arguments against the practice of mixed Communion and in support of Communion on the plan of the Apostolic Church* (London 1827), 26-7.
58 Hall, *Works*, ii, 158-9.

particularly among church members, and this illustrates the effect of the Evangelical Revival. John Ryland, minister at College Lane, Northampton, and later at Broadmead, Bristol, while President of the Bristol Academy, said in 1814 that he had supported open communion for forty-seven years, but as Hall pointed out in his reply to Kinghorn in 1818, in practice few Baptist churches would introduce open communion unless all the members agreed, so many churches retained strict communion out of deference to a minority.[59] As has been noted, Hall failed to persuade his own congregation in Leicester to adopt open communion. Nevertheless one can sympathise with Kinghorn's worry that if baptism were treated like any other opinion, it would come to be regarded as of no importance. John Stoughton, the Congregational historian, perceptively commented that 'Kinghorn might...be regarded as representing Churchmen in general, whilst Hall advocated the rights of individuals in particular'.[60]

It is interesting to note that Alexander Carson in Ireland also supported the practice of open communion. Carson never published his views on the subject during his lifetime, but told his family what they were for posthumous publication. The practice of his church at Tubbermore was never to regard obedience to baptism as an indispensable condition of admission to the Lord's Supper: indeed they received members upon evidence of their conversion with little enquiry on whether they agreed with them on the subject of baptism. As far as Carson was concerned, however, this practice did not stem from 'liberality of sentiment' but from the belief that Christ set no such condition for recognition. Writing to a church in New York in 1819, Carson regretted that they seemed 'to make baptism a term of fellowship' and entreated them to examine the subject 'recollecting that, *if it be sinful to receive any that Christ has forbidden, it also sinful to refuse any that He has invited*'.[61] He reiterated the point even more forcefully in his book on baptism of 1831, which was a response to Ewing and Wardlaw:

> Liberality of sentiment is not a phrase which I admit into my religious vocabulary; for though I love and acknowledge all who love the Lord Jesus, I hold myself as much under the law of God in embracing all the children of God, as in forming the articles of my creed. My recognition of all Christians I ground on the authority of

---

59 J. Ryland, *A Candid Statement of the Reasons which induce the Baptists to differ in opinion and practice from their Christian brethren* (2 ed, London 1827), x; Hall, *Works*, ii, 243.

60 Stoughton, *History of Religion*, vii, 267.

61 Moore, *Life of Carson*, 83-9; the quotation is from 88-9.

Jesus. To set at nought the weakest of Christ's little ones, I call not illiberal, but unchristian.[62]

In Carson, then, as with others of this group we see the separation of baptism from church—almost, one might say, the privatisation of baptism. Carson vigorously argued that baptism could only mean immersion and that the only dominical command for baptism related to believers. His emphasis on mode was accompanied by a virtually Zwinglian emphasis that baptism was a figurative representation of truth: 'The Christian has a real death, burial, and resurrection with Christ by faith. He has all these also in baptism by figure.'[63] Similarly, when talking about the subjects of baptism, Carson did not deny that infants were saved, simply that they were saved by faith. The same argument enabled him to say that nations which had not heard the gospel were not condemned by it, for it was condemnation only to those who, having heard it, failed to believe.[64] He also denied that baptism and the Lord's Supper were seals of the new covenant—the only seal was the Holy Spirit:

> When the Holy Spirit himself, in the heart of the believer, is the seal of God's truth, there is no need of any other seal. Baptism represents the belief of the truth in a figure, and takes it for granted that they are believers to whom it is applied—but it is no seal of this.[65]

For writers such as Carson, therefore, baptism was regarded as a commandment binding upon the individual, but there was no sense that the truths which it signified, such as regeneration or sanctification, were tied to it or dependent upon it in any way. Whereas the problems of sustaining such a link for infant baptism are obvious, it is noteworthy that the arguments adduced for believer's baptism in this period were not generally intended to make such a link easier to sustain. However, from a pastoral point of view the issue was rather different. In a situation where churches were growing and attracting new adherents, how were those adherents to be treated? Hall's comment that he was uncomfortable with the presence of non-communicants at the Lord's Supper expressed this anxiety. For those of Baptist persuasion, there was usually an interval betweeen someone first attending services and then making the commitment of baptism. So the intricate theological arguments which were produced also reflected the contemporary pastoral situation—and this was a very different situation from the relatively closed world of

---

62 A. Carson, *Baptism in its Mode and Subjects considered* (Edinburgh 1831), v; cf Fowler, *More Than a Symbol*, 64-5.
63 Carson, *Baptism*, 192.
64 Ibid, 209.
65 Ibid, 289.

Baptists a century before. The result was that the primary emphasis placed by dissenters on faith and evangelism tended to leave baptism as secondary; and Baptists were as much affected as Congregationalists by the subjectivism in sacramental theology which Dale so deplored.[66]

In many ways this was one of the underlying problems in the third set of issues, that concerning baptismal regeneration. One of the few things that all the writers discussed so far—Wardlaw, Ewing, Cox, Haldane, Hall, Kinghorn and Carson—were agreed upon was that baptism was not to be identified with regeneration. Many evangelical clergy in the Church of England agreed with them, as was demonstrated in chapter 2. But the development of the Oxford Movement in the Church of England from the early 1830s, which will be considered in more detail in the next chapter, heightened this contrast with the thought world of the Evangelical Revival and dissent even further. This accentuated the suspicion among Baptists in particular of any reference to baptism as a sacrament; the word 'ordinance' had been the preferred term since the late seventeenth century, but it now began to assume a more distinctly anti-sacerdotal sense.

Charles Stovel (who was to become Chairman of the Baptist Union in 1862) responded to the Oxford Movement, but sought to preserve some sacramental understanding. He gave five lectures on *The Baptismal Regeneration Controversy* in Woolwich in 1843, as a result of an exchange of tracts on the subject by local clergymen, with the objective of seeing whether the 'sacramental benefits ascribed to infant baptism and promiscuous baptism' could be supported by the Holy Scriptures.[67] Having begun by arguing that believer's baptism had a moral effect which the vicarious actions in infant baptism lacked, he criticised the Westminster Confession for what it claimed for infant baptism as strongly as the Thirty-Nine Articles or the Council of Trent, particularly the claim for '*invariable* regeneration in Baptism'.[68] But in his discussion of John 3:1-12 as it related to converted believers he was prepared to say that a new life is begun by water and the Spirit, not by one without the other but by both:

> The visible action of the water, or rather of the whole sacrament, of which it becomes the instrument, is seen in the Church; where, as an authorized act of discipline, it declares the character, and seals both the privilege and obligation of

---

66 Thus whilst it is true that 'For any covenanted community the operation of a policy of "open communion" represented considerable commitment to evangelical inclusiveness', I am not sure that Mark Smith is right in suggesting that this was 'rare among Independents before the 1830s': M. Smith, *Religion in Industrial Society: Oldham and Saddleworth, 1740-1865* (Oxford 1994), 142.

67 C. Stovel, *The Baptismal Regeneration Controversy* (London 1843), vi.

68 Ibid, 76-80.

every believer in the family of God. The action of the Spirit takes place in the mind and the heart; and, leading and sustaining the believer, reveals itself in the effects produced upon the devoted convert. Each is essential to the support of that new life, into which a believing sinner rises and enters from the moment of his Baptism.[69]

Stovel sought to justify his view by saying that regeneration and rebirth did not mean the same thing, and did not hesitate to call baptism a sacrament. Stanley Fowler concludes that 'Stovel's view of baptism was sacramental, both verbally and conceptually' and further suggests that

> if the discussion were limited to a consideration of what happens in the baptism of a repentant believer, then the rhetoric would be quite different, affirming the sacramental sense which is often present in spite of protests to the contrary.[70]

Unfortunately the discussion was not so limited, and later in the century the non-sacramental view triumphed. J.H. Hinton wrote in 1850 that 'baptism is not a means of conferring any spiritual blessings whatever';[71] C.H. Spurgeon preached a sermon on 'Baptismal Regeneration' in 1864 in which he primarily attacked the Prayer Book phrase, 'Seeing now that this child is regenerate', but also argued in relation to believer's baptism that someone 'who knows that he is saved by believing in Christ does not, when he is baptized, lift his baptism into a saving ordinance';[72] and John Clifford claimed to speak for the Free Churches generally as well as Baptists in 1888 when he wrote:

> Broadly speaking, we hold that Baptism and the Lord's Suppper are not 'Sacraments' in the ecclesiastical sense, i.e., they are not mysteries or miracles, not causes of grace, not in themselves vehicles of grace.[73]

Truly the consequences of extreme claims for baptismal regeneration had a devastating effect on the possibility of a sacramental understanding of baptism outside the Church of England.

---

69 Ibid, 127, quoted in Fowler, *More Than a Symbol*, 70.

70 Fowler, *More Than a Symbol*, 71, 72.

71 J.H. Hinton, 'The Ultimatum', *Theological Works of the Rev. John Howard Hinton, M.A.*, v (London 1865), 466, quoted in A.R. Cross, *Baptism and the Baptists: Theology and Practice in Twentieth-Century Britain* (Carlisle 2000), 12; cf Fowler, *More Than a Symbol*, 75-9.

72 C.H. Spurgeon, 'Baptismal Regeneration', *Metropolitan Tabernacle Pulpit*, x (Pasadena 1981), 326, cf Fowler, *More Than a Symbol*, 79-83, where Fowler tries to rescue some sacramental understanding from this sermon.

73 J. Clifford, *The Ordinances of Jesus and the Sacraments of the Churches* (London 1888), 4, quoted in Walker, *Baptists at the Table*, 188; cf Cross, *Baptism and the Baptists*, 12-14. Clifford acknowledged that people like R.W. Dale affirmed that the ordinances were not only declarative and symbolical of the central facts of Christianity 'but also *acts through which Christ dispenses grace mystically*' (italics original).

CHAPTER 4

The Oxford Movement and After

On 26 November 1826 John Henry Newman wrote to his friend Samuel Rickards, suggesting that it would be useful to write a summary of the opinions of the 'old worthies of our Church' (about whom Rickards knew a good deal).

> The leading doctrine to be discussed [he wrote] would be (I think) that of regeneration—for it is at the very root of the whole system—and branches out in different ways (according to the different views taken of it) into church of Englandism, or into *Calvinism, anti-paedobaptism, the rejection of church government and discipline*, and *the mere moral system*. It is connected with the doctrines of freewill, original sin, justification, holiness, good works, election, education, the visible church etc.[1]

This letter was written at just about the time when Newman gave up his former evangelicalism. The stages by which that happened will be considered presently but the significant point is that the marker Newman used was his adoption of the principle of baptismal regeneration. Similarly, the *Christian Observer*, in its comments on a letter by Newman in defence of the *Tracts for the Times* in March 1837, described baptismal regeneration as 'the very foundation of the Oxford Tracts'.[2] R.W. Church likened Pusey's tracts on baptism of 1835 (numbers 67 to 69) to 'the advance of a battery of heavy artillery on a field where the battle has hitherto been carried on by skirmishing and musketry'.[3] This chapter considers the way in which the Anglican controversy over baptismal regeneration was carried forward by the Oxford Movement. The first part will describe the essence of the 'orthodox' position at the end of the controversy begun by Richard Mant's tracts by considering Alexander Knox and Bishop Bethell. The second part will examine the positions taken up by Newman and Pusey from 1825 to 1845. The evangelical and nonconformist response to the Tractarians will be considered, particularly

---

1 I. Ker and T. Gornall, *The Letters and Diaries of John Henry Newman, i 1801-26* (Oxford 1978), 310 (italics original).

2 *Christian Observer*, xxxvi (1837), 179.

3 R.W. Church, *The Oxford Movement: Twelve Years, 1833-1845* (3 ed, London 1892), 136.

as it found expression in the Gorham Case. Finally, there is the case of the tractarian who came to believe that the Gorham Judgement had been right—J.B. Mozley. One striking feature of the discussion as it proceeded is the way in which it opened up and clarified this question: can the biblical language about baptism, which is based on the baptism of believers, be applied to the baptism of infants without entailing a view of regeneration in which faith is irrelevant?

In the discussion of Mant's tracts on regeneration and conversion in chapter 2, the emphasis fell mainly on those who criticised him. But Mant had his defenders, though they used more moderate language. Two who are of particular interest are Alexander Knox, the Irish lay theologian who has often been called a 'forerunner of the Oxford Movement', and Christopher Bethell, Bishop of Bangor, whose book on the *Doctrine of Regeneration in Baptism* went through four editions between 1822 and 1845. Bethell's book does not seem to have been read by Newman or Pusey: there is no reference to it in Newman's journals and correspondence, and Bethell himself thought that Pusey had not read it.[4] Knox's work, though written in 1820, was not published until 1834, after his death. Newman makes only passing references to Knox's work, suggesting that though he read it he did not use it.[5] He does say that Pusey read Knox attentively but, according to Liddon, Pusey said that

> The Tractarians felt that they could not claim him as a whole; and they certainly were not indebted to him for anything that they knew of Catholic antiquity or Catholic truth.[6]

Newman thought it remarkable that laymen like Knox and Coleridge should bear witness to 'Church principles', and it is significant that he and Keble, in different ways, criticised Knox for making his own judgements about church history rather than automatically siding with authority.[7]

Knox did not regard the Methodist revival as an unmitigated evil and in 1816, when the Mant controversy was at its height, criticised 'the present champions for what they think high Church orthodoxy' for their

---

4 C. Bethell, *A General View of the Doctrine of Regeneration in Baptism* (4 ed, London 1845), xxxiii.

5 He notes it in the preface to *Lectures on Justification* (3 ed, London 1874), vi-vii, and also 81; I. Ker and T. Gornall, *Letters and Diaries of John Henry Newman, iv 1833-1834* (Oxford 1980), 325.

6 H.P. Liddon (ed J.O. Johnston and R.J. Wilson), *Life of Edward Bouverie Pusey*, i (London 1893), 262; A. Mozley, *Letters and Correspondence of John Henry Newman*, ii (London 1891), 133.

7 Mozley, *Letters of Newman*, ii, 93; J.T. Coleridge, *Memoir of the Revd John Keble* (3 ed, London 1870), 250-51.

indiscriminate attack on 'those movements of piety, which belong to the mind and heart'. He lamented that the Prayer Book was 'used, without being felt', that the Bible was 'distributed, without being understood', and that religious controversy was becoming 'more and more rancorous, while neither party distinctly apprehends the nature of the dispute, nor the strict points to be established'.[8] It was in this spirit at the end of 1819 that he wrote his essay on the doctrine of baptism in the Church of England. He explained to John Jebb that he attempted 'briefly to prove the doctrine of baptismal regeneration (in the case of infants) to be that of the Church of England', and added that he stated 'unpalatable truths, which both sides will, on different grounds, equally disrelish'.[9] Jebb said he was glad to hear this, since it was 'a subject, on which both parties are, with few exceptions, lamentably in the dark'.[10]

Knox's essay is clear and delightfully short (forty pages). He began by showing with reference both to the Fathers and to the Prayer Book that the Church of England made a distinction between

> baptism, as an indelible badge of the Christian profession. and the retention of that inward grace, or spiritual regeneration, which this holy sacrament is intended to convey.[11]

The next question, therefore, was under what circumstances do the external sacrament and the inward grace go together. In relation to adults Knox believed that concurrence to be conditional, in so far as repentance and faith were required for the effectual reception of baptism. In the case of infants, however, the concurrence of baptism and spiritual regeneration is clearly unconditional, not only because of the strong language of the service, which went beyond a 'charitable hope', but also because the equivalent language in the service of baptism for adults introduced in 1662 was explicitly unconditional and therefore the earlier service could not have been left unaltered by accident. Nevertheless, Knox insisted that the spiritual grace given to infants in baptism could

> remain only in minds, where it is in some measure yielded to and cherished; but that, where...it is resisted and repelled...[it] is actually (though, through the tender mercy of God, not irrecoverably) forfeited and lost.[12]

---

8 'On the Situation and Prospects of the Established Church', 4 June 1816, *Remains of Alexander Knox, Esq.*, i (London 1834), 58, 59, 61.

9 Knox to Jebb, 3 January 1820, in C. Forster (ed), *Thirty Years Correspondence between John Jebb and Alexander Knox*, ii, (London 1834), 403.

10 Jebb to Knox, 9 January 1820, in ibid, 409.

11 *Remains of Knox*, i, 451.

12 Ibid, 467.

In a revised version of his essay, Knox added three practical consequences which he believed to follow from the doctrine he had stated. The first was that in this light the language of the Prayer Book would be seen always to be concerned with preserving the state of grace and resisting the power of sin, something which some of those who contended zealously for baptismal regeneration seemed to forget when they almost implied that there was no discernible line between the spiritually living and the spiritually dead. Secondly, the Church provided a simple and common sense way for the individual to engage in self-examination. Thirdly, a Church of England teacher would not regard the mass of an ordinary congregation as little better than heathens, but would be concerned to call forth good rather than denounce evil whilst always making clear what is needed for salvation. He went on to suggest that the great advantage of infant baptism was that a child was brought up with a foundation 'for an entire life of religion; for a choice of it, from joyful preference, rather than relentless necessity', whereas an adult convert was more likely to be fleeing from evil and therefore to begin his spiritual life 'in the depth of mental gloom'.[13] What is striking about Knox is his refreshing lack of polemic, and his transparent concern for practical religion which he related so lucidly to sound doctrine. He wrote with the air of someone who knew what he was talking about spiritually as well as theologically.

Christopher Bethell's book was obviously different—in style as well as in length. The history of its various editions in 1822, 1836, 1839 and 1845, with the various prefaces, constitutes a commentary in miniature on the controversy. He was at pains in 1845 to point out that baptismal regeneration was not simply a Tractarian doctrine.[14] Bethell firmly grasped one nettle at the outset—what regeneration meant:

> If Regeneration takes place in Baptism, it cannot, upon principles of common sense, be *an entire change of mind*: if it is an *entire change of mind, a radical change of heart and soul*, upon principles of common sense and experience, it cannot take place in Baptism.[15]

If the value of Knox's essay lies in the spiritual implications of his analysis, then the interest of Bethell lies in his discussion of the Calvinist theory and why he rejected it.

---

13 *Remains of Knox*, ii, 426-53, especially 450-1.
14 Bethell, *Regeneration*, 293-4.
15 Ibid, Preface to 1st ed, xiii (italics original): cf Preface to 4 ed, xi: 'For if the change signified by this Scriptural term takes place in Baptism, it cannot be such a change as is contended for by the opponents of this doctrine. If it is such a radical and complete change of heart and soul as is included in their definition of the word, it does not take place in Baptism.'

For Bethell the basis of baptism was the covenant of grace in Mark 16:16: 'he that believeth and is baptized shall be saved'. He was critical of the Calvinist tendency to identify baptism with circumcision, and to appropriate the promise to Abraham as the basis for baptism. Instead, he argued that scripture made regeneration dependent on baptism, though faith and repentance were necessary qualifications wherever the subject is capable of them.[16] Nevertheless God's action was primary:

> Now, though no adult can partake of these blessings without being previously qualified by faith and repentance, it is certain that they are mere acts of free grace and mercy, which must...be made over to the soul at some determinate moment, and are not the effects of any *immediate* exercise of the moral nature of man, and of that principle of self-action which God has implanted in us.[17]

Similarly, neither an adult nor an infant was declared regenerate in baptism on the presumption that he or she would act rightly after it, so it was not possible to argue against regeneration in the case of infants on the ground that it was claimed for adults because of the promises they made. Bethell argued that the departure from the primitive doctrine of baptismal regeneration had come about because of an over-reaction to the *ex opere operato* understanding of the way in which grace was conferred by the sacraments, characteristic of Roman Catholic scholasticism. Because they objected to the view that grace would be conferred without any corresponding act on the part of the recipient, provided there was no obstacle of wilful sin, they had swung to the opposite position which maintained that everyone who believed was justified and regenerated, whether baptized or not. Furthermore, because the Calvinists identified regeneration with final salvation, and because it was evident that final salvation was no necessary consequence of baptism, they shifted their emphasis from baptism to the moment of effectual calling.[18] This theoretical error led, 'in the hands of the unthinking, the injudicious and the passionate', to fanatical notions of 'a new birth, distinctly perceivable by the conscience and feelings of the individual, accompanied by throes and agonies, and bearing in every respect a close analogy to natural birth'.[19] Like Knox, Bethell was suspicious of the emphasis on total depravity, because it led to an estimate of human nature based on the worst rather than the best in man; but he also refused to go as far as Pusey in risking any identification of the grace conferred in baptism with 'conversion, repentance, faith, or any of those Christian virtues or holy habits which are the fruits and evidences of the Spirit's

---

16 Ibid, 32, 44, 53-4, 150, 59-62.
17 Ibid, 121 (italics original).
18 Ibid, 102-3, 130, 140-7, 163.
19 Ibid, 169.

influence'.²⁰ He would go no further than to say that 'that principle of life contains the germ of those graces', a position he took from Waterland.²¹

Such, then, was the kind of position on baptismal regeneration which moderate high churchmen were taking in the years just before the Oxford Movement. It is perhaps noteworthy that both Knox and Bethell would have had a more extended acquaintance with the Evangelical Revival than Mant did before he arrived in Coggeshall. Knox was familiar with Methodism and Presbyterianism in Ireland, and Bethell encountered West Country Methodism, as Bishop of Exeter before he met Welsh Calvinistic Methodism as Bishop of Bangor after 1820.

On the day he was ordained priest, 29 May 1825, John Henry Newman reflected on the change that had taken place in his views in the year since he had been made deacon:

> Then I thought the *onus probandi* lay with those who asserted an individual to be a real Christian; and now I think it lies with those who deny it. Yet I do not even now actually maintain that the Spirit always or generally accompanies the very act of baptism, only that the sacrament brings them into the kingdom of grace, where the Spirit will constantly meet them...²²

He was, in other words, starting to lose the rather precious evangelical habit of deciding whether someone really had been converted. What is particularly interesting, however, is that he attributed this change 'principally or in a great measure' to the fact that 'in my parochial duties I found many, who in most important points were inconsistent, but whom yet I could not say were altogether without grace'.²³ Like John McLeod Campbell at Row at almost exactly the same time, he found his evangelical theology cracking under the strains of real life. Theologically he had been prompted by Edward Hawkins, who was then Vicar of St Mary's, Oxford, and a Fellow of Oriel. Soon after his ordination he reported a conversation with Hawkins on real and nominal Christianity in which Hawkins had said that the majority of his congregation would not be touched by his preaching 'for they would be conscious to themselves of not doing *enough*, not of doing *nothing*'.²⁴ It was after this that Hawkins gave him Sumner's *Apostolical Preaching*, which, he said,

---

20 Ibid, Preface to 2 ed, xxix.
21 Ibid, xxx.
22 H. Tristram, *John Henry Newman: Autobiographical Writings* (New York 1957), 206, dated 29 May 1825.
23 Ibid, 206, 17 July 1825.
24 Ibid, 201, 21 July 1824 (italics original).

threatened to drive him either into Calvinism or baptismal regeneration.[25] By 1826, as was indicated at the beginning of the chapter, his movement was complete.

There was also another element in the situation, which is less often noticed.[26] At some time in 1826 (when is uncertain) he was engaged in a keen debate with his brother Francis, whose opinion was moving in exactly the opposite direction. And this led him in 1827 to prepare a sixty-six-page defence of infant baptism for his sisters.[27] Francis Newman is interesting in this context because the path he took was very similar to that taken by those Anglican clergy involved in the 'Western Schism' referred to in chapter 2, namely a rejection of infant baptism because it seemed incompatible with evangelical doctrine. Francis moved to Dublin in 1827 and came under the influence of J.N. Darby, who was one of the founders of the Brethren: so he may also be seen as having links with the kind of search for a primitive Christianity that characterized the Haldanes' movement in Scotland. Francis described his problems in his spiritual autobiography, *Phases of Faith*. Like his brother's *Apologia Pro Vita Sua*, *Phases of Faith* may be described as 'emotion recollected in tranquillity', and is therefore not an absolutely reliable guide to Francis's feelings at the time: but it is illuminating nevertheless.

Francis felt that John was cold towards those whom Francis regarded as spiritual persons; and he was 'startled and distressed' by John's adoption of the doctrine of baptismal regeneration and his working out of views which Francis regarded 'as full-blown "Popery"'. He, therefore, gradually ceased to confide in John on deep religious matters. But he did not find evangelical authors such as Thomas Scott any more satisfactory. When he subscribed to the Thirty-Nine Articles for his BA degree, he was embarrassed by the question of infant baptism, but even if he could have reconciled himself to that, he saw the greater difficulty of baptismal regeneration behind it,

> For any one to avow that Regeneration took place in Baptism, seemed to me little short of a confession that he had never himself experienced what Regeneration is...for it was as clear as daylight to me...that the High Church and Popish fancy is

---

25 Ibid, 202, 24 August 1824, cf. J.H. Newman, *Apologia pro Vita Sua* (London 1959), 101.

26 It is not mentioned in either I. Ker, *John Henry Newman: A Biography* (Oxford 1988), or S. Gilley, *Newman and his Age* (London 1990).

27 *Letters and Diaries*, ii, 4-5; Sheridan, *Newman on Justification*, 128-33; Tristram, *Autobiographical Writings*, 211, 21 February 1828.

a superstitious perversion, based upon carnal inability to understand a strong spiritual metaphor.[28]

Nor was he impressed by an evangelical clergyman he consulted, who admitted that he did not approve of infant baptism either, but practised it because it was his duty to obey established authority. It is clear that Francis only had to communicate a fraction of this to John in order to alarm him, and the sixty-six pages John spent convincing his sisters that infant baptism was justifiable becomes understandable. It may also be that the argument which John used so often that the abandonment of the doctrine of baptismal regeneration led inexorably to socinianism was powerfully reinforced by the fact that this was exactly the road trodden by Francis.

The stages by which John reached his final position in 1828 with his sermons on infant baptism, and his unpublished manuscript, 'Remarks on the Covenant of Grace, in connection with the doctrines of Election, Baptism and the Church', have been carefully expounded by Father Sheridan and need not be repeated here.[29] They provided the basis for the kind of theology expounded in the *Tracts for the Times*. Before that is considered, however, something should be said about the background to Pusey's position, before he wrote Tracts 67 to 69. Pusey seems to have come from a fairly orthodox Anglican background, and never went through an evangelical phase in the way that Newman did. Newman got to know him well at Oriel since Pusey was elected a Fellow shortly after Newman in April 1824. In the Michaelmas Term 1824 they lodged in the same house, and Newman noted their conversations in which he was inclined to separate regeneration from baptism, while Pusey doubted that separation.[30] Pusey indeed may have played some part in that change as well as Hawkins, since Newman's next journal entry on 13 January 1825 noted some reasons for changing his view—the first one being, 'unless God is likely to vouchsafe grace in baptism, why ordain it for infants?'[31] Then Pusey went to Germany and with his marriage in June 1828 he had to give up his Oriel fellowship. In November, however, he returned to Oxford as Regius Professor of Hebrew.

Their friendship continued, though they found themselves on opposite sides during the controversy over Roman Catholic emancipation in 1829 when Peel failed to secure re-election as MP for Oxford University. In

---

28 F.W. Newman, *Phases of Faith* (6 ed, London 1860: reprinted, ed. U.C. Knoepflmacher, Leicester 1970), 7-10, cf. W. Robbins, *The Newman Brothers* (London 1966), 25-9.

29 Sheridan, *Justification*, 154-77.

30 Tristram, *Autobiographical Writings*, 203, cf. 191, 'I fear he is prejudiced against Thy children' (17 May 1824).

31 Ibid.

February 1832 Newman baptized Pusey's third child, Katherine, and when she died in November Newman wrote to him in these words:

> You have done for her what you could—you have dedicated her to God, and He has taken the offering. For me, I have had a great privilege in being the means of her dedication. It is our only service which we dare perform with a rejoicing conscience and a secure mind; and in the recollection it becomes doubly precious, and a festival-work, when, as in the case of your dear little one, we have the certainty of our prayers being accepted.[32]

He also added a note in his own copy after 'secure mind' as follows: 'N.B. I mean that the belief in the *opus operatum* saves one from feeling that one's own sin has mingled in it.'[33] The exchange of letters is significant because here were two men sharing a theological conviction and using it as consolation at a time of particular personal grief. Once again the early death of a child was the occasion. But this probably illustrates the kind of pastoral help that Newman would be accustomed to give in situations of this sort, which were obviously common. It is not surprising, therefore, that when Pusey cast his lot in with the infant tractarian movement in the last days of 1833 he soon showed a concern that something should be said about baptism.

In the spring of 1834 (24 February is the agreed date) Pusey wrote to Newman on the eve of his departure for the Isle of Wight to recover from an illness that he had wished to talk to him especially about the sacrament of baptism:

> Men need to be taught that it is a sacrament, and that a sacrament is not merely an outward badge of a Christian man's profession. And all union must I think be hollow which does not involve agreement in principles at least to the Sacraments. Great good also would be done by showing the true doctrine of Baptism in its warmth and life: whereas the Low Church think it essentially cold. Could not this be done, avoiding all technical terms?[34]

Pusey seems to have made a first sketch of the tract at this time. He really got down to work in the summer of 1835, prompted by the fact that a pupil of his 'was on the verge of leaving the Church for Dissent, and on the ground that the Church taught Baptismal Regeneration in the Prayer

---

[32] I. Ker and T. Gornall, *Letters and Diaries of John Henry Newman, iii, 1832-1833* (Oxford 1979), 21, 114, cf. Liddon, *Pusey*, i, 223. Compare also Pusey's letter on the death of another young child, Liddon, *Pusey*, i, 316-7.

[33] *Letters and Diaries iii*, 114, cf Mozley, *Letters of Newman*, i, 278. These words are not in the copy sent to Pusey, as printed by Liddon.

[34] Liddon, *Pusey*, i, 287-88; Mozley, *Letters of Newman*, ii, 27; *Letters and Diaries*, iv, 194.

Book'.[35] So he entitled his tract, *Scriptural Views of Holy Baptism*, to show that the doctrine was found in scripture too.

Pusey's tract was a turning point in the history of the Oxford Movement. Newman had been wondering whether to stop the tracts altogether, and he decided to print Pusey's tract in four parts during the autumn to give a breathing space while they decided what to do next.[36] Even in their first edition Pusey's tracts were longer than the previous average, running to nearly 300 pages in all. Pusey subsequently revised Tract 67 for its second edition, when it grew from forty-eight pages to 400: Tracts 68 and 69 never were revised, and so they are not usually to be found in the collected series of the Tracts, which was based on the second edition. Another consequence of this development was that the tract which Newman had written on baptism, at Pusey's request, never appeared in the series at all, and ended up by being used as material for numbers 18 to 20 of the third volume of the *Parochial and Plain Sermons*.[37] The enthusiasm with which his friends greeted Pusey's tract restored Newman's confidence; and he decided to carry on with the tracts, but to aim at longer works and less frequent publication. The old monthly schedule was abandoned, and in Newman's words the tracts became 'much more treatises than sketches'.[38]

It would be tedious to attempt a summary of Pusey's tract, even in the first edition. Owen Chadwick remarked that despite its massed information it

> succeeded only in clouding the issue for his successors; for amid all the texts and quotations about regeneration, he nowhere considered the meaning of the word *regeneration* itself...and thereby removed almost all permanent value from the volume, apart from its use as a work of reference.[39]

Certainly, if the published sermons are an adequate guide, Newman's tract would have been more useful. The essential features of the developed tractarian position, therefore, may be best described by drawing on both sources. The advantage of Newman is that it is clear what he was saying: the usefulness of Pusey is the way he related patristic teaching to scripture and his clear exposition of what he saw as the weakness of Reformed theology.

---

35 Liddon, *Pusey*, i, 323-4, 345.
36 Mozley, *Letters of Newman*, ii, 124, 133.
37 Mozley, *Letters of Newman*, ii, 113; Sheridan, *Justification*, 214-5. Sheridan is surely wrong in saying that it was Sermons 16-18.
38 Church, *Oxford Movement*, 135; Liddon, *Pusey*, i, 354-8; Mozley, *Letters of Newman*, ii, 135-8, 142-3, 150, 152-3, 157, 159.
39 W.O. Chadwick, *The Mind of the Oxford Movement* (London 1960), 47.

Having spent Tract 67 in expounding scripture and the Fathers, Pusey proceeded in the second part of Tract 68 to criticise Zwingli as the source of the errors of Reformed sacramental theology. At root Pusey believed this flaw in Zwingli to stem from his distrust of authority and his decidedly rationalistic frame of mind. More specifically, he explained, Zwingli's problem in this way:

> He had in his mind constantly the two truths, that the Sacraments could not *in themselves* convey grace, and that CHRIST alone was the author of all grace and spiritual influence, and he could not find the central point wherein the old Catholic doctrine might yet hold good with both these truths; namely that CHRIST conveyed His grace through His Sacraments.[40]

In Tract 69 Pusey traced the effects of Zwingli on Calvin's system and described the consequences as follows:

> Whatever general terms they may use of Baptism, when they begin to explain themselves, they always resolve its benefits into the sealing or attesting past promises, or the shadowing forth of subsequent regeneration, and this to be effected by the hearing of the word, not by the influence of Baptism: they declare that by *seals* they do not mean instruments of conveying grace: they deny that Baptism is the means of remitting original sin, or of obtaining justification; they assert that those who are truly baptized have the substance of Baptism before they are baptized, and have been regenerated: that the gift of Baptism they have already received; have already been made members of CHRIST'S Church; they deny that *all* are born in original guilt; they regard it as grievous error, to suppose that we are regenerated by the act of baptizing: Baptism, according to them, does not make persons children of GOD, but attests them to be so: the Sacraments do not confer grace: nay, they seem to regard the Sacraments as extolled, if they place their efficacy on a level with that of GOD'S written word, (which has, doubtless, also a mystical power, as being GOD'S word, and operates as such on the human soul, independently of, and above its containing Divine truth, yet is not a direct means of union with GOD in CHRIST): the Sacraments are in no other way efficacious, contribute nothing in addition to the written word: the words of consecration are of no other avail than by teaching; by teaching alone does the dead element begin to be a Sacrament.[41]

This summary, despite its massive justifying footnotes, does not do justice to the position Pusey was describing. Whether wilfully or ignorantly, Pusey failed to see the difference between the sacramental doctrine of Zwingli and Calvin: the most likely explanation is that he came to the text with a prejudice that Calvin's doctrine was identical to Zwingli's, and simply interpreted it in that way. For example, where he had to

---

40 E.B. Pusey, *Scriptural Views of Holy Baptism* (London 1836), 91 (italics original).
41 Ibid, 115-24 (italics original).

acknowledge that Calvin contradicted Zwingli, he said the difference was in words.[42] Significantly also he emphasized that Socinianism arose directly from the heritage of Zwingli and Calvin; this had been a regular part of high church rhetoric for at least half a century, though it was hardly the only direction which the heirs of Zwingli and Calvin had moved. Against this position Pusey set out what he regarded as the Catholic one:

> We admit, however, that Baptism *is* a Sacrament; and if so, it must convey the grace annexed to it, whenever no obstacle is placed in its way by the unworthiness of the recipient. For this has been the notion of the whole Christian Church, that the Sacraments are not bare signs, but do convey that which they signify... And since infants are all alike incapable of opposing the Divine benefits, and the wilfulness which they might hereafter show, has no place there, and God in His Word has given us no ground for making any distinction between them, we must conclude, as the whole Antient Church did, that the benefits of Holy Baptism are by virtue of the Sacrament itself, and of the Divine Institution, imparted to all infants.[43]

So he also defends the *ex opere operato* understanding of the sacraments as expounded by Bellarmine, saying that it 'contains nothing which our Church, as well as the Lutheran, does not equally hold, whereas the school of Zuingli (sic) and Calvin cannot'.[44]

In view of this, it is quite clear why Pusey and Newman denied that baptism was identical with circumcision. Newman claimed that the parallel between baptism and circumcision was resorted to precisely because people wished to deny that baptism effected regeneration, and they therefore sought an alternative explanation which had the convenient merit of being 'a proof that a divinely-appointed ordinance need not convey grace, even while it admits into a state of grace'.[45] The first reason for baptizing infants, said Newman, was that the Church had ever done so. Furthermore, there was always the danger of minimising the effect of the new covenant: for Pusey and Newman the regeneration given to Christians in baptism was something that even the patriarchs and prophets of the Old Testament had never received.[46]

This was the point at which the question of what regeneration meant pressed hardest, for both writers acknowledged that the patriarchs and prophets were sanctified. Here Pusey was either vague, or mysterious

---

42 Ibid, 110. Sumner showed more knowledge of Calvin than Pusey, but this is not surprising.
43 Ibid, 83-84 (italics original).
44 Ibid, 193.
45 J.H. Newman, *Parochial and Plain Sermons* (new ed, London 1881), iii, 275; cf Pusey, *Scriptural Views*, 108, 135-7.
46 Newman, *Parochial Sermons*, iii, 230, 259; Pusey, *Scriptural Views*, 137.

depending on one's point of view; whilst Newman was much more explicit.

> As every one, who has been duly baptized, is, in one sense, in the Church, even though his sins have since hid God's countenance from him; so, if a man has not been baptized, be he ever so correct and exemplary in his conduct, this does not prove that he has received regeneration, which is the peculiar and invisible gift of the Church. What is Regeneration? It is the gift of a new and spiritual nature; but men have, through God's blessing, obeyed and pleased Him without it.[47]

Elsewhere he described this gift as the glory of God, which 'is imparted to every member on his Baptism', or as the Holy Spirit himself.[48]

If this was the gift in baptism, then wilfully to deprive children of it was indeed to be deplored. The only way in which parents could remove the distress they were bound to feel on reflecting that their child was 'shapen in iniquity, conceived in sin and born a child of wrath' was to bring that child for baptism. As Newman said, 'He receives by birth a curse, but by Baptism a blessing, and the blessing is the greater.'[49] Moreover we may be confident that there is no uncertainty about whether children are in the elect:

> He has expressly assured us that children are in the number of His chosen; and, if you ask, whether all children, I reply, all children you can bring to Baptism, all children who are within reach of it.[50]

Both Newman and Pusey criticised the view that baptism should be confined to the children of believing parents, and faced without flinching the alleged *reductio ad absurdam* that this would justify baptizing the children of the heathen. 'It would, indeed, prove nothing, if true;' wrote Pusey, 'for why should it follow, in the spiritual, any more than in the natural world, that because a gift was rendered useless for want of cultivation, therefore it had never been given?'[51] And it is interesting that Newman's final argument here returned to the question of infant mortality: in meeting the argument that children's hopes ultimately seemed to rest on their parents' faith, prayers and careful training of them, he responded,

> Is there no difference between a chance and a certainty? How many infants die in their childhood? is it no difference between knowing that a child is gone to heaven,

---

47 Newman, *Parochial Sermons*, iii, 230.
48 Ibid, 266, 271.
49 Ibid, 294.
50 Ibid, 292.
51 Pusey, *Scriptural Views*, 164, cf 158-64; Newman, *Parochial Sermons*, iii, 294-7.

or that he has died as he was born? But supposing a child lives, is not regeneration a real gain?[52]

Finally, it should be noted that Pusey in Tract 68 raised the problem of post-baptismal sin, drawing attention to its seriousness, since no further regeneration after baptism was available. When he came to revise the tract, he felt that he had to wait until he had read more about absolution and 'the absolving influence of the Holy Eucharist'.[53] Thus it was that the famous sermon of 1843 came to be preached, 'The Holy Eucharist a Comfort to the Penitent'. It is significant that the Baptist, Charles Stovel, in his discussion of the baptismal regeneration controversy in the same year, saw that sermon as bringing out into the open the *opus operatum* doctrine held in the Church of England, which he regarded as never having been discarded at the time of the Reformation. Thus Stovel regarded baptismal regeneration as 'the first principle of the Tractarian heresy' which 'sustains the whole system'. He acknowledged that the origin of the *opus operatum* view lay in the wish to make the efficacy of the sacrament independent of the character of the priest, but he moved very swiftly to say that it was fundamental to the doctrine of infant baptism, since an infant cannot have faith.[54]

Pusey's tract on baptism, therefore, served to accelerate evangelical fears of the Oxford Movement, an ironical result since part of Newman's hope in writing his unpublished tract was to conciliate evangelicals.[55] But the mess he got into over inviting Golightly to be his curate at Littlemore only then to find him preaching elsewhere in Oxford against Pusey's tract is a small illustration of his inability sometimes to see danger ahead.[56] Thomas Biddulph in 1837 published a pamphlet on baptismal regeneration, which was substantially the reply he had written to Richard Mant in 1816, except that now the tract was described as a tool of papist penetration into the Anglican citadel.[57] This kind of language indeed loomed large in the comments made by the *Christian Observer* on a letter written by Newman in defence of the Tracts. Some of it was good knockabout stuff, as when the *Observer* defended itself against the charge of making concessions to dissenters by saying that at least it did not call them 'in the classical language of the Oxford Tracts, "a mob of Tiptops, Gapes, and Yawns (!!!)" with many other equally calm and well-chosen expressions, which we beseech Mr Newman to reflect upon before he again charges the *Christian Observer* with using strong language towards

---

52 Newman, *Parochial Sermons*, iii, 297-8.
53 Letter to Harrison, Liddon, *Pusey*, i, 353.
54 Stovel, *Baptismal Regeneration Controversy*, iv-v, vi, 23-5, 217.
55 Sheridan, *Justification*, 216.
56 Mozley, *Letters of Newman*, ii, 102-5.
57 Fox, *Biddulph*, 294-9.

the Oxford writers'.⁵⁸ More seriously, it argued that however sophisticated a sacramental doctrine a Pusey, a Keble, a Newman, a Fenelon, a Bellarmine or a Borromeo might devise 'the rude multitude will transmute every thing to gross materiality and soul-deluding superstition'.⁵⁹ Only the preaching of justification by faith could stand against that. On baptism in particular, said the *Observer*,

> The whole of this confusion arises from applying to persons baptized in infancy, but who when they come to age are living in unbelief and ungodliness, the glowing language of the Sacred Writers respecting believing adults.⁶⁰

The system of the Oxford Tracts in their simplicity, it concluded, was 'the very spirit of that Popery against which the Reformers protested, and from which, through the mercy of God, this nation has for nearly three centuries been delivered'.⁶¹ What comes through these various charges, however, are the underlying fears of evangelicals: and it needs to be remembered that the *Christian Observer* was a journal for moderate evangelicals, precisely those whom Newman might have hoped to persuade.⁶²

Not surprisingly the *Tracts for the Times* were regarded by most nonconformists as a manifestation of popery. But Wesleyans in particular reacted against the apparently Roman tendencies of the Tractarians because they had always regarded themselves as sharing an essentially Anglican theology; and a series of tracts and books were published in reply. This also exposed the diversity of views among Wesleyans on the matter. Richard Watson's *Theological Institutes* of 1829 probably reflected the position closest to that of the Book of Common Prayer. Many took a middle position which tried to balance the emphasis on regeneration with an appropriate recognition of what was begun in baptism. But by the later 1830s some were much more trenchant in their criticism of the Church of England. In May 1837 the Revd John McLean, who had been a probationer under Jabez Bunting, wrote to him from Sheffield to criticize a tract in a series published by the Book Room, entitled *Baptism not the new Birth*, on the grounds that it was at variance with Wesleyan and scriptural theology:

> That Baptism *is not* the new birth is true; that Baptism and the new birth do not *invariably* go together is true also; but that an infant *as such* is *incapable* of the new birth as this tract attempts to prove, is a most cruel and God-dishonouring

---

58 *Christian Observer* (1837), 173.
59 Ibid, 166.
60 Ibid, 183-4.
61 Ibid, 197.
62 P. Toon, *Evangelical Theology, 1833-1856* (London 1979), 6-7, 31-3.

notion—a notion repudiated by Mr Wesley, by the Church of England, by primitive antiquity, and above all by the scriptures of truth.[63]

Two or three years later George Cubitt, assistant Connexional Editor, in a letter to Bunting lamented a tendency towards what he called a 'low Arminianism' in theology which detracted from evangelism and also contained a low view of the sacraments. He referred to a meeting of the Book Committee at which someone had said that they were 'getting fast on to Oxford Tractism', citing as evidence the fact that a preacher before the Conference had spoken about 'the grace given in Baptism!'[64] In 1842 the Book Committee decided to publish a series of ten anonymous *Wesleyan Tracts for the Times* to combat high church claims: John Hannah, who was President in 1842, wrote one on 'Wesleyan Methodism *not Schism*' and Cubitt one on 'Justification by *faith* an essential doctrine of Christianity'.[65] The combination in 1843 of the Disruption of the Church of Scotland and Sir James Graham's Factory Education Bill pushed many Wesleyans to resist the establishment and affirm their protestantism. A letter to Bunting from Abraham Farrar, Superintendent of the Liverpool (North) circuit, at the end of March 1843 claimed that the Church of England wished to assert its exclusive rights and that a century's work in building chapels and gathering Sunday schools deserved 'only to share the fate of the Socialism and Chartism of the day—and ought to be swept aside to make an open platform for the full operation of the Oxford Tractarians!'[66]

Alfred Barrett represented the most substantial Wesleyan reaction to Tractarianism. His *Catholic and Evangelical Principles*, published in 1843, captured in its title the feeling on the part of many Wesleyans that they affirmed their position as part of the Catholic Church whilst distancing themselves from any Romeward movement. In his letters on baptism he began by justifying the practice of infant baptism along the lines developed in William Wall's *History of Infant Baptism* (1705), arguing that baptism was connected with grace but not regeneration. He said that infants were '*declaratively* accepted' in baptism, and 'as their acceptance is grounded on the christian covenant, and not on the natural benignity which God bears to all his creatures, the christian sacrament is devoutly to be regarded as the expression of this acceptance'.[67] Somewhat trenchantly he asserted that 'the living Church has no interest

---

63 W.R. Ward (ed), *Early Victorian Methodism: the Correspondence of Jabez Bunting, 1830-1858* (Oxford 1976), 187.
64 Ibid, 237-8.
65 Ibid, 270-1.
66 Ibid, 283-4.
67 A. Barrett, *Catholic and Evangelical Principles viewed in their present application to the Church of God in a series of letters to a friend* (London 1843), 72 (italics original).

in dying infants beyond that of following with a spiritual eye their certain and direct flight to the paradise of God'.[68] Quoting Wesley's *Journal*, he affirmed that regeneration was a response to faith rather than the application of water. He cited Hooker in support of this position, and argued that even the baptism of adults was promissory:

> this sacrament is an infallible pledge to the faithful soul that pardon and all things necessary to salvation shall be given, while on the part of the recipient it is a voluntary engagement to submission, obedience, faith and holiness in whatever degrees they may be obtained.[69]

Barrett argued that Calvin had got things right, significantly quoting his *Commentaries* rather than the *Institutes*, not least in his rhetorical question, 'what are sacraments other than signs of the word?'[70] Moreover he dismissed the Tractarian doctrine of the church as a body with 'a life distinct from that of its individual members' as 'a figment of the imagination'.[71]

Barrett denied that evangelicals depreciated sacraments in order to exalt faith. In his penultimate letter on baptism he suggested that the problem was that the Fathers, influenced, he thought, by the tradition of Hellenistic Judaism in Alexandria, resurrected the Jewish idea of a new birth associated with proselyte baptism and applied it to Christianity, despite the apostolic distinction. But his knock-down argument was that even Augustine said that '*the sacrament of baptism is one thing*, and (conversionem cordis) *the conversion of the heart another*: but that the salvation of a person is completed by both of them'.[72] He concluded that,

---

68 Ibid, 73.
69 Ibid, 82.
70 Ibid 91-3, quoting Calvin's *Commentary on the Epistle to the Ephesians*. The Latin 'quid enim sunt Sacramenta, quam verbi, sigilla?' is rendered 'What else are the sacraments but seals of the Word?' in the edition edited by D.W. Torrance and T.F. Torrance (Edinburgh 1965), 207. Barrett cited Augustine, 'Take away the word, and the water is neither more nor less than water', *Tractate 80 on the Gospel of St John*, §3 in P. Schaff (ed), *Select Library of the Nicene and Post-Nicene Fathers*, vii (1888, reprinted Grand Rapids 1983), 344; this is also cited in Bishop Jewel's *Treatise of the Sacraments*: J. Ayre (ed), *The Works of John Jewel, Bishop of Salisbury*, ii (Cambridge 1847), 1105. In the next sentence Augustine described the sacraments as 'a kind of visible word'.
71 Barrett, *Catholic and Evangelical Principles*, 96.
72 Ibid, 105, 107-13. The quotation is on p 113, and the italics are Barrett's; it comes from Augustine, *On Baptism, against the Donatists*, Bk iv, ch 25 in P. Schaff (ed), *Select Library of the Nicene and Post-Nicene Fathers*, iv (1887; reprinted Grand Rapids 1979), 462. Barrett took it from Wall, *The History of Infant Baptism*, i, 256.

> If conversion of the heart after baptism be needed, then their regeneration cannot be regarded as in itself effecting much, and on this single point they take common ground with the most enthusiastic Methodist that ever lived.[73]

Interestingly Pusey conceded this point in a letter to the press in 1849 following the Gorham Judgement. In response to a comment by William Goode that an adult is not necessarily in a state of spiritual regeneration because he was baptized as an infant, Pusey said,

> If Mr Goode means by this that an adult is not necessarily in a state of grace, and so may require a solid and entire conversion, notwithstanding the gift of God in Baptism, no Christian instructed in the first principles of the Faith would contend with him.[74]

One almost wonders what all the fuss was about!

It is striking how again and again the issue of dying infants returns. Barrett saw that much of the problem could be explained by the application to infants of an understanding of baptism originally developed in relation to adults; but he rejected the Roman *ex opere operato* solution:

> Original sin does exist in infants, and it must be washed away. If they die in infancy this washing is effected by the Spirit's application of the atoning blood and his own sanctifying energy pledged in baptism, and if they live it is removed at the same time with the blotting out of their actual transgressions, which is the justification of their persons, and if they are never justified from actual transgression it is never removed. But to assert the new birth to be effected solely and simultaneously with the application of water by episcopal administrators, irrespective of the moral chacter or the spiritual apathy of the responsible parties, is to have here before us the Romanist doctrine on the subject. There is no *via media* here, however the Tracts may attempt to explore such a path; sacraments are either those 'moral instruments of salvation', which Hooker speaks of, or else they are charms.[75]

Barrett, therefore, defended Wesley's amendments to the Book of Common Prayer on the grounds that even in adults 'the outward sign and the inward grace are not always concomitant' and the blessing infants receive is not regeneration but intended to lead to that in later life.[76]

A final letter on baptism and justification suggested that the Tractarian doctrine of the doubtfulness of pardon after baptism was likely to drive

---

73 Barrett, *Catholic and Evangelical Principles*, 113.

74 H.P. Liddon, *Life of Edward Bouverie Pusey*, iii (London 1894), 236; cited (without source) by C.C.J. Webb, *Religious Thought in the Oxford Movement* (London 1928), 103-4, and J.M. Turner, *Conflict and Reconciliation* (London 1985), 153.

75 Barrett, *Catholic and Evangelical Principles*, 118-9.

76 Ibid, 126.

the awakened conscience to despair. But he noted that the doctrine of the Spirit's direct witness to our adoption was regarded as fanaticism, and asked why it was not fanaticism to believe that the Spirit could 'awaken alarm, and give godly sorrow which worketh repentance to salvation'. The Methodist pleaded for one part of this experience and the high churchman for the other. 'Both are equally opposed to the experience of the unawakened worldling.'[77] So he concluded that 'evangelical doctrine provides far more efficiently than what is called Anglicanism, for the existence and spread of holiness'.[78]

It is interesting that Barrett returned several times to the notion of covenant underlying infant baptism, and despite his evangelical Arminianism was ready to cite Calvin in support. Hence he said that infant baptism could not legitimately be administered 'to other than the children of believing parents', because of 'the covenant character of the rite'.[79] Barrett's open-mindedness contrasts with Pusey's tunnel vision. He wrote an interesting letter to Jabez Bunting in 1845 about the newly-formed Evangelical Alliance, expressing the hope that it really would be a 'constant exhibition to the world of Christian unity'. Holding as he did 'the sentiments of evangelical Arminianism', he had been 'delighted in intercourse with Calvinist brethren to find in them an approximation to my own views which I did not previously suspect, and in some instances a use of scripture phraseology which was juster and more emphatic than that to which I had been accustomed'.[80] But he also worried lest it become simply an 'Anti-Popish confederation'. On the whole Barrett was a more temperate critic of the tractarians than other nonconformists, but the bluntness of his language cannot be missed, in effect representing Wesleyan disappointment that the Oxford Movement was moving away from what had previously been regarded as a common Reformation heritage with the Church of England.

It will now be clear what George Cornelius Gorham was trying to avoid when in the *Ecclesiastical Gazette* for 8 September 1846 he placed the following advertisement:

> A Curate is wanted by the resident Incumbent of St Just, Cornwall. He must be an active, pious man, free from all tendency to what is well understood by the term Tractarian error, &c.[81]

---

77 Ibid, 138.
78 Ibid, 142.
79 Ibid, 128.
80 Ward, *Early Victorian Methodism*, 334, 337.
81 G.C. Gorham, *Examination before Admission to a Benefice by the Bishop of Exeter* (London 1848), 6.

Henry Phillpotts, the Bishop of Exeter, rebuked Gorham for his choice of words, and indicated that he would wish to examine the person appointed. When Gorham found a suitable candidate, Phillpotts said he needed to satisfy himself 'of the soundness of his views on the great points of Christian doctrine, especially on Baptism, the foundation of all'.[82] Gorham indicated that his potential curate's views were identical with his own, and after an episcopal examination Phillpotts granted a licence. Gorham then wrote to Phillpotts, complaining of his treatment, drawing attention to his long service, and pointing out that when he had come to St Just the chancel was 'crowded with Popish furniture' and the services affected 'a Popish model'.[83] All this had been the result of the influence of men like Newman and Oakeley who had recently seceded to Rome. When later in 1847 the Lord Chancellor presented Gorham to the vicarage of Brampford Speke in Devon, Phillpotts firstly declined to counter-sign Gorham's testimonial on the ground that he had written contrary to the discipline of the Church, and that what he had said made Phillpotts think that he also held what was contrary to its doctrine. Then, after the Lord Chancellor had persisted in his presentation, Phillpotts summoned Gorham for an examination of his doctrine on baptism, lasting for five days in December and three days in March 1848 and consisting of 149 questions in all. The upshot was that Phillpotts ruled that Gorham's doctrine of baptism was unsound, and he declined to institute him.

The key questions in the examination were numbers five to seven in which Phillpotts asked whether Gorham held that infants properly baptized were made children of God and born again of water and of the Holy Ghost. Gorham's answer was that Articles 25 and 26 made it clear that worthy reception, as well as right administration, was essential if the sacraments were to be effectual signs of grace, hence 'where there is no worthy reception, there is no bestowment of grace'.[84] This meant that the Church's affirmation that the child was a member of Christ etc. was based on a 'charitable hope'. 'Regeneration, therefore, in Baptism', continued Gorham, 'is affirmed *absolutely* in words, but *conditionally* in meaning; it *may not* have taken place, and is, therefore, to be *implored* in after years.'[85] From this position Gorham refused to be budged, and supported his position by arguments from the Homilies and the Reformers. When Phillpotts refused to institute him, he appealed to the Court of Arches, where in August 1849, Sir Herbert Jenner Fust ruled that since Gorham had denied that grace was conferred by baptism or through baptism, he had maintained opinions contrary to the Church, 'as the

---

82 Phillpotts to Gorham, 25 November 1846, ibid, 9.
83 Gorham to Phillpotts, 28 January 1847, ibid, 18, 24-26.
84 Ibid, 68-9.
85 Ibid, 70-1, 74 (italics original).

doctrine of the Church of England undoubtedly is, that children baptized are regenerated at baptism, and are undoubtedly saved if they die without committing actual sin'.[86] Gorham appealed to the Judicial Committee of the Privy Council. J.C.S. Nias has examined the arguments presented in considerable detail, so it is sufficient to cite the main conclusions of Lord Langdale's judgement, given on 8 March 1850. His first point was that the case had to be decided from the Articles and Liturgy, as interpreted by the normal legal rules of interpretation. Secondly, he declared that the Articles did not determine what was signified by right reception of a sacrament, nor what was the distinct meaning and effect of the grace of regeneration. Thirdly, the Prayer Book was to be interpreted by the Articles, and not *vice versa*. Finally, he declared that since men such as Jewel, Hooker, Ussher, Jeremy Taylor and others had maintained opinions not significantly different from Gorham, the judgement in the Court of Arches ought to be reversed.[87]

The results of this judgement were many and various. There were still a number of legal devices which had to be gone through before Gorham was instituted on the *fiat* of the Archbishop of Canterbury, with the Bishop of Exeter declaring that he would not hold communion with anyone who instituted Gorham. The judgement also provoked a second wave of secessions to Rome, as well as a declaration from the high church party against it. The legal principles for determining the doctrine of the Church of England laid down in the Gorham Judgement, however, proved to be long-lasting. The most significant theological consequences were twofold. On the one hand, evangelical suspicions of baptismal regeneration were intensified, even though Pusey still believed that the difference between high church and low church was not as great as some of the more alarmist high churchmen had claimed.[88] Archbishop Sumner published the ninth edition of his *Apostolical Preaching* with a new preface in which he reaffirmed that the Church of England considered that baptism conveyed regeneration, but also drew attention to the variety of opinions which the Church had historically allowed. Although he did not share all those opinons, he did not doubt that a minister of the Church might justly maintain them because there was no definitive word of scripture on the matter: 'Scripture declares the general necessity of baptism, without determining the actual effect of infant baptism.' The Church's formularies were framed 'on the principle of charitable presumption'.[89] Nevertheless, Peter Toon has suggested that evangelicals developed 'such a fear of baptismal regeneration *ex opere operato* that

---

86 Quoted in G.C.B. Davies, *Henry Phillpotts, Bishop of Exeter, 1778-1869* (London 1954), 237; J.C.S. Nias, *Gorham and the Bishop of Exeter* (London 1957), 60-73.
87 Nias, *Gorham*, 97-104.
88 Liddon, *Pusey*, iii, 263-4.
89 Sumner, *Apostolical Preaching* (9 ed), v, ix-xi.

gradually all views involving full baptismal regeneration were given up'.[90] Secondly, the Gorham Judgement still had not defined what the Anglican doctrine of baptismal regeneration was: it had simply declared that Gorham's position, which need not in any case be regarded as an absolute denial of regeneration, was not contrary to Anglican doctrine.

In conclusion, therefore, it is instructive to consider the view taken by J.B. Mozley. James Mozley was a younger brother of Thomas Mozley, a friend of Newman who became a Fellow of Oriel in 1829. James himself went up to Oriel in October 1830 and became a pupil of Newman. He is generally regarded as one of the middle group of tractarians, alongside R.W. Church, and also as one of the ablest minds of the movement, next to Newman himself. John Tulloch said of him that 'as a theologian [he] is really great, although somewhat hard and polemical'.[91] There can be no doubt about Mozley's enthusiasm for and commitment to the Oxford Movement, but it is interesting that in 1838 he commented in a letter to Thomas that he had never read Pusey's *Baptism* 'in a regular way'.[92] It was also Mozley in an article in the *Christian Remembrancer* for January 1846, who remarked that it was doubtful whether Newman had ever fully identified himself with the life and work of the Church of England, because he energised as an author rather than as a parish priest: though it should be noted that he wrote at the time that it was the most disagreeable article he had ever had to write.[93]

When the Gorham Judgement was announced, Mozley took a cautious line, seeing 'nothing immediate coming to alarm people'. He said that those who wished to push matters to extremes were not men of weight or influence, 'intellectual or moral'. Nor was he prepared to commit himself to an opinion on whether Gorham was 'really an actual heretic or not'. He did not believe that the matter could be decided solely on the basis of statements in the Baptism Service, and he saw changes and modifications in the doctrine coming out in history, as allowable within the Church.[94] He then spent the next four years in further reading on the subject, which led to the writing of two books, or rather one book in two parts: *The Augustinian Doctrine of Predestination*, and *The Primitive Doctrine of Baptismal Regeneration*, published in 1855 and 1856 respectively. These books represented a 'very decided change of opinion' on the doctrine of baptismal regeneration, and consequently he felt duty bound to give up

---

90 Toon, *Evangelical Theology*, 195.
91 J. Tulloch, *Movements of Religious Thought in Britain during the Nineteenth Century* (London 1885: reprinted, ed. A.C. Cheyne, Leicester 1971), 121; Chadwick, *Oxford Movement*, 60, 174.
92 A. Mozley, *Letters of the Rev. J.B. Mozley, D.D.* (London 1885), 73.
93 *Christian Remembrancer*, xi (1846), 179; Mozley, *Letters of Mozley*, 173.
94 Mozley, *Letters of Mozley*, 202-3.

the editorship of the *Christian Remembrancer*, which was identified with the high church party.

> I now entertain no doubt of the substantial justice of the Gorham decision on this point (he wrote). Practically I have no wish to separate myself from those with whom I have hitherto acted. The Tractarian body is *now* the one with which, on the whole, I most sympathise... But when a particular doctrine has been made the watchword, and people have been considered to take their sides, according as they thought one way or another upon it, a disagreement with the party with which one has hitherto acted upon it cannot be ignored by one's-self.[95]

When he published his *Review of the Baptismal Controversy* in 1862, the separation was more apparent and even extended within the family, because the *Christian Remembrancer* took a strong line against the book; but his brother John refused to allow James to dissociate the family name from the title page of the periodical.[96]

The great value of Mozley's work lies in enabling us to see how the theological method of the tractarians was modified in such a way that it was able to survive. To read through Mozley's pages is, as it were, to enter a new world—the modern world. Newman wrote rather sourly and unjustly, 'Poor James Mozley never had a grain of Catholicism in him—he is as hard as a stone. Curious, that his hardness and Pusey's softness should issue in the same result.'[97] Nevertheless, with an easy confidence and lucidity Mozley moves through the controversy making a series of points which one is surprised to reflect have not really been made before, despite the many words written.

Two points in particular may be emphasized. The first is a general one, concerned with the use of language and the use of sources in theology. Mozley pointed out that it was not sufficient to discuss in general terms whether biblical statements should be interpreted literally or in some other way: in either case their meaning could only be understood by reference to the system of thought which they assumed. So he criticised the way in which Augustine had been quoted frequently but with little appreciation of his overall theological system. Similarly, it was a mistake to collect as many patristic assertions of baptismal regeneration as possible: 'a statement is not explained by simply being repeated; the question still remaining to be answered—What is the meaning of it?'[98] For Mozley the key to the meaning of the word 'regenerate' lay in the

---

95 Ibid, 227-8 (italics original).
96 Ibid, 253-4.
97 Newman to W.G. Todd, in C.S. Dessain (ed), *The Letters and Diaries of John Henry Newman, xvii, 1855-57* (London 1967), 205.
98 Mozley, *Baptismal Regeneration*, xl.

predestinarian language of scripture. Failure to see this had led people to construct

> a forced and artificial meaning of the term regenerate, as signifying a capacity only,—a meaning based upon the doctrine of free-will, and representing that doctrine; whereas the term regenerate does not represent the free-will side of Scripture doctrine, but the predestinarian one.[99]

On the other hand, it followed from this that the assertion that regeneration was given in baptism had to be hypothetical rather than literal. Was it not odd, he asked, that the defenders of a literal interpretation began by asserting that people who were manifestly wicked were actually regenerate? And then he drove the sword deep into the wound by saying that a careful reading of Pusey's tract must lead to the conclusion that it almost anticipated the Gorham Judgement, since the language cited from the Fathers had to be taken hypothetically rather than literally. In fact, he argued, the position taken by the high church party in the Gorham Case made two serious mistakes. One was the assertion that it is necessary to believe that God gives all baptized persons a grace or spiritual power sufficient for them to attain salvation—because the Church's tolerance of predestinarianism shows that it has always been an open question whether God gives all Christians this sufficient grace at all. The second mistake was to call this grace 'regeneration', and he pointed up this remark by wondering whether if the word in dispute had been 'election' rather than 'regeneration', as in terms of the formularies it might well have been, there would have been the same fuss, or the same refusal to define what regeneration meant.[100]

The second point which Mozley made, which is worth emphasizing, concerns infant baptism. Arguing that infant baptism is not an article of faith but a Christian custom, he noted that there is no proof in scripture for infant baptism, and therefore obviously there cannot be proof for infant regeneration either. He also pointed out that William Wall, whose *History of Infant Baptism* (1705) was still the standard work, had argued that it should be treated as an open question, not dividing members of the same church; and he condemned the Baptists not for their opinions but for dividing the Church over the matter.[101] The main problem facing the Church in its doctrine of baptism was that whereas the institution was primarily designed for adults, and only secondarily for infants, the practice of infant baptism had come to be so completely the general rule that it was popularly regarded as primarily for infants and only secondarily for adults. In the case of adults, and indeed of infants if they

---

99 Ibid, xxiv.
100 Ibid, xxxi, xxxii, xlvii-lxi.
101 J.B. Mozley, *Review of the Baptismal Controversy* (London 1862), 22, 370-1.

were seen as potential adults, the assertion of regeneration was hypothetical. But the Church had customarily made an absolute assertion of regeneration in the case of infants: why? The answer was partly that although, as he put it, infants 'get baptism on one ground, they keep it on another', and it was impossible to separate the grace of baptism from the one baptized. But, more important, if one looked to see why Augustine so confidently asserted that baptized infants dying in infancy are certainly saved, the answer is that their early death saves them from actual sin.

> The gift of early death is in the Augustinian system one form of the grace of final perseverance: the same God who secures the elect adult from the bad effect of trial, saves the elect infant from meeting it, and gives victory in the one case, innocence in the other.[102]

However, by this time an alternative view of baptism had been advanced by F.D. Maurice, who turned away completely from the arguments over post-baptismal sin. This will be the theme of the next chapter.

---

102 Ibid, 126-35.

CHAPTER 5

'A Spiritual and Universal Kingdom'

Towards the end of his life Frederick Denison Maurice wrote an autobiographical letter to his son in which he described how he had come to write his book, *The Kingdom of Christ*:

> I had been much impressed in my Bubbenhall curacy among labourers and farmers; I was still more impressed in the midst of this London population of sick men and women, with the language of our Catechism—that language which caused most offence to the Evangelical school. It seemed to me that except I could address all kinds of people as members of Christ and children of God, I could not address them at all. Their sin, it seemed to me, must mean a departure from that state; it must be their true state, that which Christ had claimed for them. I thought I had no Gospel for the sufferers in Guy's Hospital, if it was not that... I felt therefore much sympathy with those who spoke of baptism as bearing witness of the state into which men are redeemed; I felt the worth of that direct appeal to the hearts and consciences of men which had distinguished the Evangelical preachers of the last century from the dry moralists, but I thought they had become weak, because they assumed sin, and not redemption, as the starting point. The new form of churchmanship which was set forth in the Oxford Tracts had so far an attraction for me that it appeared to treat of a regeneration as dependent on the will of God and the death of Christ, not the individual faith of men... With that part which concerned baptism I dreamed for a while that I should have a real point of union. That dream was entirely scattered by Dr Pusey's tract on Baptism. Instead of affording me the least warrant for the kind of teaching which appeared to me alone Scriptural and practical, it made such teaching utterly impossible. The baptised child was holy for a moment after baptism, in committing sin it lost its purity. That could only be recovered by acts of repentance and a system of ascetical discipline. I remember to this day the misery which this tract caused me as I read it in a walk to one of the London suburbs; I saw that I must be hopelessly and for ever estranged from this doctrine and from those who taught it, unless I abandoned all my hopes for myself and for the world.[1]

There in a nutshell is a description and an explanation of Maurice's theology of baptism. *The Kingdom of Christ* was in a sense his answer to Pusey, setting out his vision of the relationship of the world and the Church, both alike under the kingship of Christ. In looking for the signs

---

1 F. Maurice, *Life of Frederick Denison Maurice* (London 1884), i, 236-7.

of the existence of the Church on earth, he asked 'whether Baptism be not the sign of a spiritual and universal kingdom?'[2]

Though there are a number of references to the effect Pusey's tract had on him, Maurice nowhere pinpoints the precise passage to which he objected. It could be part of the discussion in Tract 68 of the effects of post-baptismal sin: referring to baptism as God's seal put upon us, Pusey wrote:

> If we have broken that seal and resisted that Spirit, we cannot be as if we had kept it safe and listened to His warnings... Let us bless God that, although that first and more joyous way of Baptismal faithfulness may no longer be open to any of us, another, though more rugged and toilsome and watered with bitter tears, is still left.[3]

A more interesting question is whether Maurice would or would not have agreed with the statement in Tract 69:

> Regeneration then, or the new-birth whereby we are made sons of God, is a privilege of the Church of Christ; and we dare not extend it where His word does not warrant us. To the Church alone in this life, it belongs to be the mother of the sons of God.[4]

Nevertheless, the significance of Maurice is that he broke away from the premise for redemption and thus for baptism that both Roman Catholics and Protestants had in common—the doctrine of the Fall. This was why the Wesleyan theologian, J.H. Rigg, spoke of what seemed to him to be Maurice's light treatment of revelation: 'He believed in God's revelation just so far as this seemed to tally with his own personal needs and convictions'.[5] Although in his own time his theology was regarded as somewhat eccentric, he was the inspiration for the incarnational emphasis made by Hort and Westcott at Cambridge, and in a rather different way by Gore and Scott Holland at Oxford, because his Platonism provided a basis for the developing interest in the Greek Fathers in the later nineteenth century. Thus, in a rather curious way Maurice became another bridge whereby the later Tractarians were able to walk away from the kind of theological foundation on which Pusey and Liddon built. So Michael Ramsey was able to speak with enthusiasm in 1948 about what could be learnt from Maurice's theology in the twentieth century, whilst adding the cautious comment that perhaps Maurice pressed the principle, 'Become what you are' so far as 'to miss the Biblical emphasis upon

---

2 F.D. Maurice, *The Kingdom of Christ* (Everyman ed, London 1906), i, 265.
3 Pusey, *Scriptural Views*, 78-9.
4 Ibid, 137.
5 J.H. Rigg, *Modern Anglican Theology* (3 ed, London 1880), 245: cf the more positive view in A.R. Vidler, *F.D. Maurice and Company* (London 1966), 48.

those *momenta* in history in which salvation is offered and accepted'.[6] There is a *de facto* universalism about much twentieth-century theology which makes a study of Maurice still relevant to the theme of this book; and his thought also illuminates that of some later nineteenth-century nonconformists, particularly in Congregationalism.

Maurice's family background seems to have influenced his attitude to baptism, as it did the rest of his theology. His father, Michael Maurice, was a Unitarian minister. In 1774 Theophilus Lindsay, himself a convert from the Church of England, published *The Book of Common Prayer reformed according to the plan of the Late Dr Samuel Clarke*. The Exhortations in the baptismal service in this book emphasised the universal character of the rite. Thus parents were told to 'Tell *him* that *he* is to love and do good to all men, because all are equally the children of God with *himself*, and the objects of his fatherly kindness and care'; whilst those being baptized as adults were told, 'By being baptized, you do not declare yourself of any religious sect or party: but a Christian'. The service also permitted the use of either the traditional trinitarian formula (because it was biblical) or baptism 'into the name of Jesus Christ' (following Acts 2:38 and 19:5).[7] Michael always baptized 'in the name of the Father and of the Son and of the Holy Ghost'.[8]

Maurice's mother and sisters, however, became Calvinists, and then underwent a second baptism in order to become members of the Baptist church in Bristol where John Foster was minister. For this reason Maurice's youngest sister was not baptized as an infant. The fact that his two elder sisters should write to their father to tell him that they could no longer attend a Unitarian place of worship, and therefore could no longer hold communion with him, made a powerful impression on the young boy. To these experiences may probably be traced his emphasis on unity and horror of division, and perhaps also his rather idealised view of family relations. It also gives added poignancy to his own subsequent decision to be baptized a second time in March 1831 in order to become a member of the Church of England. Notwithstanding this he retained a close relationship with his father until his death.[9] Principal Tulloch

---

6 A.M. Ramsey, *F.D. Maurice and the Conflicts of Modern Theology* (Cambridge 1951), 36.

7 H. Davies, *Worship and Theology in England: From Watts and Wesley to Maurice, 1690-1850* (Princeton, NJ, 1961), 87-8; cf. D. Young, *F.D. Maurice and Unitarianism* (Oxford 1992), 47.

8 Michael's practice provoked Robert Hall who was a friend of his in Bristol to say, 'Why, Sir, as I understand you, you must consider that you baptize in the name of an abstraction, a man and a metaphor': Maurice, *Life*, i, 122-23.

9 Maurice, *Life*, i, 20-5, 122-3. Jeremy Morris's comment that 'This was not, officially, a *re*-baptism—at least there are no signs that it was such' perhaps indicates some embarrassment at this demonstration that high church Anglicans often did not

regarded this rebaptism as 'a truly painful incident in Mr. Maurice's career', and commented on his self-justification that he thought he was directed to do it by the Holy Spirit, 'What is this but an assertion of his own private judgment in a form which admits of no answer?'[10] The one great advantage Maurice derived from this rather stormy upbringing was an ability to see and feel various different theological positions from within, and a concern to present that truth which he was sure each contained but free from the distorting errors which surrounded it.

By the early 1830s the main outlines of his theological position were becoming clear. In a letter to his sister, Priscilla, of January 1831, he wrote of dimly seeing 'the way in which Christ, by being the Light and Truth manifested, shines into the heart and puts light there, even while we feel that the Light and Truth is still all in Him, and that in ourselves there is nothing but thick darkness'.[11] Then, in the well-known letter to his mother of December 1833 he set out his belief that Christ was in every one, that 'Christ is the Head of every man':

> Ye are children of God: ye are members of Christ. Profligates, hard-hearted sinners, yea, hypocrites, this is your condemnation, that you are. It will be your misery to find that you were so, unless you will believe.[12]

The phrase, 'Christ is the head of every man', comes from 1 Corinthians 11:3, but Maurice probably took it from Thomas Erskine's book, *The Brazen Serpent* (1831), the first edition of which he had certainly read by the beginning of February 1831.[13] The book was a critique of the penal substitutionary doctrine of the atonement; thus Erskine wrote, 'When, therefore, it is said that Christ did or does things for us, it is not meant that he did or does them as our substitute, but as our head'.[14] A few pages later Erskine said,

> This is the meaning of Christ being called 'the second Adam'. And this is the meaning of that word also, 'the head of every man is Christ'. And this is the gospel

---

consider nonconformist baptism as baptism, despite the tradition of the Church that lay-baptism was valid: J. Morris, *F.D. Maurice and the Crisis of Christian Authority* (Oxford 2005), 49-50. Chapter 1 has demonstrated that at least some Anglican clergy in the eighteenth century were prepared to recognise nonconformist baptism.

10 Tulloch, *Movements of Religious Thought*, 265-6.

11 Maurice, *Life*, i, 119.

12 Ibid, i, 155, 157.

13 Ibid, i, 121: he was writing to his sister Priscilla, and he clearly suspected that her Calvinism might have made Erskine uncongenial.

14 T. Erskine, *The Brazen Serpent* (Edinburgh 1831), 38. In the 2nd edition (1831) and the 3rd (1879) this is found on p. 45. The 1st edition has an almost breathless urgency, which is more restrained in subsequent editions.

which Paul was commissioned to preach amongst the Gentiles, 'Christ in you, (yea in every man) the hope of glory'.[15]

The phrase Maurice used to his mother is very like that used by Erskine in his second edition: 'He was indeed the head of every man, and therefore when he died, he died for every man', the conclusion of which is not part of the argument of 1 Corinthians at that point. Erskine wrote,

> Christ died for every man as the Head of every man—not by any fiction of law, not in a conventional way, but in reality as the Head of the whole mass of the human nature, which, although composed of many members, is one thing, one body, in every part of which the Head is *truly* present.[16]

Maurice's admiration for Erskine was expressed in the Dedication of his sermons on *The Prophets and Kings of the Old Testament* (1853):

> Have we a Gospel for men, for all men? ... Is it a Gospel that He has reconciled the world unto Himself? Is it this absolutely, or this with a multitude of reservations, explanations, contradictions?[17]

In a letter to Erskine in December 1852, Maurice said that he felt it a duty to express what he felt towards him 'in connection with the task which God has shown me that I am to perform for His Church, that of testifying that the grace of God has appeared to all men'.[18]

It followed from this, in Maurice's view, that the Church had a distinct reality over against the nation, even though the two went together. In July 1834, writing to his friend Acland, who had been one of the sponsors at his baptism, he said:

---

15 Ibid, 46. (I have not traced this passage in subsequent editions.)

16 T. Erskine, *The Brazen Serpent* (3 ed, Edinburgh 1879), 42. This is quoted in N.R. Needham, *Thomas Erskine of Linlathen: his Life and Theology, 1788-1837* (Edinburgh 1990), 328, but Dr Needham does not make clear the differences in wording between the first and second editions, nor indeed does Morris, *F.D. Maurice*, 52.

17 F.D. Maurice, *The Prophets and Kings of the Old Testament* (Cambridge 1853), vii; cf Needham, *Thomas Erskine*, 410-11. Significantly his dedication began by saying (characteristically) that he had come to see the positive point affirmed by the Scottish Covenanters in emphasising that God himself was king and lawgiver, but that they had undermined it by using that principle to justify any evil acts which they felt necessary for their purposes. Any acknowledgement of possible justice in the position of the Scottish Covenanters would have horrified traditional high churchmen.

18 Maurice, *Life*, ii, 150. I am more persuaded by Vidler's view that Erskine was the decisive influence on Maurice than by Morris, who sees him as shaped by 'doctrine, devotion, and institutions of the Church of England': Vidler, *Maurice and Company*, 249; Morris, *F.D. Maurice*, 53.

> I would wish to live and die for the assertion of this truth: that the Universal Church is just as much a reality as any particular nation is; that the latter can only be believed real as one believes in the former; that the Church is the witness for the true constitution of man as man, a child of God, an heir of heaven, and taking up his freedom by baptism: that the world is a miserable, accursed, rebellious order, which denies this foundation, which will create a foundation of self-will, choice, taste, opinion; that in the world there can be no communion; that in the Church there can be universal communion; communion in one body by one Spirit.[19]

The final element in this cluster of beliefs about the presence of Christ, baptism and the Church, was his conviction that the Church is a kingdom and a present reality. This, as Frank McClain pointed out, was almost certainly derived from the Revd J.A. Stephenson of Lympsham, who, as a result of millenarian influence, believed that the prophecies about the establishment of Christ's kingdom had been literally fulfilled at the fall of Jerusalem, and therefore that the kingdom already existed as a present reality.[20] In a letter to Stephenson in July 1834, Maurice wrote: 'I have found myself in all my private meditations, as well as preaching, drawn to speak of Christ as a King, and His Church as a Kingdom'.[21] In a memoir of Stephenson, Maurice wrote that he regarded the ordinances of the Church as 'the symbols of Christ's kingdom' and 'the bonds of fellowship between Christ and all the redeemed in heaven and earth'. He also attached increasing importance to apostolic succession for the same reason. But, said Maurice,

> These doctrines did not make him bigotted, or exclusive; they were in his mind the assertion of the universality of the Church—of its being a real and not an imaginary body—of its being a kingdom which is destined to rule over all. Through his life he was a striver after peace and unity.[22]

Such words might almost serve as a description of Maurice himself. It was in this context that he reacted first to Pusey's tract on Baptism and then to the Beaconite controversy in the Society of Friends.

In the early 1830s, Maurice had been regarded as moving in a tractarian direction, and it was because of this that he had been proposed in 1836 as a candidate for the Professorship of Political Economy at Oxford. It was only when he began to publish his 'Letters to a Quaker', which became in due course *The Kingdom of Christ*, that the tractarians realised the extent to which he disagreed with Pusey; as a result he

---

19 Ibid, i, 166.
20 F.M. McClain, *Maurice: Man and Moralist* (London 1972), 54-62.
21 Maurice, *Life*, i, 167.
22 Ibid, i, 151.

withdrew from the contest.²³ Maurice's son commented that Pusey's tracts on Baptism were in his father's view 'throughout life the true representative notes of the party as a party'.²⁴ In an explanatory letter of 1871 Maurice wrote that the tract 'drove me more vehemently back on what I took to be the teaching of our Catechism—that by Baptism we claim the position which Christ has claimed for all mankind'.²⁵ He also said in a letter to Acland written in 1836 that the most earnest men he knew 'especially those who to diligent theological study add parochial duty among the poor' had expressed to him 'the great distress which Dr Pusey's Tracts on Baptism had caused them'.²⁶ Maurice, therefore, resolved in August 1836 to write a series of 'Letters on Baptism', with the Coleridgean intention of showing that in each of the parties in the Church there was a great truth asserted, but that each was wrong when it became the denier of the truth of the others. He started on them three times, only to be overtaken in December 1836 by an urgent request from another friend, Samuel Clark, to write some letters on Quakerism. Thus it was that the material drafted for the 'Letters on Baptism' turned into the second of the 'Letters to a Quaker'.²⁷

It is a striking fact that among all those who have written about Maurice's theology, only two, H.G. Wood and Olive Brose, have taken any time to explain the background to the Quaker controversy into which Maurice launched, notwithstanding the fact that this precipitated what is generally regarded as his most significant work. One of the two, H.G. Wood, was, of course, a member of the Society of Friends himself. Yet this controversy provides further evidence of the way in which baptism was an issue stirring the Churches in the first half of the nineteenth century. In 1835, Isaac Crewdson, a wealthy silk and cotton manufacturer in Manchester, published a book entitled *A Beacon to the Society of Friends*. Crewdson was one of that considerable number of Friends, who had been stirred by the Evangelical Revival and felt it important that the Society should give more emphasis to the great evangelical doctrines. He was particularly critical of claims that men were taught true knowledge of God and salvation '*immediately* by the Spirit, independently of His

---

23 Newman wrote to Keble that 'Maurice has published a rambling theory of Baptism', partly in response to a letter from Acland who felt that he had misunderstood Pusey but nevertheless 'put forward some most important truth': G. Tracey (ed), *The Letters and Diaries of John Henry Newman, vi, 1837-38* (Oxford 1984), 27-28; cf. Morris, *Maurice*, 64.
24 Ibid, i, 213.
25 Ibid, i, 182.
26 Ibid, i, 205.
27 Ibid, i, 202-3; 212.

'A Spiritual and Universal Kingdom' 99

revelation through the Scriptures'.[28] This brought down the fire upon his head of those who accused evangelical Friends of deserting the traditional Quaker witness to the light within. The Manchester meeting was divided, and the London Yearly Meeting set up a Committee of Inquiry. The irony of this was that the London Yearly Meeting itself was dominated by evangelical Friends. Joseph John Gurney, brother of Elizabeth Fry, was one of those on the committee (against his will) even though he himself had written that the stress on the universal inward working of Christ was a dangerous exaggeration.[29] The Committee advised the Manchester Monthly Meeting not to take action against Crewdson for doctrinal unsoundness but also recommended that he be silent in meetings for worship, even though he was a minister. The result was that in 1836 Crewdson and some fifty sympathisers resigned from the Manchester meeting, and some two or three hundred did the same in other parts of the country.

Most of those who seceded joined other churches, but in Manchester Crewdson and his followers formed their own organization of Evangelical Friends. In December 1837 they decided to examine the New Testament carefully to see what guidance it gave on church order (thereby becoming yet another example of the early nineteenth-century attempts to recover New Testament Christianity, like the Scotch Baptists, the Haldanes, the Brethren and Churches of Christ). They rejected the ministry of women and birthright membership. despite the honoured place of both in Quaker history; they adopted a statement of faith, the singing of hymns, bible reading and preaching in worship, and most significantly of all they adopted the sacraments of baptism and the Lord's Supper. In 1837, as a result of this, a campaign began in the Society of Friends itself to introduce baptism into the Society, or at least to make it optional. The proposal was so controversial that it was not even minuted in the official records of the Yearly Meeting. Though discussion persisted for two or three years it eventually died down; and Crewdson's own movement soon died out after his own death as his supporters joined other churches. A number joined the Brethren, as indeed B.W. Newton had urged them to do.[30]

The Beaconite controversy was more complex than this theological analysis has suggested, because it provided an opportunity for the more radical Friends, who were trying to emphasize the essence of early Quakerism against what they considered to be a dangerous lapse into evangelicalism, to manoeuvre the predominantly evangelical London

---

28 Quoted in D.E. Swift, *Joseph John Gurney* (Middletown, CT, 1962), 175; H.G. Wood, *Frederick Denison Maurice* (Cambridge 1950), 38-41; O. Brose, *Frederick Denison Maurice: Rebellious Conformist, 1805-1872* (Athens, OH, 1971), 122-3.

29 Swift, *Gurney*, 174-5.

30 E. Isichei, *Victorian Quakers* (Oxford 1970), 45-53.

Yearly Meeting to take action against those who were only a little more evangelical than themselves. It was also tied up with the cross-currents already travelling across the Atlantic in connection with the campaign for the immediate abolition of slavery. But for our present purpose it is important in exposing the extent to which the question of baptism and the sacraments generally touched a raw nerve in the Society. Joseph John Gurney had gone through agonies of conscience on whether it was right to abandon baptism and the Lord's Supper, even though his exposition of the principles of Friends, which was one of the Society's authorised publications, consistently defended the no-sacraments position.[31] The temptation of many Friends of Gurney's social standing and position to become evangelical Anglicans or dissenters was considerable, and a number did so. Ralph Wardlaw wrote some *Friendly Letters to the Society of Friends* in the winter and spring of 1835-36 in support of Crewdson's arguments, only to draw the rebuke from Gurney that he had exaggerated the strength of the reformers.[32] So Maurice's intervention was more than a pedagogical device. The friend who urged him to write the letters, Samuel Clark, subsequently was ordained into the ministry of the Church of England. On the other hand, as Maurice told Julius Hare at the time, 'I write *to* Quakers, but in a great measure *for* Churchmen';[33] and looking back on things later he wrote,

> The old Quakers had spoken of the divine Word as the light which lightens every man that cometh into the world. A younger body of them, who were in strong sympathy with the Evangelicals, declared that this doctrine interfered with reverence for the written word and with the doctrine of human depravity... Reflecting much on this controversy and connecting it with what was passing in the English Church, it seemed to me that the old Quakers were affirming a most grand and fundamental truth; but that it had become narrow and contradictory, because they had no ordinance which embodied it and made it universal; that we, on the other hand, forgetting their Quaker principles, or rather the words of St. John, necessarily made baptism a mere ceremony or a charm. The two being united expressed to me the reconciliation of the High Church Baptismal regeneration with the Evangelical demands for personal faith.[34]

Maurice's letters were published monthly during 1837, and the twelve were gathered together in the three volumes of the first edition of *The Kingdom of Christ* in 1838. The edition which is most common, and which has been several times reprinted, is the second edition of 1842, which was almost completely rewritten. Maurice liked the second edition better and its publication came at the time of the baptism of his second

---

31 Swift, *Gurney*, 130-7.
32 Alexander, *Wardlaw*, 354-6.
33 Maurice, *Life*, i, 213.
34 Ibid, i, 237.

child, which was particularly appropriate.³⁵ It is less repetitive than the first. Nevertheless, as Merlin Davies remarked, the order and argument of the first edition are in some respects clearer than that of the later version.³⁶ It is also interesting that the *British Magazine*, which was a recognized organ of the tractarians, should carry a review which described the work as 'the production of no ordinary mind' which had been read with great pleasure.³⁷

The treatment of baptism, which occupies the second letter, is fuller in the first edition than the second. The argument of the first three letters, which constituted the first volume, was to show that in the Sacraments

> the idea of Christianity as the revelation of a spiritual and universal kingdom, is set forth, that it depends upon the prominence given to them, whether this idea is upheld or lost, and that with the utter loss of it all the practical fruits of Christianity will disappear.³⁸

In the first letter he had argued that George Fox's principle of the inner light was right, and an implication of Christianity, but it was not to be identified with Christianity: it was, however, to be defended against those who would set up the doctrine of justification by faith against the belief of the Word dwelling in the heart of man.³⁹ The universal Church required men to give up their individuality and become members of a body in order to claim the privileges which Christ had won for them: sects which made the notion of individual faith and particular redemption the grounds of a church were leading men astray, by being witnesses for separation rather than for union.⁴⁰

In his second letter, therefore, Maurice set out to argue that the Quaker neglect of baptism had rendered their witness to a spiritual kingdom feeble and ineffectual, and he maintained that the various strands of opinion in the Church had prevented baptism being perceived in all its clarity. He isolated three strands of opinion: the high church belief in baptismal regeneration; the evangelical belief that it marked admission into the visible church; and the opinion represented by Henry Budd and others that baptism did mean regeneration when administered to the

---

35 Ibid, i, 305, 309.
36 W. Merlin Davies, *An Introduction to F.D. Maurice's Theology* (London 1964), 21.
37 *British Magazine*, xv (1839), 203.
38 A Clergyman of the Church of England, *The Kingdom of Christ, or Hints on the Principles, Ordinances, and Constitution of the Catholic Church in letters to a Member of the Society of Friends* (London 1838), i, xxxv.
39 Ibid, i, 31.
40 Ibid, i, 46-47; cf. Erskine on the 'accepted time and day of salvation' (2 Cor: 6:2): 'It is a time when men are not treated as individuals but as members of the righteous Head', *Brazen Serpent* (1 ed), 63.

children of believing parents. It may be noted in passing that Henry Budd was a friend of Edward Bickersteth, who tried to argue for baptismal regeneration in a way which would commend itself to evangelicals, particularly in his book of 1827, *Infant-Baptism, the Means of National Reformation*. In this, he claimed that if only parents and all churchmen would accept the implications of their commitment to Christ everything that was promised in the services of the Church would come true. To the evangelicals Maurice said that the whole language of conversion presupposed that men were awakened to a realisation of their true state, instead of what might be called in a modern phrase their 'false consciousness' when they were sinners. To the high churchmen Maurice said that baptism was 'the sacrament of constant union' not 'an act done in an instant', and that their emphasis on baptism effecting a change of nature destroyed the idea of a sacrament which necessarily implied 'that all the virtue and life of the creature consists in a union with a Being above itself'. To Mr Budd and his followers Maurice said that he was not satisfied with a notion that the high honour of being called a son of God was conferred on someone because he was intended to become one, rather than because he was one.[41] But his conclusion was that each position contained some truth which was best realised in combination:

> Our Baptism is in the name of the Father, the Son and the Holy Ghost. The idea of an adopting Father is, I conceive, satisfactorily brought out by the High Churchman. He is unsatisfactory, as I think I have shown, when he speaks of our constitution in Christ, or of the gift of the Holy Ghost. The Evangelical view, rightly interpreted, explains one of the High Church omissions, but only imperfectly and implicitly recognizes the other. The idea of the Holy Spirit, personally and actually inhabiting, educating, informing the mind of the child, — of parents, schoolmasters, legislators, being his servants and fellow-workers in training the whole family, and each member of the family, to realise the privileges of their constitution, and to become acquainted with the name and will of Him who has established it, — is a grave and glorious truth, which it is a high honour to Mr Budd that he had been permitted to perceive, and which we should be very thankful to him for having, even in an inadequate manner, illustrated.[42]

In conclusion, Maurice argued that Friends needed to think more carefully before they rejected the Scripture testimony to baptism as belonging to a temporary dispensation of external observance: and he suggested that their contemporary troubles were due to their polity having been established on the basis of human faith, rather than God's ordinance.

---

41 [Maurice], *Kingdom of Christ*, 1 ed, i, 82-3, 94-7, 103-5.
42 Ibid, i, 106.

Maurice regarded baptism as affirming the fundamental relationship between God and humanity, that everyone belonged to Christ. Hence in his Lincoln's Inn sermons on *The Prayer Book* in 1848 he said,

> You speak of your baptism and dispute about it, but you do not believe your baptism, for you do not think it has sealed you members of Christ, and sons of God, and inheritors of the Kingdom of Heaven, and that God is ever with you to make this inheritance actually yours.[43]

He even affirmed that it was a witness to a redemption which comprehended those who were not baptized. Susanna Winkworth told her sister that Maurice had said that the unbaptized were God's children 'not by virtue of their natural and physical birth, but by God's taking them into His adoption'.[44] He made a similar point when preaching on *The Doctrine of Sacrifice* in 1854:

> The meaning of your baptism, of your calling to be members of a Church, is, that He makes you sharers of His own mind; that He promises you His Spirit every day and hour to overcome that in you, and you, and you, which is disposed to set up a separate mind, a mind of your own, in opposition to it.[45]

There is an echo of Erskine's emphasis that Christ died for all, not for individuals. Maurice's criticism of Pusey was that he seemed to make baptism the effective agent of regeneration, rather than seeing this as something effected by God in Christ and signified in baptism. This was not a contrast between a subjective view and an objective view, but between two different objective views. Thus Liddon was mistaken to say that Pusey's tract

> taught that baptismal regeneration meant a change of nature, produced by union with the new humanity of the Son of God, while Mr Maurice believed that it meant no more than bringing into light a relation to God which had always existed.[46]

Maurice did not believe that the relation had *always* existed, even if it had always been intended; it was created by the death of Christ. But his Platonism (like Erskine's) exposed him to the criticism that, if an

---

43 F.D. Maurice, *The Prayer Book and the Lord's Prayer* (London 1902), 233, quoted in Young, *Maurice and Unitarianism*, 261.

44 Young, *Maurice and Unitarianism*, 262, quoting M.J. Shaen, *Memorials of Two Sisters* (London 1908), 183.

45 F.D. Maurice, *The Doctrine of Sacrifice* (London 1893), 223-4, cf. Morris, *Maurice*, 188-9. These sermons were a response to the criticism of his *Theological Essays* by the Scottish theologian, Robert Candlish, and significantly in his dedication Maurice again expressed his debt to Irving and Erskine.

46 Liddon, *Life of Pusey*, i, 350.

underlying reality existed, the difference was between those who perceived it and those who did not.

This exposition has not done full justice to the complexities of Maurice's thought, but there is a detailed chapter on Maurice's understanding of baptism in Alec Vidler's *F.D. Maurice and Company*.[47] The critical question which Maurice's exposition raises is this: does anything happen in baptism? In other words, does baptism *do* anything, or is baptism essentially declaratory? This question may be considered by referring first to two contemporaries of Maurice in the Church of England, F.W. Robertson and Charles Kingsley; and then after some further examination of Maurice's own comments on this issue, turning to some contemporary Congregational theologians.

F.W. Robertson was Perpetual Curate of Holy Trinity Church, Brighton, from 1847 until his death in 1853 at the age of thirty-seven. In March 1850 he preached two sermons on baptism, which were a direct response to the Gorham Judgement. They caused a great sensation in Brighton, displeasing both high churchmen and evangelicals, but according to his biographer, Stopford Brooke, 'they reconciled to the Church many who had despaired of ever accepting the teaching of her Baptismal Services'.[48] After the first sermon the sister of a Quaker applied to him for baptism.[49] In many ways Robertson's sermon says more succinctly and more clearly what Maurice was saying: but although Robertson venerated Maurice, he decided that he disagreed with the Tractarians on baptism shortly after his arrival in Oxford as an undergraduate in October 1837, and there is no reference in his published letters to his having read anything by Maurice.[50] In his first sermon Robertson considered the Roman Catholic position and the Calvinist position before coming to what he regarded as the view of the Church of England. The Roman Catholic position had the merit of recognizing that the Church was a society and not an association, i.e. it was made by facts not by will. But he objected to it for three reasons. First, it assumed baptism to be not the testimony to a fact but the fact itself: hence it made baptism 'not a sacrament, but an event'.[51] Secondly, it was gross materialism and magic because it implied that God's action was controlled by his priests. Thirdly, it made Christian life 'a struggle for something that is lost, instead of a progress to something that lies before'.[52] For modern Calvinism Robertson could not find anything positive to say. Again he had three objections. First, the

---

47 Vidler, *Maurice and Company*, 87-109.
48 S.A. Brooke, *Life and Letters of Frederick W. Robertson* (new ed, London 1883), i, 234-5.
49 Ibid, i, 331.
50 Ibid, i, 16, 136-7.
51 F.W. Robertson, *Sermons: Second Series* (new ed, London 1884), 49.
52 Ibid, 50.

'judgement of charity' which allowed that it was right to speak of the child as God's child ended at the baptismal font, for later in life such people were 'exactly the persons who do not in after-life charitably presume that all their neighbours are Christians'.[53] Secondly, like the Roman Catholics, the Calvinist view created the fact instead of testifying to it, except that it was faith, rather than baptism, that made the child a child of God. Thirdly, by treating their children as children of the devil, Calvinists tended to make them so.

Against these two views Robertson set what he claimed was the doctrine of the Bible and the Church of England. Christ came to reveal a Name—the Father: and the revelation was that 'man is God's child, and the sin of the man consists in perpetually living as if it were false'. Baptism was 'a visible witness to the world of that which the world is forever forgetting. A common Humanity united in God.'[54] The virtues of his view were again three: first, that it prevented exclusiveness and pride by proclaiming a kingdom not for a few favourites but for mankind; secondly, it protested against the atomistic view of the Church, characteristic of Calvinism (in his view), by baptizing a separate church, 'in order that the church may baptize the race'; and thirdly, it sanctified materialism, because the things of earth were pledges and sacraments of things in heaven.

In his second sermon Robertson set out to meet two further objections: did such a doctrine make light of original sin, and did it reduce baptism to a superfluous ceremony? He argued that original sin was not just hereditary guilt but hereditary tendencies: it was in fact refusing to live as God's children and saying that we are not His children. That was why redemption was realising that one was God's child and being taken out of the life of falsehood into the life of truth and fact. Neither was baptism a superfluous ceremony, because it was something that made a doctrine into a reality, because it was the token of a universal church, and because it was an authoritative symbol.[55] In essence therefore, as Robertson wrote in a letter at the time, he argued that baptism was the visible declaration of a fact, but the fact had to be true before it was declared: hence his comparison with the coronation—that coronation can only make the Queen Queen if she is so before. 'To live as such—to believe it and realise it—is to become regenerate'.[56] Maurice's high opinion of Robertson is noted in his *Theological Essays*.

The same emphases on solidarity are to be found in Charles Kingsley. Kingsley first read *The Kingdom of Christ* at the time he took up his curacy at Eversley in July 1842. In a letter written on the first day he took

---

53 Ibid, 52.
54 Ibid, 54-5.
55 Ibid, 60-72.
56 Brooke, *Life of Robertson*, i, 330-1.

services there he rejected both the Roman view of baptismal purity and the evangelical tendency to preach to sinners as if they were heathens. He intended to preach repentance in a new way:

> I would say, 'You *have* had the grace of God given you—you *are* a Christian whether you like it or not—you have taken vows upon you, and your guilt is the greater because you have thereby swindled heaven (if I may use the expression) out of so many blessings by promising what you have not performed. You have the Holy Spirit in you striving with you.[57]

There is the same opposition to individualism: in September 1843 he wrote, 'What a thought it is that there is a God! a Father, a King! a Husband not of individuals—that is a Popish fancy—but of the Church—of collective humanity.'[58] So he was critical of all views which suggested that God was 'not the Father, nor Christ the Lord, of all men, but only of a chosen few'.[59] Likewise in his controversial sermon in 1851 on the message of the Church to the labouring man, Kingsley claimed that the church had three special possessions and treasures: 'the Bible, which proclaims man's freedom, Baptism his equality, the Lord's Supper his brotherhood'.[60] What is particularly interesting in Kingsley is his specific claim to have adopted a Logos theology based on John and developed in Clement, Alexandrinus, Philo and the Eastern Fathers. And to another correspondent in 1852 he confessed himself a Platonist.[61] Kingsley, of course, was very much more obviously influenced by Maurice, speaking of him on one occasion as beginning the great theological revelation of the day, that is, the sense of Christ living now.[62]

It is easy to see from this discussion how Maurice's doctrine of baptism and his belief that Christ was 'in every man' became the theological basis of his Christian Socialism. It helps to explain why he should devote one of the Tracts on Christian Socialism of 1850 to the implications of the Gorham Judgement. Curiously enough this tract is not referred to in Maurice's *Life*, perhaps because in it he actually raised the possibility that it might be necessary to secede from the Church if the government and the evangelicals were successful in changing the baptismal services. Even the suggestion of such a possibility seems quite out of character, but it shows how strongly Maurice was opposed to the

---

57 *Charles Kingsley: His Letters and Memories of his Life*, edited by his wife (London 1878), i, 78-9.
58 Ibid, i, 96.
59 Ibid, i, 254.
60 C. Kingsley, *Alton Locke* (with a prefatory memoir by T. Hughes: London 1887), xxxiii.
61 *Life of Kingsley*, i, 317, 325.
62 Ibid, i, 337.

evangelical position, at least as represented by Gorham. Hort recorded a conversation at this time when Maurice was full of Gorham with scarcely a word on Socialism. Hort was convinced that lay communion rather than secession was the answer, since it seemed schismatical to leave the body of the Church. Maurice said he thought the middle classes would strongly resist a proclamation that their children were sons of the devil. But when Hort pressed him what he would do if the worst came to the worst he said he would give up the emoluments of the Church but not cut himself off: on the other hand, he agreed with the view that if the services were altered those who made such an alteration would be cutting themselves off from the Church 'inasmuch as they would be professing that the ground of their communion was not union in the body of Christ, but the accident of their holding intellectually the same opinions'.[63] Hort's conversation with Ludlow on the same day was entirely about the Working Men's Associations.

Hort posed the critical question about Maurice's doctrine. In July 1848 he wrote to John Ellerton:

> I believe we agree in thinking that Maurice's view, so far as we enter into it, is the true one, though I, at least, — and I should be surprized were it otherwise, — am still rather *in nubibus* about some points relating to it; chiefly concerning the relation of the baptized to the unbaptized. Is the Holy Spirit given only in baptism (I mean, of course, *not till* baptism), or given before but increased in baptism, or lastly, is it given to every human creature, and is baptism only its seal and assurance? This is a point on which I should much like to have a long talk with Maurice.[64]

Unfortunately there is no record that he ever did.

Alec Vidler accumulated an impressive selection of quotations which illustrate Maurice's view of the declaratory character of baptism.[65] 'Baptism tells me that I am God's child, and may live as if I were', he wrote to a friend in 1854.[66] A letter to Kingsley in October 1855 brought out the problem. Kingsley was still bothered by the phrase in the Catechism that by baptism we are '*made* the children of grace'. Maurice's response was that any alternative word to 'made' was likely to sacrifice a different part of the truth. He noted the parallel case of the way illegitimate children are called natural children, and then pointed out that to change the word would be to to lose 'the testimony that there is a higher bond between human beings, spiritual creatures, than the natural one'. Similarly to take away the word 'made' would be to lose 'the

---

63 Hort, *Life and Letters of Hort*, i, 160-1.
64 Ibid, i, 76.
65 Vidler, *Maurice and Company*, 104-6.
66 Maurice, *Life*, ii, 242.

witness of men being above nature, above their law of the ordinary birth', and, he continued,

> I do not know if we exchanged it for any other that we should not slide back into the very notion against which our whole lives are a fight, that we are in our flesh, merely as animals, sons of God, which is in fact the Rousseau, French Revolution inversion of the Christian Universality and leads to unlimited selfishness, to every man's hand being against his brother's.[67]

Or, as he put it earlier in the letter, men are not animals plus a soul, but spirits with an animal nature. This is as near as Maurice came to saying that men are not by nature sons of God, that they become so by baptism, and thus that baptism effects what it declares. In a letter to Sara Coleridge in 1843, he made it clear that he did not regard baptism simply as the affirmation of what was already true:

> the character of the state itself is an answer to the question why it cannot be spoken of as a birth state...man's proper state must be felt to be God's gift... Let the man say it is mine by right as a man and he utters either the greatest truth or the greatest falsehood...the greatest falsehood, if he suppose it in any respect an independent matter of course, a possession—a state of nature.[68]

But he resolutely refused to explain: in the first edition of *The Kingdom of Christ* he denied that there was a change of nature, and distinguished between the high church *idea* 'that the child is taken into covenant with God, and that it is really and truly a spiritual creature, redeemed by Christ, and adopted into union with Himself' and the high church *explanation* which he said was rendered unnecessary 'by the declaration, that the child's reception into the Ark of Christ's Church, *is* its deliverance from the evil of a fallen world'.[69] Something does seem to happen, therefore, but the understanding of what happens is closely tied to the Platonic philosophy which underlies Maurice's theology.

It remains briefly to note some of the implications of this within nonconformity. Alexander Mackennal, who was one of the early ecumenical pioneers in English Congregationalism, wrote in 1901 that he suspected that the abiding influence of Maurice would be seen not on English Churchmen but on English Congregationalists; whilst Dr F.J. Powicke, who left Spring Hill College, Birmingham (subsequently Mansfield College, Oxford) in 1877, said that he thought a majority of the younger ministers in 1877 'bore the Mauricean stamp'.[70] This is a

---

67 Ibid, ii, 274.
68 Quoted in McClain, *Maurice*, 91.
69 [Maurice], *Kingdom of Christ*, 1 ed, i, 114 (italics original).
70 A. Mackennal, *Sketches in the Evolution of English Congregationalism* (London 1901), 206: F.J. Powicke, 'Frederick Denison Maurice (1805-1872): A Personal

very interesting indication of the speed of the collapse of Calvinism in nineteenth-century Congregationalism. In Chapter 3 reference was made to the teaching of Greville Ewing and Ralph Wardlaw in Scotland, and in particular to Wardlaw's argument that baptism should be confined to the children of believing parents on classical Calvinist grounds. Even in the 1820s Wardlaw was aware that English Congregationalists were more relaxed on this point than those in Scotland, though Wardlaw's line was embodied in the Declaration of Faith of the Congregational Union in 1833 (in the compilation of which Wardlaw participated).[71] In England John Pye Smith took the Wardlaw line, but he recognised that most pastors took 'a sort of middle course', which his biographer described as being willing to baptize children 'of the piety of whose parents he had a good hope, though they might not make what is called a public profession'.[72] In 1844, however, Robert Halley, who had been a pupil of Pye Smith and then Professor at Highbury College before going in 1839 as minister to Mosley Street Chapel, Manchester, delivered the Congregational Lecture (in fact, a series of seven) on baptism.

Halley's lectures set the tone of Congregational practice for the rest of the century. His biographer said that 'they gave the death-blow to the custom, prevalent in many of our churches, of refusing baptism to the children of parents who were not church-members'.[73] Halley understood sacraments to be 'significant rites—emblems of Divine truth—sacred signs of the evangelical doctrine—designed to illustrate, to enforce, or to commemorate the great and most important truths of the Gospel'. In this context, therefore, he saw baptism as 'the sign of purification on being admitted into the kingdom of Christ; but neither the cause nor the seal of it'. So the 'evangelical doctrine, and not the sacrament, the truth, and not the symbol, the spirit, and not the letter, gives life and sanctity to the recipient'.[74] Indeed, he believed both baptismal regeneration, and a belief in baptism as the seal of grace, were subversive of justification by faith. Halley's indifference to form was strikingly illustrated in his discussion of immersion: he himself justified sprinkling as the mode of baptism, but his objection to those who said that only immersion was right was that this

---

Reminiscence', *Congregational Quarterly*, viii (1930), 172; quoted in Wood, *Maurice*, 1-2.

71 Declaration of Faith, Church Order and Discipline: Principles of Religion, xviii, in A. Peel, *These Hundred Years* (London 1931), 72.

72 J. Medway, *Memoirs of the Life and Writings of John Pye Smith* (London 1853), 504.

73 R. Halley, *A Short Biography of the Rev. Robert Halley, together with a Selection of his Sermons* (London 1879), lxxxiii.

74 R. Halley, *The Sacraments: An Inquiry into the nature of the Symbolic Institutions of the Christian Religion usually called the Sacraments. Part 1, Baptism* (London 1844), 94-5.

was 'to invest the sign, which may be conveniently changed, with the importance of the immutable truth'. He continued:

> If I eat what I honestly believe to be the Lord's supper, even though I should use rice for bread, or the juice of the currant for the fruit of the vine, that to me is the act of submission to the legislation of Christ in commemorating his death; and so if I observe what I believe is Christian baptism, even though I may be mistaken, that observance is to me the act of submission to the legislation of Christ, in receiving what I believe to be the authorised symbol of Christian truth.[75]

Halley's anticipation of the 'biscuits and orange juice brigade' in relation to the Lord's Supper reveals an essential subjectivism. It also probably explains why some Congregationalists in the nineteenth and twentieth centuries have found it easy to move into the Society of Friends. Similarly, his argument for not restricting baptism to the children of believing parents was that Jesus's commandment to baptize all nations should be taken literally. Since the reason for baptism was obedience to the command, there was nothing else to say. 'Can I hesitate a moment', he said, 'in conferring a sign of external privilege (baptism is nothing else) upon the children of the Gentiles, the new branches of the good olive?'[76] The force of Halley's comment in his preface, that he did not see any reason for collision with the Baptists, may now be seen:

> As these opinions prevail, (he wrote) the two denominations will unite upon the principle, not of open communion churches whose principle is toleration of error—Baptists allowing Independents, or Independents allowing Baptists to commune with them—but upon the higher principle of unsectarian churches, whose principle would be a disavowal of the authority to determine in such a controversy, the members baptizing how, and when, and where, and whom they please.[77]

By the middle of the century open communion had become the norm among Baptists, symbolised appropriately by the Norwich Chapel Case of 1860 when in a suit brought against George Gould, the minister of Kinghorn's old Baptist church in Norwich, the Master of the Rolls ruled that strict communion was not a fundamental principle of the faith of Particular Baptists.[78] Although most Baptists were not prepared to go quite as far as Halley wished, his exposition does explain why baptism could come to be regarded almost as a matter of private conviction in the later nineteenth century. Halley, like Wardlaw, did not regard baptism as a church ordinance, and although one was baptized into the kingdom of Christ, it was still necessary to join the church, i.e. the local congregation,

---

75 Ibid, 293-4.
76 Ibid, 553.
77 Ibid, vii-viii.
78 Payne, *Baptist Union*, 87-9; Walker, *Baptists at the Table*, 36-41.

by a voluntary act of faith. If Mauricean seeds were sown in this ground, the flowers were likely to look rather different from the 'sacramental socialists' of the Church of England.

Halley has been discussed because he was typical of many Congregationalists. R.W. Dale stands as one who embodied the influence of Maurice, but who moved back towards a more objective position. Dale defined sacraments as 'revelations of Christ in *acts*, not in *words* or in *things*';[79] and he criticised Halley's definition of sacraments as 'emblems of Divine truth' as omitting what was essential to the very idea of a sacrament, namely the idea of action. 'The spectators may learn some great truths from Baptism; but something is *done* to the person who receives it; and what is done to him is done by the authority of Christ.'[80] This is a stronger statement than any to be found in Maurice, but when Dale expounded the nature and design of baptism the influence of Maurice and Robertson was clearer:

> In baptism Christ claims us not only as His subjects, but as those whom He has redeemed.... In baptism, Christ gives us the assurance that He loves us with an infinite love, and will do His part towards saving us from sin, and bringing us to eternal glory. Baptism does not create a new relationship between Christ and the baptized person; it affirms a relationship which already exists.... Its deepest significance lies in the fact that it does not, in the case of an adult, express the faith or feeling of the baptized person; or, in the case of a child, the faith or feeling of its parents; but that in both cases it is a revelation of the authority and grace of Christ.[81]

Dale also used the image of the coronation which Robertson had used:

> Kings are not made kings by being crowned; they are crowned because they are already kings: their coronation is only the assurance that the power and greatness of sovereignty are theirs. And it is not by baptism that we are made Christ's inheritance; it is because we are Christ's inheritance that we are baptized.[82]

Writing to his Anglican friend Dr Wace at about the same time, he said:

> I sometimes appeal to Baptism in connection with remission of sins and all the blessings of Christian Redemption, but in another way—a way which I suppose Mr Maurice would have approved. I remind my congregation that Baptism was the personal, direct assurance to them that they belong to the race which is Christ's own, for which He died, which He has redeemed, which He defends, over which He

---

79 R.W. Dale, *A Manual of Congregational Principles* (London 1884), 123 (italics original).
80 Ibid, 123-4 (italics original).
81 Ibid, 127-8.
82 Ibid, 139.

reigns; and that Redemption is therefore theirs—only they can reject and despise it. I find it very useful to talk to my children's class in this way.[83]

The weakness of the coronation analogy is that it overlooks how kings do become kings—by hereditary succession; its appeal is that it bases the claim to be God's children in birth, rather than in any ecclesial act. Whether this is sustainable is a question which goes to the heart of any sacramental theology.

A comparison of Maurice with Halley and Dale obviously indicates that Halley's theology is essentially subjective. But it serves also to sharpen two questions about Maurice. Does his understanding of baptism flow out of the nature of the sacrament itself, or is it rather to be read into the sacrament as though baptism were an inherited institution waiting to be filled with new meaning? Secondly, in the absence of a strong sacramental tradition, would Maurice's theology create one? The evidence of Dale suggests that in his case Maurice's ideas were built on to a different foundation, namely Dale's great theological work on the atonement.

Finally, there was one other respect in which nonconformists found it impossible to go all the way with Maurice. One of the main planks in Maurice's platform was that the Church and society were coterminous in extent—this is one hint of a reason why Hort worried over what the difference was between the baptized and the unbaptized. Nonconformists believed in a gathered church. In 1848 the Hon. and Rev. Baptist Wriothesley Noel of St. John's Chapel, Bedford Row, left the Church of England and became a Baptist, taking up a ministry at John Street Chapel, where the Revd J.H. Evans of the Western Schism had ministered. He was perhaps the most socially distinguished seceder from the Church of England in the century. What eventually drove him out was the conviction that the link between church and state could not be justified, though he was never one of those who led the nonconformist political agitation against the establishment.[84] In 1882 Edward White, a Congregationalist who had rejected infant baptism in 1850 and caused some controversy by his 'advanced' theological views, gave one of the Congregational Union's Jubilee Lectures on 'Broad Church Doctrine and Independency'.[85] He was critical of what he regarded as the theological degeneracy of the post-Maurice school in respect of authority in religion, but he especially criticised the tendency to assert 'the solidarity of the race in spiritual things'. In scripture, by contrast, the spiritual classification of mankind was invariably dualistic:

---

83 A.W.W. Dale, *Life of R.W. Dale* (London 1905), 529-30.

84 Payne, *Baptist Union*, 74; cf B.W. Noel, *Essay on the Union of Church and State* (2 ed, London 1849).

85 R.T. Jones, *Congregationalism in England, 1662-1962* (London 1962), 240.

> The prophets of God, and the apostles of Christ, and the Son of God Himself speak of the righteous and the wicked as of creatures differing not superficially but in the root-principle of their being.[86]

There is an echo here of J.B. Mozley's remark about the language of regeneration belonging to the predestinarian strand in scripture. So White feared above all else the broad church schemes of comprehension, which he thought had a particular attraction for certain kinds of Congregationalist. Against this 'all-comprehending Churchmanship', White tried to assert the principles of classic Independency, but there is an indefinable sense that he realized that this was a broken reed. The problem, however, was a real one. Was there a Catholic doctrine of the Church which could avoid the bland identity of Church and society that seemed to follow from broad church teaching? White did not refer to baptism anywhere in his lecture. But it was the search for a new doctrine of the Church which was to provide the context for the twentieth-century debate about baptism, which is the subject of the next chapter.

---

86 *Congregational Union Jubilee Lectures* (London 1882), ii, 160-1.

Chapter 6

The Twentieth-Century Debate

In his study of religion in the Industrial Revolution in South Wales Canon E.T. Davies described the Rhymney Baptismal Fair which took place in November 1844. A public debate had been arranged between the Baptists and the Independents, and on the appointed day the roads to Rhymney were crowded with people. There were two stages on wagons outside the Clarence Hotel and two chairmen were appointed. 'The rules laid down that baptism only was to be discussed; that each protagonist should speak for seven minutes; that no appeal for support should be made to the crowd, and that good order must be maintained throughout the meeting.' However, the rules were broken and the meeting got out of hand. 'The wagon of those who upheld infant baptism was attacked and removed, and as many of the crowd as were able adjourned to a nearby chapel where pandemonium again broke loose.' The debate continued on the next morning, but despite the urging of one of the ministers present that the meeting should end 'for the honour of Nonconformity', an afternoon meeting was held, which also 'became a shambles, with cries of "Twm Paine", and "Pull him down, pull him down"'. In their report, the Independents

> denied the accusation that three co-religionists had spat tobacco in the face of the Baptist champion; while the Baptists ... claimed that these proceedings had led to an increase in baptism in Rhymney and they reasserted the charge levelled against the Independents of trying to extinguish Baptist oratory with tobacco juice. The more responsible Nonconformists deplored these performances, declaring that the learning of the debaters was superficial and that such proceedings could only result in bitterness and bad feeling; yet all the Nonconformist churches were in a turmoil in those days over the matter of baptism.[1]

Anyone who has read such debates will readily agree that the kind of arguments used were tedious in the extreme, consisting very often of detailed and repetitive examination of bibical texts. Often, too, the question of whether baptism should be only by immersion took up as much time as whether infants or believers should be baptized. Moreover,

---

1 E.T. Davies, *Religion in the Industrial Revolution in South Wales* (Cardiff 1965), 51-2.

even if they did not end in near-riots as the one in Rhymney did, such debates did relatively little to advance agreement on the matters under discussion. It is, therefore, particularly interesting that in the twentieth century the whole question should have been opened up again, largely in the first instance as a result of the work of paedobaptist scholars. This chapter considers how and why this took place.

Bishop Westcott prophesied at the turn of the century that the next great theological controversy would be about baptism, and Alec Vidler commented that when he was editor of *Theology* (1939-64) he had more manuscripts submitted to him on that topic than any other.[2] Westcott's remark also reflected the way in which baptism had receded from the forefront of theological debate after the early 1860s. There were a number of reasons for this. First and foremost was the fact that the Gorham Judgement of 1850 produced a virtual stalemate as far as baptismal doctrine in the Church of England was concerned. Had the Convocation of Canterbury begun to meet regularly again a few years earlier, there might have been more formal ecclesiastical reaction to the Judgement. As it was, the Judgement acted as a stimulus to the revival of synodical action in the Church—the Bishop of Exeter himself convened a diocesan synod to discuss it—but when the Convocations did meet again, baptism did not figure largely on their agenda. This was probably due to the second reason, namely that controversy over the Eucharist became more widespread in the 1850s with the development of the ritualist movement. In so far as the baptismal controversy in the first half of the century had been one between catholic and 'calvinist' sacramental theology, this division was more sharply focused in the second half of the century over Holy Communion. Antipathy to the Mass, the real presence and transubstantiation was more easily mobilised than suspicion of baptismal regeneration. A third reason for the fading of the baptismal question was the decline of Calvinism in nonconformity and its replacement by an evangelical theology that attached relatively little importance to the sacraments. As noted in Chapter 5, the open communion controversy among Baptists was virtually settled by the Norwich Chapel Case in 1860, and the practice of open membership, whereby it was not necessary to be baptized as a believer to become a member of a Baptist church, began to spread. One odd effect of this development was that it became possible to be a member of a Baptist church without being baptized at all. The same practice also became more common among Congregational churches. Finally, the development of bibical criticism and historical scholarship began to undermine some of the simpler defences of existing baptismal practice and thereby to force a

---

2 G.W.H. Lampe, *The Seal of the Spirit* (2 ed, London 1967), vii; Vidler, *Maurice and Company*, 87.

reappraisal of the basis of sacramental theology in all the Churches. In the long term this was undoubtedly the most significant development of all, since nothing is more striking about the way infant baptism was justified in the twentieth century than the different use made of the bibical and historical material.

The changes which have taken place may be discussed most conveniently first by tracing the development of Anglican sacramental theology into the 1920s, then by considering the revival of sacramental theology among nonconformists, especially as illustrated by the work of P.T. Forsyth, and finally by examining what happened after the second world war and Karl Barth's call for the abandonment of infant baptism.

The essay on 'Sacraments' (the absence of the definite article was presumably deliberate) in *Lux Mundi* (1889) illustrated the shift in the way sacramental theology was justified in the Church of England. It was written by Francis Paget, Regius Professor of Pastoral Theology at Oxford, and was not really about either baptism or Communion as such. Rather it was concerned with the sacramental principle in religion, and in particular with the question of whether the Church's sacramental system matched its environment in human life. Paget's essay contained all the characteristic themes of *Lux Mundi*: the incarnation, discernment of God in creation, and the significance of social solidarity:

> It does seem deeply significant that when the Word was made flesh and dwelt among us, He took up the lines of a history replete with forecasts of the consecration of material things... The consecration of material elements to be the vehicles of Divine grace keeps up on earth that vindication and defence of the material against the insults of sham spiritualism which was achieved for ever by the Incarnation and Ascension of Jesus Christ.[3]

Or again:

> By Sacraments men are to be taken out of the narrowness and isolation of their own lives, out of all engrossing preoccupation with their own state, into the ample air, the generous gladness, the unselfish hope of the City of God: they are to escape from all daily pettiness, all morbid self-interest, all preposterous conviction of their own importance, into a fellowship which spans all ages and lands.[4]

Thus, the sacraments became a foretaste of glory and an assurance of where grace is to be found. Paget's essay picked up themes concerning the sacramental principle that were found in the *Tracts for the Times*, but it had now become a more autonomous justification for the nature of the Church.

---

3 C. Gore (ed), *Lux Mundi* (15 ed, London 1904), 302, 309.
4 Ibid, 307.

A very similar emphasis was found a year earlier in A.J. Mason's *The Faith of the Gospel*, dedicated to Lightfoot and Westcott, which was intended as a manual of Christian doctrine. The root of the sacramental principle, wrote Mason, lies in 'the relation which subsists from the beginning between creation and the Word, or even in the nature of the Word Himself'.[5] So the incarnation itself was a sacrament. It was this which marked the advance of Christianity over Judaism, for Christians are presented with 'signs which not only speak of spiritual mysteries, but convey the things they speak of'.[6] Hence, as Article 25 declared, the sacraments are 'not only badges and tokens of Christian men's profession', as Zwingli made them. Rather, by the sacraments Christ 'brings out the true dignity of the visible creation, and still further glorifies it'.[7] Coming to the doctrine of baptism in particular, Mason argued that the blessings of the gospel—justification, sanctification, etc—were promised to those who are in Christ. Our union with Christ depended on the act of Christ himself. 'Without faith on our part, our union with Christ remains inoperative, but our faith does not constitute the union.... Admission into Christ is the great gift of Baptism.'[8] Two main blessings flowed from baptism: remission of sins, and eternal union with Christ through being made children of God. Mason denied that such language implied, as F.D. Maurice thought, that human beings were not children of God before:

> All men are children of God, in one sense, by virtue of their humanity; and though they are justly banished from the filial privileges in consequence of their sins, they still retain a natural kinship with the Divine. But in Baptism we receive, by membership in the Incarnate Son, a new kind of filiation altogether, in comparison with which the unbaptized might rightly be said not to be children of God... Each baptized person is...like a kind of fresh incarnation of Christ.[9]

Infant baptism was justified on the ground that all ages are suitable for baptism, the only condition being that there should be sponsors; and confirmation was regarded as 'one Sacrament with Baptism', a sealing with the Spirit. Mason's exposition, coming as it did from a Cambridge rather than an Oxford stable, indicates how the emphasis on patristics and the incarnation in the tradition of the Cambridge trio of Westcott, Lightfoot and Hort produced a result very close to the liberal Catholicism of the *Lux Mundi* group.

---

5 A.J. Mason, *The Faith of the Gospel* (London 1888), 257-8.
6 Ibid, 259.
7 Ibid, 261-2.
8 Ibid, 267.
9 Ibid, 273, 275.

The emphasis by Mason on the integral relationship of baptism and confirmation also led in another direction which was not really arrested until Geoffrey Lampe published *The Seal of the Spirit* in 1951. Mason's book, *The Relation of Confirmation to Baptism*, was published in 1891, and in it he argued that the separation of confirmation from baptism in the Western Church had led to many of the blessings of confirmation being attributed to baptism; and that this had been responsible for some of the problems felt about baptism. After a lengthy review of the New Testament and patristic evidence, Mason concluded,

> first, that if we are to be guided by primitive antiquity, Confirmation is an integral part of Holy Baptism, in such a sense that what we usually call Baptism is, without it, an unfinished fragment, although conveying priceless blessings; and secondly, that the *res sacramenti*, the objective bounty extended by God for our acceptance, in this crowning part of Baptism, is that which bears the title of the gift of the Holy Ghost. In so special and unique a sense does this gift belong to Confirmation, that, notwithstanding all previous operations of the Holy Ghost upon the soul, the baptized but unconfirmed believer may, unless the Divine action depart from its ordinary course, be truly said not to have received the Holy Ghost.[10]

He went on to develop the significance of the various gifts of the Spirit in a detail which need not be examined here. But the significance of his general argument may be seen by his conclusion that 'the main difficulty lies less in defining what Confirmation adds to Baptism, than in defining what Baptism confers apart from Confirmation'.[11] Mason's conclusions were not, of course, uncontroversial, but they illustrate very clearly the way in which discussion of the matter was changing at a number of levels. First, the way in which Mason went behind the sixteenth-century origins of the Prayer Book, and indeed behind the medieval tradition of the Latin Church, indicated a new role for patristic scholarship in the discussion. In particular the study of the liturgical development of baptism and confirmation was used in much more detail to support conclusions about contemporary policy. This bridging of the gap between the New Testament and the Reformation inevitably involved a more critical approach to the Reformation itself, not out of any preference for the Roman Catholic tradition, but in the more general context of church history. Secondly, the concern for confirmation came at the end of half a century when the bishops of the Church of England had worked with considerable success to reform and renew the significance attached to it within the ordinary life of the Church. The number of confirmation centres had been increased; the expansion of the episcopate (by the introduction of suffragans and the further division of dioceses) had made

---

10 A.J. Mason, *The Relation of Confirmation to Baptism* (2 ed, London 1893), 414.
11 Ibid, 455.

it possible to reduce the numbers confirmed at any one time; much greater emphasis had been laid on the whole process of preparation for confirmation.

The way in which Mason's argument buttressed confirmation was an important source of strength to those campaigners for church reform who wanted to create institutions of self-government within the Church, with a franchise based on confirmation rather than baptism. Such a movement, however, inevitably involved bringing out the way in which the Church was a community distinct from the nation as a whole, since the number confirmed had never been as high a percentage of the population as the number of those baptized. In party terms this enabled the more liberal evangelicals to make common cause with the more liberal Anglo-Catholics, the former group finding in the emphasis on confirmation some mitigation of the difficulties posed by a general assertion of baptismal regeneration, and the latter finding the whole sacramental emphasis on baptism, confirmation and communion congenial to their understanding of churchmanship. This combination was later important for the Life and Liberty Movement in its work for self-government after 1916, even though in the end a baptismal franchise rather than a confirmation franchise was adopted.

The space devoted to the sacraments in the collection of essays entitled *Liberal Evangelicalism* (1922) was quite small, but it indicated the kind of movement which had taken place. The necessity of the sacraments was still defended in terms of their institution by Christ, which, it was noted, modern criticism had failed to disprove. But this point was immediately amplified by a more general appeal to the existence of similar acts in all religions, suggesting that sacraments met 'a fundamental need in human nature'; and also by the observation that the sacramental principle whereby material things expressed spiritual meaning was part of the whole of life. Sacraments did not create the fact they symbolised, but they did foster the maintenance and development of the spiritual state out of which they arose and of which they were an expression. So baptism was not a mere act of enrolment in the Church, but 'an effectual sign, which helps the individual to grasp what God offers'. The twelve pages on the sacraments did not make any reference to confirmation.[12] Three of the contributors, including H.B. Gooding, the author of the essay referred to, were members of the Archbishops' Commission on Christian Doctrine, which sat from 1922 to 1938, and the fact that they were able to adhere to the fuller statement on sacraments contained in *Doctrine in the Church of England* (1938) was perhaps more significant than the small space and content of the statement in *Liberal Evangelicalism*.

---

12 *Liberal Evangelicalism*, by Members of the Church of England (London n.d.), 153-61.

One of those who played an important part in drafting the statement on the sacraments in the 1938 report was Oliver Chase Quick, whose own book, *The Christian Sacraments*, was first published in 1927 and went through four editions in five years. He developed the important distinction between 'significance' and 'instrumentality'. A discussion of the efficacy of sacraments simply in terms of the impact they made as signs, he suggested, would always be inadequate. Nor would it be adequate to interpret their operation as means of grace in terms of the change of status which, say, baptism, might confer. Hence he went on to ask,

> Why then should we not suppose that God uses an appointed sacramental action so as to be, not only the sign of a presence and gift to be realised through conscious appreciation of what the sign signifies, but also the direct means of a bestowal, the reality of which *makes* the sacramental action significant? In other words, I would suggest that it is not more true to say that the efficacy of a sacrament depends on its significance than that its significance depends on its efficacy.[13]

Quick's discussion of sacraments in general made a number of distinctions which help to clarify the way different views had been developed. The distinction he drew between instrumentality and significance as the fundamental type of relation between God and the world was particularly helpful:

> The theologian who thinks in terms of instrumentality will emphasise the truth that in some particular sacrament God really acts and does something; while he who thinks in terms of significance will teach rather that in particular sacraments God's universal presence and activity are more readily apprehended and made known.[14]

This difference could also be expressed by saying that the first group valued sacraments, and the second sacramentalism. Such a distinction certainly helps to illuminate the relationship between Maurice and the tractarians.

Quick also distinguished between aesthetic and ethical sacramentalism:

> Ethical sacramentalism moves in a world of change and action. To it outward things are instruments and therefore the value of none is finally fixed. For the value of everything, being instrumental, depends upon what can ultimately be made out of it, and that we see not yet. The only fixed goodness is that of the divine ideal and of the will which seeks to realise it... Aesthetic sacramentalism on the other hand is bent upon apprehending a world of expression, a world of values embodied in outward symbols, which as such are unalterable. It does not seek to change anything, but rather to penetrate towards a fuller knowledge of the reality which the

---

13 O.C. Quick, *The Christian Sacraments* (4 ed, London 1948), xv.
14 Ibid, 17.

outward seems to veil even in revealing. For it to make demands upon an unknown future to reverse the values of the present would be rank treachery to its fundamental faith.[15]

The value of this preliminary groundwork was seen when Quick came to discuss baptism. Defining baptism as 'essentially the sacrament of the divine Fatherhood', he went on to observe that in no sacrament were the symbolic and instrumental aspects more likely to come into conflict. Either one said that God was the Father of all, so that baptism seemed purely declaratory, or one said that in baptism a real gift of new life was bestowed, which seemed to lead to the view that God was 'King of all and the Father of some'. The New Testament evidence was also ambiguous. Both the Gospels and the Pauline Epistles spoke only of God as Father of believers, yet one of the characteristics of the children of God seemed to be the recognition that their Father's loving purpose extended to all sinners.[16] The way through this dilemma seemed to be by reference to the Christian theory of life as a whole, which Quick had already considered earlier. On this theory holiness was understood as a separation from common life in order that all life might be included in a purified form:

> The separateness of the child of God from other men is always to be measured by his capacity to represent in himself something which is true of them also and in so doing to elicit it effectively from them.[17]

The modern difficulties about the nature of baptism, concluded Quick, had arisen from the failure of both the orthodox and their critics to realise that the shift in the Church's practice from adult baptism to infant baptism should also have involved a shift of emphasis from the instrumental to the symbolic aspect of the sacrament. For Paul, 'baptism only effects the beginning of a process of which it symbolises the end and the whole',[18] but the understanding of the full significance of this had been beyond the mental grasp of the early Church as a whole. Infant baptism could not be regarded as an instrumental rite in the same way in which the baptism of converted adults could be: the attempt to do so had resulted in the development of the doctrine of original sin. But even this was ineffective, since 'so far as experience can show the sinful tendencies or spiritual defects of a baptized and of an unbaptized child are very

---

15 Ibid, 49, 50.
16 Ibid, 161, 167.
17 Ibid, 168.
18 Ibid, 169.

much the same'.[19] So Quick was led to postulate a radically different defence of infant baptism in symbolic rather than instrumental terms:

> Nevertheless the Church's rule of baptism is quite capable of rational defence if we will frankly abandon the claim that the baptized individual must necessarily possess some spiritual privilege or power which the unbaptized individual necessarily lacks. The rational justification for Baptism ultimately rests not on the explicit appointment of Jesus, probable though it be that He did appoint it, nor upon the mistaken idea that Baptism bestows anything—even a guarantee—which for the individual is otherwise unobtainable, but rather upon a whole conception of that plan for the salvation of mankind which God revealed through Jesus Christ and carries on in the life of His Church.[20]

Quick admitted that the main difficulty in this method of interpretation was that it changed the emphasis of New Testament theology: but he was content to justify this by referring to 'the peculiar and necessarily transient conditions under which the New Testament was composed'.[21] He also added a note on confirmation, in deference to the work of Mason and others, in which he said that whilst there was a strong case on theoretical and historical grounds for bringing confirmation and baptism together again, he thought that for practical and pastoral reasons this would not happen, and that, therefore, the Church of England had to stick to the justification of confirmation as a secondary requirement in the Christian life in the way that Western theology had understood it since the middle ages.

The lucidity with which Quick expounded his view and the frankness with which he discussed its theological implications are admirable. But it will also be clear that he crystallized the dilemma which confronted the Church of England. An instrumental view of baptism, when applied to infants, could no longer be maintained, so wishing to retain infant baptism Quick argued for a symbolic emphasis. The opposite possibility, that an instrumental view could be retained by abandoning infant baptism was not considered. His treatment of confirmation made it plain that he put practical and pastoral reasons first. But the argument that the New Testament was the result of transient conditions made it more than ever necessary to depend upon the tradition of the Church as the main theological justification for the practice, an appeal which was, of course, circular in its effect.

It will come as no surprise to discover that *Doctrine in the Church of England* was more cautious in its treatment of baptism than Quick had been, even though Quick was a member of the Commission. The

---

19 Ibid, 172.
20 Ibid, 177.
21 Ibid, 179.

Commission grounded its doctrine of the sacraments in the redemptive work of Christ (perhaps as a result of the influence of J.K. Mozley, who wrote much of the report). On the question of dominical institution the Commission was cautious:

> The bestowal of grace by means of sacraments has in Christian theology been held to rest upon divine appointment, which thus supplies the basis of assurance to the worshipper. Divine appointment may have been effected in various ways, and need not be restricted to explicit institution by our Lord Himself; it may also be found in the action of the Apostolic Church taken under his authority and guided by His Spirit.[22]

The Commission agreed that the sacraments were 'effectual signs':

> As signs they represent the gifts of grace offered through them; as effectual they are instrumental means whereby God confers those gifts on worshippers who receive them with faith.[23]

This statement seems to bear the influence of Quick upon it. But the Commission was divided on the manner in which the sacraments conveyed grace, some believing that grace was directly conferred, others that opportunities of grace were conveyed which the recipient had to appropriate, and yet others preferring to say that the sacraments expressed and confirmed a state of mind and will which fitted the recipient to receive God's gift.

When the Commission came to baptism, Quick's influence may perhaps be discerned in the way it argued that baptism admitted to the eternal fellowship of the Church:

> Baptism, standing at the beginning of the Christian life, on the one hand signifies a state of salvation which is fully reached only through the whole process of life, and on the other hand effects forthwith the necessary first stage of that life.[24]

The rest of the section, however, was strikingly defensive, proceeding to elucidate baptism by reference to difficulties which had been felt about it. The problem of what infant baptism cleansed the recipient from was dealt with by referring to 'Original Sin' (in inverted commas) as those influences which predispose to sin. The fact that the infant is unaware of what is happening was met by the statement that

> an infant is a personality in germ—as a brute animal is not—and the practice witnesses, as nothing else can, to the universality of the Gospel of the Love of

---

22 *Doctrine in the Church of England* (London 1938), 128.
23 Ibid, 130.
24 Ibid, 137.

God, including all persons, Jew or Gentile, black or white, child or grown-up, legitimate or illegitimate. The witness to this fundamental truth compensates for the loss of the greater impressiveness of adult Baptism.[25]

This seems to be a clear case of the adage 'argument weak, shout louder'. The section concluded with a rather tangled attempt to explain how one could still maintain that baptism was a necessary means of incorporation into the body of Christ if one was comparing a baptized person without Christian training with an unbaptized person who had been trained as a disciple. It is not so much that what was said in the report was less convincing in itself than what had often been said before, but the whole section breathed an atmosphere of defensiveness. Significantly, after a three-page discussion of baptism the report proceeded to a forty-eight page discussion of Holy Communion. When the topic of confirmation was reached, the report avoided Mason's argument that Confirmation confers the gift of the Holy Spirit for the first time, but it did describe it as 'the rite which expresses the completeness of Church-membership and of its obligations'.[26]

Such was the position reached by the Church of England when the Second World War broke out. By this time also some significant changes had taken place among nonconformists, as may be seen in the work of the Congregationalist, P.T. Forsyth, and the Baptist, Henry Wheeler Robinson. 'Who is this P.T. Forsyth?', asked R.W. Dale, in a famous remark: 'He has recovered for us a word we had all but lost—the word Grace.'[27] The attempt of R.W. Dale to give a dynamic interpretation to the sacraments among English Congregationalists was described in chapter 5. P.T. Forsyth, who was Principal of Hackney Theological College for twenty years from 1901 to 1921, became the most notable Congregational theologian of the twentieth century. He is best remembered for his thoroughgoing attempt to build a modern theology on the basis of the atonement and the doctrine of redemption. In 1917 he published his *Lectures on the Church and the Sacraments* in which he attempted to offer a view of the sacraments which was neither Zwinglian memorialism nor High Catholic, but which treated the sacraments as symbols 'not as mere channels, but in the active sense that something is done as well as conveyed'.[28] When he came to discuss baptism Forsyth began characteristically by lashing contemporary practice:

We neglect Baptism and we cosset the child... Many of the child-lovers are among the careless about Baptism. This is only one of several current indications how the

---

25 Ibid, 137-8.
26 Ibid, 189.
27 P.T. Forsyth, *The Work of Christ* (London 1959), xv.
28 P.T. Forsyth, *Lectures on the Church and the Sacraments* (London 1917), vii.

cult of the child in the Church may destroy the worship of the Gospel... I have been at many Sunday School anniversaries...when all the singing, even of the morning service, is on these occasions given up to children's, not to say babies' hymns, with music to correspond, while Baptism was of little moment, or was hidden away in the home.[29]

But the sacrament was the acted Word, signs which were more than signs, Christ's love-tokens to the Church; they not only suggested him but also conveyed him to the Church.

On the origin of baptism Forsyth made the important claim that 'Baptism was instituted by the ascended Christ through the Apostles as His will for the Church. It was not, like the Supper, expressly set up by the earthly Jesus.'[30] He dismissed Mark 16:16 as not genuine and thought Matthew 28:19 a rather fragile base. Hence he was able to make the bold claim (for a Free Churchman) that *'the Sacraments are valid not chiefly because they were instituted by the command of Christ, but because they arise from the nature of His Gospel in the Church'*.[31] This marked an important break with the kind of justification offered by all his predecessors, and indicated the impact of bibical criticism.

Another strong emphasis made by Forsyth was that the sacraments were corporate acts:

Baptism is not primarily an act of the parent nor of the child, but of the Church, and of Christ in the Church. It is our individualism that has done most to ruin the sacrament of Baptism among us... Baptism is not there primarily for the individual, nor for the family, but for the Church, to confess before God and man the Word of Regeneration.[32]

Because baptism was into Christ's death, it necessarily involved the idea of new birth or regeneration. In fact, like the other sacraments baptism 'declared and enacted the whole Gospel, and not merely an initiatory stage of it'.[33] This was very similar to what Quick said later, though Quick nowhere made any reference to Forsyth's book. It may also be that the similar emphasis in the 1938 *Doctrine* report came from Mozley, who thought very highly of Forsyth, rather than Quick. Baptism was also *holy* baptism, that is to say it affected the soul and conscience of a moral being, by God's moral action in Christ. Grace was a relation of active persons, not an infusion of vital substance:

---

29 Ibid, 161.
30 Ibid, 185.
31 Ibid, 186. The italics are Forsyth's.
32 Ibid, 166.
33 Ibid, 179.

> The spiritual virtue of a Sacrament is not drawn from the ethereal action of the Word made flesh for us, but from the moral action of the Word made sin for us, and unto us righteousness.[34]

The redemptive, rather than the incarnational, emphasis is clear. The gift of forgiveness and eternal life was given both by the Word and by the sacrament: but the one did not take the place of the other, since baptism became the act of final committal. But Forsyth stressed once more that baptism was 'an act of the Church even more than of the individual, and of God, of the Spirit, most of all'.[35] Baptism did not make people Christian:

> The converts were Christian before Baptism. They became Christian by an act of their native personality responding to God's mercy in Christ. Before Baptism they were Christ's. Therefore they were baptized. After it they were openly in the body of Christ.... We cannot think of regeneration apart from a Church.[36]

There is clear continuity here with Dale's use of the coronation image, mentioned in the last chapter; but the emphasis upon the Church is stronger. Moreover, said Forsyth, 'it is Christ that receives you, not a friendly society'.[37] The term 'friendly society' was presumably used in its technical sense of a voluntary organisation for charitable purposes; but it will immediately be seen that this contrast itself put the emphasis in the understanding of the Church firmly on the initiative of Christ rather than human action. Throughout his exposition Forsyth insisted on the priority of the Word of God, shown and active in Christ's death and resurrection.

Hence, Forsyth regarded adult baptism as the norm in the New Testament. Infant baptism was within the principle of the gospel, but was not part of New Testament practice because the New Testament church was a missionary church. So he could say that 'a Baptism *unto* the confession of the Church faith may be as true to the Gospel Grace as a Baptism *upon* it, and less individualist'.[38] His rejection of individualism may have been influential here. He also conceded to those whose sympathies lay with adult baptism that every infant baptism should be sympathetically an adult baptism: those present should understand themselves to be assisting, not simply watching but renewing their own baptism in spirit. It is curious that this emphasis should not come under the censure of individualism, even though it emphasised what people felt about the sacrament. It is also unclear how people whose only experience

---

34 Ibid, 183-4.
35 Ibid, 191.
36 Ibid, 193, 194.
37 Ibid, 195.
38 Ibid, 169 (italics original).

of baptism was infant baptism were to set about identifying themselves as adults with a rite of which they had no memory. But he stressed that much misunderstanding had been caused by transferring things which were only possible for the adult experience to the unconscious child, thereby turning them into magic, and robbing the sacrament of its moral power. Nevertheless, Forsyth did not believe that Christianity would be reformed by abolishing infant baptism: rather both infant and adult baptism should be accepted side by side. A child brought up in a Christian home was not like someone converted as an adult: why then should the child not have the sign of belonging to the Church as well as the blessings of a Christian home? It was important to see the sacraments testifying not to the priority of faith, but the priority of grace. Infant baptism was wrong when it was administered without any prospect of Christian nurture: so it was also important that there should be an opportunity for confirmation, i.e. the personal assumption of responsibility by the one baptized. Confirmation was not to be regarded as a second sacrament, and certainly not as conveying a second gift, but it did realise the gift and grace that were assigned in baptism. When Forsyth's book was reissued in 1947 J.K. Mozley wrote an Introduction—it was indeed one of the last things he ever wrote. In it he acknowledged that Forsyth's exposition was not in line with Catholic method; yet it was a sustained attempt to base the sacraments on the Cross, and to get away from any view which implied that they were 'signs or pictures or mere memorials, promises of what God will do or reminiscences of what Christ has done'.[39] In this sense Forsyth took a significant step towards a catholic emphasis.

Nor was he alone. His general approach to grace received much support from the work of theologians like John Oman in *Grace and Personality* (1917) and W. Fearon Halliday in *Reconciliation and Reality* (1919). Some believer baptists were also starting to move in this direction. Among Churches of Christ, William Robinson, following Forsyth, argued in his *Essays on Christian Unity* (1922) that the Free Churches needed to recover a sense of the sacraments, and that in believer's baptism as the rite to mark conversion a truly sacramental understanding of baptism could be found.[40] But for Baptists the situation was complicated by reactions to the Lambeth Appeal of 1920. This will be discussed in more detail in the last chapter, but something needs to be said here to explain the context for Baptist thought in the inter-war period.

J.H. Shakespeare, General Secretary of the Baptist Union from 1898 to 1925, was a pioneer in the formation of the Federal Council of the

---

39 P.T. Forsyth, *Lectures on the Church and the Sacraments* (ed J.K. Mozley: London 1947), xi.
40 W. Robinson, *Essays on Christian Unity* (London 1922), 169-89, 203-48.

Evangelical Free Churches in 1919, and was keenly involved in the discussions between the Federal Council and the Church of England, following the Lambeth Conference of 1920. However, his overt support for episcopacy and his perceived readiness to accept a compromise on the status of Free Church ministers fuelled opposition both to the reunion proposals and to him personally within the Baptist Union. T.R. Glover was elected as President of the Union for 1924, mainly because of his public opposition to Shakespeare.[41] In fact, baptism as such did not loom large in the Lambeth discussions, rather disappointingly; but Glover had long ago reached the conclusion that Jesus did not intend to found the Church and did not institute any sacraments. He did not find these developments surprising, because of the world in which the early Christian community was set—'a world without natural science, steeped in belief in every kind of magic and enchantment, and full of public and private religious societies, every one of which had its mysteries and miracles and its blood-bond with its peculiar deity'.[42] In a later book, published at the time of the reunion discussions, he was even more forthright in criticising what he called 'the victory of organization and the sacramental interpretation of religion', which he regarded as 'entirely alien' and 'antithetical' to the mind of Jesus: 'salvation came to be associated more and more automatically with the Church and its sacraments; apart from the Church there was no salvation; all must be in it for safety; conviction was of less consequence'.[43] Glover's thought had developed a long way from the time he spent listening to the preaching of Forsyth in Cambridge as an undergraduate, but it fitted with the interest he displayed in the Society of Friends in the early twentieth century.[44] However, his standing as an ancient historian and as a layman made him the perfect defender of what had come to seem to be the Baptist tradition in the nineteenth century; it also explains the apparent paradox of the theological liberal leading an opposition to ecumenical involvement that was primarily supported by conservative evangelicals.

This was the context in which Henry Wheeler Robinson, Principal of Regent's Park College, addressed the ministers' session of the London Baptist Association in June 1922 on 'The Place of Baptism in Baptist

---

41 H.G. Wood, *Terrot Reaveley Glover* (Cambridge 1953), 151-5; cf R. Hayden, 'Still at the Crossroads: Revd J.H. Shakespeare and Ecumenism', K.W. Clements (ed), *Baptists in the Twentieth Century* (London 1983), 31-54.

42 T.R. Glover, *The Conflict of Religions in the Early Roman Empire* (London 1909), 158; cf A.R. Cross, *Baptism and the Baptists: Theology and Practice in Twentieth-Century Britain* (Carlisle 2000), 107.

43 T.R. Glover, *Jesus in the Experience of Men* (London 1921), 164, 165.

44 Wood, *Glover*, 81-6.

Churches To-day'.⁴⁵ Wheeler Robinson was to become one of the leading exponents of a sacramental understanding of baptism among Baptists in the first half of the twentieth century. After a brief discussion of the problems (as he saw them) of the practice of infant baptism in other churches, he went on to warn against making immersion the essence of the matter, for that would 'gravely imperil our real witness to baptism as a personal profession of repentance and faith, an act at once moral and religious, an act of human personality entering into conscious fellowship with the divine'.⁴⁶ (The emphasis on believer's baptism as a moral action goes all the way back into the nineteenth century, at least as far as Charles Stovel's lectures.) He was more concerned about the possibility of open membership churches leading to a neglect of baptism altogether, asking whether all Baptist ministers were convinced Baptists. His fear was that 'we have been so driven to the assertion of *believers'* baptism, as against the baptism of infants, that we have failed to maintain the not less important emphasis on believers' *baptism*, in the fulness of the New Testament meaning, a baptism of the Holy Spirit'.⁴⁷ The reason for the neglect of the latter lay, he thought, in an unconscious fear that so much was made of it by those who believed in baptismal regeneration, which had led to an emphasis on baptism as 'a personal and human profession of repentance and faith'. It was that, 'but the uniquely ethical character of our baptism safeguards us from the risk of misunderstanding, and leaves full room for the evangelical sacramentalism of the New Testament'.⁴⁸ Thus Baptists needed to avoid baptism having little meaning, as it did among Congregationalists, because it would then drop out; but in order to avoid the errors of Catholicism, which made baptism central, they had to put the whole New Testament truth into it. The contrast between this view and that advanced by Glover is obvious, and the lecture was given before Glover became President of the Union.

In his later book on *Baptist Principles*, first published in 1925, Wheeler Robinson encouraged Baptists not to be frightened of the word 'sacraments', even if they distrusted sacramentarianism. He repeated that baptism was more than an act of personal obedience, but had value as an ethical act by the individual, as a powerful symbol of conversion, and as an acted parable in the mode of immersion acting out the verbal confession of faith.⁴⁹ He made much of the ideas of prophetic symbolism

---

45 Fowler claims that 'all the essential aspects of his renewal of baptismal theology were present' in this address: Fowler, *More Than a Symbol*, 90.

46 H. Wheeler Robinson, 'The Place of Baptism in Baptist Churches To-day', *Baptist Quarterly*, i, 5 (January 1923), 212; cf Fowler, *More Than a Symbol*, 89-97.

47 Ibid, 214 (italics original).

48 Ibid, 216-7.

49 H. Wheeler Robinson, *Baptist Principles* (3 ed, London 1938), 11-31; H. Wheeler Robinson, *The Life and Faith of the Baptists* (2 ed, London 1946), 69-81.

drawn from his own work as an Old Testament scholar, which he developed in a later address to the London Baptist Association in January 1939. Here he reviewed the New Testament evidence in much greater detail, and addressed the question of how Paul and his colleagues interpreted the function of water-baptism. He did not hesitate to argue that the spiritual is always mediated by the material: that was the 'very principle of the Incarnation, when the Word became flesh'. But the truest answer, he thought, was in terms of prophetic symbolism which meant much more than an 'acted parable': 'The prophets of the Old Testament did not simply proclaim a word of the Lord; they sometimes began to put it into operation by identifying themselves with it in a personal act, which was already a fragment, as it were, of the whole act of God which they proclaimed.'[50] Such an interpretation would remove baptism from 'the baser sacramentarianism on the one hand, as it does from otiose "symbolism" on the other'. So he concluded that Baptists needed to move in this direction if they were to be true to the New Testament: 'Baptism is there not only a necessary profession of repentance and faith; it is also a sacrament of grace, as truly as is participation in the Lord's Supper'.[51] His worry, however, remained that of 1922: did Baptists really believe this? If they did not, he felt that they had no contribution to make to the universal Church of the future, whatever form it might ultimately assume.

An unexpected twist to these developments was given by interventions from two of the most distinguished Reformed theologians of the period, Emil Brunner and Karl Barth. In 1937 Brunner gave the Olaus Petri Lectures at Uppsala, which he subsequently revised and published as *Wahrheit als Begegnung*—'Truth as Encounter': the title lost some of its force when translated into English in 1943. As the German suggests, the lectures were about the Christian understanding of truth. Brunner argued that there was a necessary dialectic between objectivism and subjectivism in theology: he identified the Catholic Church with an exclusive emphasis on objectivism, but noted that the subjective reaction represented by the Reformation was rapidly turned into a new kind of protestant orthodoxy, which reinforced the objective understanding. In his final chapter on 'the Biblical Understanding of Truth and the Church', he first criticised objectivism in doctrine, which equated or failed to distinguish between God's Word and doctrine. Then, he criticised objectivism in the understanding of the sacraments, particularly in relation to baptism. Catholic doctrine and practice had separated it from its biblical meaning by removing the act of confession which stemmed from God's act of

---

50 H. Wheeler Robinson, 'Believers' Baptism and the Holy Spirit', *Baptist Quarterly*, ix, 7 (July 1939), 394.
51 Ibid, 395.

grace. The effect of indiscriminate infant baptism was that most contemporary neo-pagans and members of atheistic societies had been baptized as infants. (One wonders how far this reflection was prompted by developments in Nazi Germany.) Thus

> Infant baptism, which has its good points in an entirely Christian fellowship—that is to say, a fellowship of persons who all joyfully profess Jesus Christ as their Lord—becomes a highly questionable arrangement where it is requested more from consideration of custom than from conviction of faith.[52]

But his conclusion was stronger still: 'The contemporary practice of infant baptism can hardly be regarded as being anything short of scandalous.'[53] The reason for the strength of his language was that the question of infant baptism was not one among many in relation to the Church, but the decisive one, because baptism was the basis of church membership: the discrepancy between the 'gigantic Church of those baptized and the tiny Church of those assenting to confession' was one of the chief causes of the current difficulties of the Church in all places.[54]

Karl Barth was even more publicly associated with the Confessing Church in Germany, before he had to take refuge in Switzerland. In 1943 he delivered a lecture on 'The Teaching of the Church regarding Baptism', which was translated into English by Ernest Payne in 1948. Baptism, said Barth, was the picture, witness and sign of God's gracious activity towards man in Jesus Christ, but it was no dead or dumb representation. Its power lay in the free act of Christ himself. But baptism was not the cause of redemption, any more than faith was: rather it was cognitive.

The new ground in what Barth had to say came in the last part. He suggested that the order and practice of baptism in the Church left much to be desired: partly this had to do with the rather casual way in which it was often administered, but more significantly it had to do with the fact that the baptism of infants, those who had nothing to say in baptism because they were not able to speak, produced not a mere chink but a hole in the teaching of all the great Christian confessions. Luther and Calvin, he thought, had landed themselves in hopeless confusion on the subject. A number of arguments had been devised to support infant baptism, one of the strongest being that it illustrated the free antecedent grace of God. But such an argument had not been used by the Reformers

---

52 E. Brunner, *The Divine-Human Encounter* (London 1944), 131.
53 Ibid, 132.
54 Ibid, 135.

themselves, and only carried conviction if the rightness of infant baptism could be proved another way.[55]

> Am I wrong [concluded Barth] in thinking that the really operative extraneous ground for infant-baptism, even with the Reformers, and ever and again quite plainly since, has been this: one did not want then in any case or at any price to deny the existence of the evangelical Church in the Constantinian *corpus christianum*—and today one does not want to renounce the present form of the national church (*Volkskirche*)? If she were to break with infant-baptism, the Church would not easily any longer be a people's church in the sense of a state Church or a church of the masses.[56]

Yet the Church need not cease to be a Church *of* the people by ceasing to be a Church *for* the people, and as a minority Christians might be a healthy Church.

Did this lecture reflect the influence of Kierkegaard's attack upon Christendom, or a similar disillusionment with the *Volkskirche* concept to Brunner, as a result of Barth's experience in Germany in the 1930s? Certainly, the implications of these works for the traditional concept of Christian civilization were appreciated very quickly by the Scottish theologian, John Baillie, Professor of Divinity at Edinburgh. In his Riddell Memorial Lectures for 1945, '*What is Christian Civilization?*', he was one of the first theologians to address the issues raised by Brunner, Barth and indeed Kierkegaard (before Barth's lecture had been translated into English). He devoted a significant part of his second lecture to the significance of infant baptism—or rather 'the baptism of families'—as a characteristic of Christian civilization; and he regarded it as no coincidence that an attack on this practice characterized most protest movements in the Church from Montanism to Anabaptism. 'The insight enshrined in this doctrine and practice [i.e. infant baptism]', he wrote, 'is that the most likely way to bring men to an individual decision for Christ is to nurture them within a Christian community.' This applied both to the family and larger social units.

> Just, therefore, as it is wrong to think meanly of the Christianity of children before they reach the age of personal decision and are confirmed in the faith, so I believe it wrong to hold as of no account the Christianity which pervades the life of a community before it is confirmed in the personal decision of every individual citizen.[57]

---

55 K. Barth, *The Teaching of the Church regarding Baptism* (London 1948), 14-16, 27, 36-52.
56 Ibid, 52-3.
57 J. Baillie, *What is Christian Civilization?* (2 ed, London 1947), 42.

The second edition of Baillie's lectures contained a new Appendix, which discussed in more detail the arguments of Kierkegaard, Brunner and Barth on the practice of infant baptism. It concluded with a long quotation from the Report of the Commission for the Interpretation of God's Will in the Present Crisis, presented to the General Assembly of the Church of Scotland in 1943. After referring to the Westminster Confession and affirming the importance of baptism 'in the face of the congregation', the Statement went on to state the need for personal profession of faith:

> Opinions may differ as to the precise form the act should take and as to the age at which it should be expected; but what is important is the recognition that there is an age to which such individual testimony is proper, and also an age before which it would be unnatural and hurtful to demand it, and that, nevertheless, those of earlier age may be just as truly beloved servants of Christ, yielding to Him the only kind of service of which they are capable or which at that age He desires from them, and accepted by Him as cherished members of His Mystical Body.[58]

Thus the reaction to the German Church conflict could take very different forms on each side of the North Sea. The significance of Baillie's view for the later discussions of the Church of Scotland on baptism was considerable.

There was a time-lag in the translation into English of the books of both Brunner and Barth, accentuated by the war. Nevertheless, despite the hopes of many believer-baptists their arguments were not taken up; and it is worth emphasising that the question both were really raising concerned the nature of the Church. As indicated earlier, Brunner was prepared to accept infant baptism in a community of believers. Barth subsequently modified his position further, and the final fragment of the *Church Dogmatics* (1967) dealt with his mature view of the matter. In this he set out 'to present Christian ethics as the free and active answer of man to the divine work and word of grace'.[59] His original plan was to consider baptism, the Lord's Prayer and the Lord's Supper, but only the first part was ever written. In the light of the book by his son, Markus, on baptism in the New Testament (significantly never translated into English)[60] he abandoned the 'sacramental' understanding of baptism, which he had still held in 1943, but his new view did not imply a weakening, but rather a confirmation, of his opposition to 'the custom, or abuse, of infant

---

58 Ibid, 86, quoting *God's Will for Church and Nation* (London 1946), 80-1; see also J.A. Whyte, 'Church and Society in the Thought of John Baillie', D. Fergusson (ed), *Christ, Church and Society: Essays on John Baillie and Donald Baillie* (Edinburgh 1993), 237-44.

59 K. Barth, *Church Dogmatics, iv, The Doctrine of Reconciliation, Part 4* (Edinburgh 1969), ix.

60 M. Barth, *Die Taufe—ein Sakrament?* (Zürich 1951).

baptism'. But while he did not suppose that its abandonment would be the solution to the healing of the Church, he asked how the Church could be or become 'an essentially missionary and mature rather than immature Church, so long as it obstinately, against all better judgment and conscience, continues to dispense the water of baptism with the same undiscriminating generosity as it has now done for centuries?'[61] However, he emphasised that baptism as the foundation of the Christian life was infinitely more important to him than his objection to the predominant baptismal practice. His English editors, G.W. Bromiley and T.F. Torrance, suggested in their Preface that Barth expounded Christian baptism 'not as a sacrament or even as a work of divine grace but as man's liturgical work in recognition of what God has already done for us in Christ and in obedience to the commission laid upon us in the reconciling work of Christ'. Barth, they argued, held that there was only one sacrament—Jesus Christ himself; baptism and the Lord's Supper were not sacraments 'since they are not recurrent actualisations of the incarnation or means through which supernatural power is infused into believers'.[62]

Barth himself wrote that this book would leave him 'in the theological and ecclesiastical isolation which has been my lot for almost fifty years'.[63] He was right. Professor Torrance, who was one of Barth's main supporters in Britain, showed no sign of commending him on this matter, and indeed was Convener of the Church of Scotland's Commission on Baptism in the 1950s, which made much of precisely the arguments Barth rejected. However, one of the results of his work was a flowering of New Testament scholarship designed to show how much infant baptism harmonized with New Testament theology. Oscar Cullman published a reply to Barth, translated into English in 1950 under the title *Baptism in the New Testament*; and in 1958 Joachim Jeremias published his *Infant Baptism in the First Four Centuries* which was developed from a pamphlet originally written in 1938. Jeremias also found himself engaged in a separate controversy with Kurt Aland of the University of Munster. In England, the Methodist scholar W.F. Flemington published his *New Testament Doctrine of Baptism* in 1948. That book was one of the most systematic studies of the New Testament material made by an English scholar, and it included in the last chapter a justification of infant baptism as a legitimate development from New Testament practice in terms of the priority of God's gracious action. Indeed, Flemington went so far as to wonder (in a suitably muffled rhetorical question) whether

---

61 Barth, *Church Dogmatics*, iv, *4*, x-xi.
62 Ibid, v.
63 Ibid, xii.

those who made their insistence on the necessity of *faith* a reason for denying any objective efficacy to infant baptism are themselves betraying a lack of faith concerning the method of divine revelation and the power of God to fulfil his own promises.⁶⁴

It was perhaps a sign of the defensiveness of those who argued for infant baptism that there was an increasing tendency to argue that faith on the part of the recipient of baptism might be a positive disadvantage. R.W. Dale had suggested in 1884 that the fact that the consent of the adult was necessary to baptism 'may suggest a false conception of the rite'.⁶⁵ Forsyth's worry that believer's baptism might foster individualism has already been noted. The Church of Scotland Commission's *Interim Report* of 1955 read at one point as follows:

> Apart from repentance and faith Christian Baptism is unthinkable. The Gospel calls men to account, to decision, and to confession of the name of Christ, and all that is focussed in Baptism. But Baptism which takes place in a Covenant relation between God and His people and requires faith and obedience, declares that it is not by our believing that we are saved, but by God alone. We cannot be saved apart from faith, if we grow up into responsible life, but faith relies entirely upon the faithfulness of Christ.⁶⁶

The Commission concluded that baptism should not be seen as a sacrament of our faith, or of our repentance, but as a sacrament of the gospel in which salvation is bestowed upon us from beyond by pure grace. One consequence of this strong doctrine, of course, was to increase the pressure to explain why infant communion should not be practised also. The Commission's initial suggestion was that communion was essentially self-offering whereas baptism was not self-administered. This was hardly convincing, since both sacraments are administered to individuals and involve their self-offering; to choose one emphasis for one sacrament and another for the other is entirely arbitrary.

It is interesting that both the established Churches in Britain should have had Commissions sitting on the subject of baptism in the post-war years. The Church of Scotland's Commission was set up in response to a request from the Edinburgh Presbytery in 1949 that a clearer definition be given of the Church's requirement that the parents of a child presented for baptism should 'profess the Christian religion'. When it became clear that, although the words might be changed, the problem of definition could not be so easily resolved, a Commission was appointed to

---

64 W.F. Flemington, *The New Testament Doctrine of Baptism* (London 1948), 136 (italics original).
65 Dale, *Manual of Congregational Principles*, 128.
66 *Church of Scotland: Interim Report of the Special Commission on Baptism, May 1955* (Edinburgh 1955), 50.

examine the whole doctrine of baptism. In the Church of England Joint Committees of both Convocations were appointed in 1942, originally to consider problems arising out of the decline in Church schools and the 'grave disparity between the numbers of children presented for Baptism and those brought to Confirmation and Communion'. Hence the Joint Committees' first report in 1944 was on *Confirmation Today*; in 1949 their second report was entitled *Baptism Today*. In each Church the underlying problem was the sense of a widening gap between the Church and society as a whole, which was precisely the issue Barth subsequently identified as central.

Ironically, the two Churches seemed to move in opposite directions. The Church of Scotland did have a formal requirement appropriately supported by its Reformed theology that infant baptism should be confined to the children of professing Christians and did not require sponsors; it produced a report which asserted the primary importance of the faith of the Church, and suggested that faith on the part of the family was relatively unimportant. On the other hand, the Church of England, which because of the system of sponsors made no formal requirements of parents at all, was trying to cope with an increasing number of clergy who wished to limit the availability of infant baptism. The Church of England Joint Committees declined to adopt the extreme view of the importance of Confirmation, exemplified in Dom Gregory Dix's lecture of 1946 on 'The Theology of Confirmation in relation to Baptism' which argued that baptism was incomplete without confirmation.[67] But they did adopt the language of 'Christian Initiation' to cover the cycle of rites which begins with baptism and ends with first communion, and did much to popularize this approach to the problem. Geoffrey Lampe provided the theological answer to Dix in *The Seal of the Spirit* (1951). Baptism, he argued, was the sacrament of the whole gospel: but it was not surprising that particular aspects of its meaning should have become associated with some of the subsidiary rites; and he did not find the arguments put forward for the restoration of the primitive practice compelling. So, although the Church of England Liturgical Commission proposed in 1958 that a newly designed service for the baptism of adults and confirmation should become the archetypal service for the revised services of baptism and confirmation, the suggestion was not received with enthusiasm. Nevertheless, this was done when the *Alternative Service Book* was published in 1980, and has been retained in *Common Worship* (2000). But the dilemma over the practice of infant baptism remains, and the baptismal discipline required of parents can now vary considerably from parish to parish in England.

---

67 G. Dix, *The Theology of Confirmation in Relation to Baptism: A Public Lecture in the University of Oxford delivered on January 22nd 1946* (London 1946).

Perhaps one of the most interesting signs of the changed mood in this area, however, was Donald Baillie's posthumously published book on *The Theology of the Sacraments* in 1957. In itself it said nothing that was new, though it was elegantly and clearly written. What is significant is that a Church of Scotland theologian, nurtured in the Free Church tradition, was seriously worried about the problem of 'the death of the sacraments' (to quote Paul Tillich's phrase) and was not particularly impressed by the solution Tillich offered in *The Protestant Era* (ET 1951). Baillie wanted to recover a sense of the vitality of the sacraments for Christian faith and life. The clue lay, he thought, in seeing the personal character of grace — an emphasis already noted in Forsyth and Oman, and it was true of T.F. Torrance in the Church of Scotland's Commission on Baptism as well. Interestingly the person he appealed to was Baron von Hügel, quoting the following words from his *Essays and Addresses*:

> I kiss my child not only because I love it; I kiss it also in order to love it. A religious picture not only expresses my awakened faith; it is a help to my faith's awakening.

And Baillie added, 'All such are "means of grace", methods employed by the graciousness of God to express and develop a gracious personal relationship between Him and us.'[68] By the 1950s, therefore, baptism in particular and sacramental theology in general had become an ecumenical concern. They were no longer the property of any one school of thought in the Church. Most fascinating of all, the concern over baptism owed next to nothing to the discussion of the subject among the defenders of believer's baptism. Such a development had been foreshadowed by Forsyth. The ecumenical implications of this will be explored in the last chapter; but before that it is necessary to return to the question of the relationship between theological developments and popular belief and practice.

---

68 D.M. Baillie, *The Theology of the Sacraments and other papers* (London 1957), 54, quoting F. von Hügel, *Essays and Addresses, First Series* (London 1921), 251.

Chapter 7

Popular Belief and Practice

In 1847 the Revd J.C. Atkinson was presented to the living of Danby-in-Cleveland in North Yorkshire. One day, as they were talking about arrangements for the transfer, his predecessor said, 'I hope you will be kind to my people... I have been very kind to them, but they have not been very thoughtful or considerate about me.' And he went on to explain what he meant:

> I mean that when a child is born, they send for me to baptize the bairn; and I go. A fortnight afterwards, they send for me to 'church the mother'; and I go; and I think they might be content with that. But they are not, for a fortnight later they send for me to 'christen' the child. And that is surely a little too much.[1]

This story illustrates the gap which existed between popular belief and practice and the theological controversies about baptism discussed in the previous four chapters. This chapter, therefore, returns to the themes of chapter 1, in order to see what had changed and what remained the same in the nineteenth and twentieth centuries. If anything the gap between ecclesiastical and popular expectations seemed to widen as a result of attempts to reform baptismal practice.

It is probable that concern over the popular understandings of baptism was part of the background to those controversies. Reference was made in chapter 4 to the fear expressed by the *Christian Observer* in relation to the Oxford Tracts that however sophisticated the theology and devotion of the leaders might be, the 'rude multitude' would always 'transmute everything to gross materiality and soul-deluding superstition'. It continued:

> The wafer will be a sacred charm; holy water will sanctify evil deeds; fasts and alms will atone for sin; priests will be feared, though perhaps not loved, as mediators between God and man; and the hardened and dying profligate of an English village will send, with ensnaring hope, in his last hours, to his parish pastor, as the divinely authorized dispenser of some miraculous viaticum—just as the Italian assassin, or the Spanish leader of a troop of banditti, does to his priest for extreme unction, when he is perishing from his wounds, or on the scaffold, and can pursue his crimes no longer. Compare the conduct of an unlettered peasant, or a civic

---

1 J.C. Atkinson, *Forty Years in a Moorland Parish* (3 ed, London 1907), 45.

artisan, among the Methodists, whom the Anti-Jacobin ridicules, with the miscreant in a corresponding scale of society in Ireland, who goes to mass one day, commits murder the next, and does penance and gets himself shriven the third; and you will see the difference in moral effect between 'spiritual' and 'physical' religion.[2]

The criminal or violent examples chosen probably reflect an underlying concern about the relationship between religion and public order—this was the period when the Chartist agitation was getting under way. But the emphasis on faith was related to religious morality: the fear is that what the *Christian Observer* called 'physical religion' is actually morally subversive. If one asks why it was acceptable for evangelicals to preach a universal atonement to hardened sinners, but unacceptable for high churchmen to preach baptismal regeneration to the same people, the answer must lie in the moral response required in the former case, and the genuine concern that sinners might be deluded into believing that they were safer from eternal damnation than they were. The high church position was regarded as magical; the evangelical approach was seen as rational and moral.

In investigating the nature of popular belief and practice in relation to baptism, there are important problems over the evidence which need to be noted. One is that evidence is inevitably sporadic, coming from widely scattered places and unevenly distributed over time. It is difficult to speak with confidence about 'typical' beliefs, and generalisations about changes in attitude over time need to be hedged about with caution—though sometimes there do exist statistics over a reasonable period. This problem is not an unusual one for the historian, and was true of the evidence used in chapter 1 as well. The second problem is more intractable. In chapter 1 the main sources used were diaries and visitation returns; similar evidence is used here, except that generally visitation returns are less helpful. Most of the evidence used in this chapter comes either from nineteenth-century clergymen or twentieth-century sociologists. For different reasons, neither of these groups is likely to say much about religious beliefs about baptism. The remarks of clergymen used here were usually written down precisely because they were striking, or out of the ordinary—no clergyman was likely to make a special point of noting that Mrs Smith had a firm belief in the doctrine of baptism contained in the Prayer Book, unless that itself was unusual! Sociologists, by contrast, have often rested content with noting a superstitious element in beliefs about baptism without feeling any necessity to consider the relationship between those beliefs and religious beliefs. This is particularly so if nonconformists are being considered since it is assumed that nonconformist religion is essentially non-sacramental. For example,

---

2 *Christian Observer* (1837), 166.

Robert Moore in his fascinating study of four Durham mining villages stated, without further amplification, that the prevalence of 'superstitious' beliefs about baptism was well-established for the mining villages of County Durham, but developed his discussion on the assumption that such beliefs must be essentially separate from Methodist religious beliefs since Methodism is a 'felt' religion, stressing personal religious experience.[3] This can lead to an implicit reductionism, whereby only superstitious elements in baptismal belief and practice are discussed, and the conclusion which emerges not surprisingly is that at the popular level baptism is seen in primarily superstitious terms. It is, of course, easier to state this problem than to resolve it. However, in recent years much more work has been done in the area of oral history, and a greater sensitivity to understanding popular beliefs in their own terms has been apparent.

Before any discussion of the popular understanding of baptism, it is necessary to sketch the general changes in baptismal practice in the nineteenth century, particularly as they were affected by the pastoral revival in the Church of England on the one hand and the growth of towns on the other. Chapter 1 showed that popular neglect of baptism had begun by the eighteenth century, and the problem of private baptisms indicated in the extract from Atkinson's memoir at the beginning of this chapter shows that little had changed in that respect either. In chapter 2 it was noted that Richard Mant discovered that a large number in his parish had not been baptized when he first arrived in Coggeshall in 1810. Among these were not only those who were Baptists, but also 'many professing to be members of the Church of England'.[4] In 1852 Benjamin Armstrong completed a visitation to certain outlying parts of his parish of East Dereham in Norfolk (to which he had been inducted two years before) and discovered 'only fourteen children unbaptized' among a hundred families.[5] By contrast, in 1858 the Revd T.J. Rowsell told a House of Lords Select Committee that when he went to Stepney fifteen years before many children died without being baptized.[6] Whatever the particular explanations for these situations, it remains the case that the time had long gone when it could be assumed that England (or Wales, or Scotland) was a homogeneous society in which the rites of passage were universally observed. A folk belief in baptism was not universal, as has sometimes been assumed.

Nor was baptism always celebrated with the dignity that might have been expected. Francis Kilvert recorded what he had been told by the

---

3 R. Moore, *Pit-men, Preachers and Politics* (Cambridge 1974), 94-5.
4 Berens, *Memoir of Mant*, 64.
5 H.B.J. Armstrong (ed), *Armstrong's Norfolk Diary* (London 1963), 32.
6 *Report of Select Committee of the House of Lords on the Deficiency of Means of Spiritual Instruction and Places of Divine Worship in the Metropolis*, H.C. 387 (1858-59), 72, qq 1000-2.

Vicar of Fordington in Dorset about the state of things there when he had arrived in the 1820s:

> One day there was a christening and no water in the Font. 'Water, Sir!' said the clerk in astonishment. 'The last parson never used no water. He spit into his hand.'[7]

The Sarum Rite prescribed that the priest should spit in his hand to touch the ears and nose of the infant, but this was not the baptism.[8] However, Kilvert himself did not seem too put out by having to baptize a baby with ice in the font on a frosty day at Bettws in February 1870.[9] Sometimes in the early part of the century there was not even a font in the church at all. Archdeacon Hodson on his primary visitation of the archdeaconry of Stafford in 1829-30 found twelve churches out of 167 without fonts, and another thirty-one in need of basins. In four cases the font was in the churchyard, and at Lapley it was said that the former vicar had used it for feeding his calves.[10] Atkinson explained the same neglect, when commenting on the poor state of the font at Danby, by the fact that private baptism had become very common, but the evidence from chapter 1 suggests that the problem went back further.[11]

The towns faced the opposite problem, because of the rapid growth of population. A correspondent wrote in the *British Magazine* for February 1837,

> Let any one visit the churches of our populous parishes on the Sunday afternoons, when this holy rite is performed, and I think his feelings will be shocked by witnessing the abuse of his holy solemnity. The crowd of sponsors, obviously unknown to the minister,—they may be infidels or anything else,—dropping in during the sermon, as if they had no concern in the services of the church; their frequent inability to answer the questions in the order without being prompted by the clerk; the utter ignorance of the parents and sponsors of the nature and privileges of baptism;—these circumstances all mark a practical corruption in this important point.[12]

When Walter Hook became Vicar of Leeds in 1837 he found that the vicar, one curate and a clerk in orders had to conduct all the baptisms, marriages and burials for the whole town: they baptized and churched twice every day and in 1842 and 1843 had just over 1,800 baptisms a

---

7 W. Plomer (ed), *Kilvert's Diary*, ii (London 1939), 442.
8 E.C. Whitaker, *Documents of the Baptismal Liturgy* (London 1970), 237.
9 W. Plomer (ed), *Kilvert's Diary*, i (London 1939), 34-5.
10 D. Robinson (ed), *Visitations of the Archdeaconry of Stafford, 1829-1841* (London 1980), 53.
11 Atkinson, *Forty Years*, 45.
12 *British Magazine*, xi (1837), 168.

year.¹³ (In 1764 Leeds had 5,000 families, and catechising was confined to Lent.¹⁴) Dr Joseph Baylee of Holy Trinity, Birkenhead, explained to the House of Lords Select Committee that the Liverpool Working Man's Church Association had been formed to provide clergy in populous districts to undertake the pastoral work that an incumbent had no time to do because he was so busy with baptisms and churchings.¹⁵ By contrast Armstrong in East Dereham had 148 baptisms a year—though even that is slightly more than two a week.

By the 1850s baptisms on the scale of Leeds and Birkenhead reflected a greater concern on the part of the clergy, though the problems of keeping the services orderly still remained. In 1858 the rector of St. Clement Danes, with a parish population of 17,000, was baptizing between 300 and 400 a year, whilst the minister of St. Matthew's, Bethnal Green, with a population of 10,000, baptized between thirty and forty per week. However, St. Matthew's was known as a church which was popular for baptisms, and not all those brought came from the parish. It seems that the first incumbent of the church used to take the poor out into the country on excursions, and they became attached to the church in that way. In Stepney baptisms took place on Sundays, Wednesdays and Fridays, whilst in St Pancras the busy days were the two in the week when no fee was charged for registration.¹⁶ It was partly the fear of a rise in fees after the new Registration Act that led to the baptism of 360 children aged from infancy to six or seven in a single afternoon at Manchester Collegiate Church on the last Sunday in February 1837.¹⁷ Charles Stovel cited a letter to *The Times* which said that the average number of baptisms per year in Bethnal Green was 257 fewer in 1838-40 than in 1835-7 despite the growth in population. He added that the clergy were worried about the potential loss of fees as a result of civil registration, and this was the real reason why they were emphasising baptismal regeneration!¹⁸

One great inhibition working-class parents apparently felt in bringing their children to baptism was the problem of sponsors. The scale of this problem seems to have been a new development since the previous century, although William Holland, Vicar of Over Stowey in Somerset, noted an occasion when there were not two godmothers for a female child and they had to wait for someone else to arrive. He once rejected a

---

13 W.R.W. Stephens, *Life and Letters of Walter Farquhar Hook* (7 ed, London 1885), 222, 329.

14 Annesley and Hopkins, *Archbishop Drummond's Visitation Returns*, ii, 112.

15 House of Lords Select Committee (1858), 386, q 5049.

16 House of Lords Select Committee (1858), 115 q 1470; 40-41 qq 543-9; 72 qq 1006-9; 202 q 2750.

17 *British Magazine*, xi (1837), 475.

18 Stovel, *Baptismal Regeneration Controversy*, 224-5; the date of the letter was not given.

former servant of his as a godmother because she had not been baptized, even though on another occasion he had had to accept a dissenter as a godfather, much to his chagrin.[19] One cannot help wondering whether it was easier to turn away a godmother than a godfather! There was keen debate on this matter in the Church of England in the 1850s and 1860s. The Prayer Book rubrics required that there should be three godparents for each child, and Canon 29 required them to be communicants. Many clergy felt that this requirement was a major disincentive. The Revd T.T. Bazely of All Saints, Poplar, said that although he had 500 baptisms a year this was only about half the average. The reason for this was the difficulty of obtaining sponsors, and he got round it by transgressing the canon and allowing parents to be godparents.[20] At the same time Charles Lowder at St. Peter's, London Docks, was calling on the Sisters of Mercy who worked at the Mission to act as godparents: later he asked members of communicant guilds to do the same.[21] Some alleged that this requirement encouraged parents to take their children to nonconformist chapels for baptism, as the Bishop of Lincoln did when proposing a revision of Canon 29 in the Convocation of Canterbury in February 1860. Although the proposal was eventually accepted, the royal assent was never given.[22] Not all clergy were convinced of the genuineness of this argument: the vicar of Sapcote, Leicestershire, said in his Visitation Return for 1882:

> Some of the people say they take their children to be christened at the Chapel because there they do not require Godfathers and Godmothers but I think this an excuse—I do not hear it so often now they bring their children to Church.[23]

Lincolnshire, of course, was a more strongly Methodist county than Leicestershire, and Bishop Jackson's view was doubtless based on comments made by his clergy. In the neighbouring diocese of Ely, the vicar of Great Stukeley, Huntingdonshire, said in 1873 that 'among the poor the profession of sponsorial obligations at baptism is greatly looked on as a *sham*'.[24] Another reason given was that parents could not afford

---

19 J. Ayres (ed), *Paupers and Pig Killers: The Diary of William Holland, a Somerset Parson, 1799-1818* (Harmondsworth 1986), 63 (3 January 1802); 185-6 (19 November 1809); 229 (19 January 1812).
20 House of Lords Select Committee (1858), 183 qq 2442-7.
21 L. Ellsworth, 'Charles Lowder and the Ritualist Movement', unpublished Cambridge Ph.D. thesis 1974, 115.
22 P.J. Jagger, *Clouded Witness* (Allison Park, PA, 1982), 83-4.
23 Peterborough Episcopal Visitation Returns, 1882, Sapcote.
24 F. Knight, *The Nineteenth-Century Church and English Society* (Cambridge 1995), 89.

to treat the godparents after the ceremony.²⁵ It is not clear why this should have become a greater problem since the previous century. Nevertheless, despite the difficulties, the indications are that the proportion of baptisms in the Church of England was rising in the later nineteenth century.

What then did baptism mean to the increasing number of parents who brought their children to the font? The popular view was that baptism gave a child a name and entitlement to Christian burial.²⁶ Each of these beliefs concerned the identity of the child: the name provided an identity within the community; Christian burial guaranteed an eternal identity. Both were thus religious beliefs in the most elementary sense.

The significance of giving a name was apparent in the discussions surrounding the bill for the civil registration of births, marriages and deaths in 1836. This bill was intended to provide a measure of relief to dissenters, since the legal validity of any registration of births, marriages and deaths which was not in a parochial register was a matter of uncertainty in the eighteenth century, despite various attempts to establish it.²⁷ On the Committee stage of the bill in the House of Commons, Henry Goulburn, MP for Cambridge University, complained that the tendency of the bill 'would be to dissociate the naming of the child from the baptism' and would therefore lead to neglect. He believed that

> There were many among her professing Members, who, from ignorance, did not fully appreciate the benefits which the rite of baptism conferred upon their children, and who were now only led by the temporal consideration of the necessity of giving those children names.²⁸

Sir Robert Peel supported this view on the third reading, saying that the separation of naming from baptism would be bad for the lower classes and that it was the duty of the House to indicate the necessity of the religious sense of baptism where it did not exist: and in the House of Lords the Archbishop of Canterbury also objected to the separation of naming and baptism.²⁹ These protests were mild compared with Thomas Mozley. He had written to Newman in 1834, when civil registration was first mooted:

---

25 J. Obelkevich, *Religion and Rural Society: South Lindsey 1825-1875* (Oxford 1976), 128.

26 Ibid, 272.

27 B.L. Manning, *The Protestant Dissenting Deputies* (ed O. Greenwood, Cambridge 1952), 254-71.

28 *Parliamentary Debates*, xxxiv 133.

29 *Parliamentary Debates*, xxxiv 1017; xxxv 83.

> This new act of *compelling* parents to *name* their children as a civil process as soon as they are born, and compelling them to adhere to that name in baptism seems to me as bad as anything yet meditated against the Church.[30]

The protests were to no avail, and the Registration Act came into force in 1837. Some clergy, such as George Wilkins, Archdeacon of Nottingham and Vicar of St. Mary's Nottingham, devised a shorter 'naming' ceremony. 'This involved the babies being brought to the vestry by their parents or nurses, and then "named" by the sprinkling of water, the use of the baptismal formula and the inclusion of one or two prayers.'[31] There were no sponsors, but the child was registered, a certificate was issued and paid for. Wilkins defended this practice in a letter to the Bishop of Lincoln as a way of offsetting the effects of the Registration Act.

For many years Anglican clergymen continued to blame the Act for reducing the number of parents bringing their children for baptism. The religious press was filled with letters advising clergy of ways in which they could point out that the Act had not done away with the need for baptism. In 1851 a correspondent claimed in the *Guardian* that in nine cases out of ten the Act did discourage parents.[32] William Cotton, who had been involved in the work of the Incorporated Church Building Society since its inception in 1818, attributed the neglect of baptism in Bethnal Green to this fact in 1858:

> I am sorry to say that many now consider going before the registrar sufficient. In one district parish in one year, 800 men, women and children were baptized; and lately, when an opportunity was given to the poor to be baptized, in Mr Rowsell's parish, which adjoins Bethnal Green, I think there were upwards of 300 baptisms.[33]

However, as has been noted already, there may have been other factors determining the popularity of particular churches in the East End. Unfortunately, since the registration of births was compulsory, it is not so easy to identify a preference between religious and non-religious ceremonies, and also between different types of religious ceremony, for baptisms in the way that Olive Anderson did in her study of the effect of the Registration Act on civil marriage.[34] Dr Anderson concluded that the variations she found in the incidence of civil marriage reflected widely

---

30 Ker and Gornall, *Letters and Diaries*, iv, 291.
31 Knight, *The Nineteenth-Century Church and English Society*, 87.
32 Jagger, *Clouded Witness*, 62-4.
33 House of Lords Select Committee (1858), 10 q 87.
34 O. Anderson, 'The Incidence of Civil Marriage in Victorian England and Wales', *Past and Present* 69 (1975), 50-87; cf R. Floud and P. Thane, 'The Incidence of Civil Marriage in Victorian England and Wales', and O. Anderson, 'Rejoinder', *Past and Present* 84 (1979), 146-62.

dissimilar social cultures and were not 'the expression of individual conscientious scruples or of spreading de-Christianization'[35] — a conclusion which would be of considerable importance if it could be extended into the area of baptism.

The significance of baptism as a naming ceremony is also illustrated by the fact that 'naming' became a vernacular term for baptism, and James Obelkevich found a clergyman using the term in correspondence.[36] Until recently also there has often been a sense that the name of a child is not finally determined until baptism, however clearly the parents say that they have made up their minds, though in North Yorkshire and in East Anglia it was considered unlucky to reveal a name before baptism, and also to change it once decided.[37] On the other hand, this must be seen in the context of the interval between birth and baptism. In the early Church and in the early middle ages baptisms were confined to the seasons of Easter and Pentecost, unless there was danger of death. But from the eleventh century ecclesiastical opinion increasingly came to favour baptism within a week of birth, and from the thirteenth century this view was embodied in conciliar and episcopal decisions. Naming at the church door was all that remained of the old catechising process.[38] In 1552 this was abandoned and the whole service took place at the font; and in 1662 the words 'Name this child' were introduced as the first injunction to the parents. Although early baptism may have become the norm, it certainly did not become the rule. In the House of Commons debate on the Registration Bill, Dr Lushington said that it was notorious that baptism did not take place within a month, or six months, or even twelve months of birth.[39] In such circumstances naming could not have been tied to baptism, even though baptism might be understood as naming.

The second staple of popular belief was that baptism was essential for a Christian burial. This was legally true in that the Prayer Book Funeral Service could not be used for any who died unbaptized, excommunicate, by their own hand, or in the act of committing violent crime. Since this had been the rule of the Church for so long, it is difficult to judge how

---

35 Anderson, *Past and Present* 69 (1975), 87.

36 Obelkevich, *Religion and Rural Society*, 128 n 3.

37 R. Blakeborough, *Wit, Character, Folklore and Customs of the North Riding of Yorkshire* (reprinted Wakefield 1973), 113-14; E. Porter, *The Folklore of East Anglia* (London 1974), 22.

38 J.D.C. Fisher, *Christian Initiation: Baptism in the Medieval West* (London 1965), 109-19, 149-57.

39 *Parliamentary Debates*, xxxiv 140. At Horsley, Gloucestershire, between 1786 and 1812 the interval 'between births and baptisms ranged from 2.5 to 41 weeks and the median interval was 18.5 weeks': A.M. Urdank, *Religion and Society in a Cotswold Vale: Nailsworth, Gloucestershire 1760-1865* (Berkeley 1990), 139.

far popular belief reflected the legal situation and how far it reflected even more ancient beliefs about the relationship between the rituals surrounding birth and death. Chapter 1 has already illustrated the extent to which this was a live issue from the Reformation onwards. Francis Kilvert reported the vicar of Fordington's conversation with some villagers about the meaning of baptism in which some said that 'we must go to Church at last so we may as well go there at first':

> The rest said they understood that if a child died without a name he did flit about in the woods and waste places and could get no rest.[40]

The belief that such a child would flit about and get no rest may be a relic of the Roman Catholic belief that unbaptized children went to limbo, but equally it could be related to the belief in the southern counties of Scotland that unbaptized children were at the mercy of fairies.[41] It should also be noted that the villagers referred to a child dying 'without a name'. In Lincolnshire it was believed that the souls of the unbaptized wandered endlessly in the form of wild geese.[42] Clearly this talk of restless and wandering spirits is not far from beliefs about the origins of ghosts and haunting; and there may be a link here with the fact that pre-Reformation baptismal orders included exorcism.[43]

Professor Williams, when investigating the Cumberland village of Gosforth in the early 1950s, said that,

> It was very difficult to obtain statements of reasons why people had their children baptized. Most people could give no reason at all. Some said it was because they 'believed in the Church of England'; others because they 'believed in God'; and a few because they 'wanted their children to go to Heaven'. Everyone, however, agreed that to bury a child without baptism was a terrible and shocking thing, to be avoided at all costs, and in commenting on this many people who had found it impossible to say why they had their own children baptized were stimulated into expressing opinions. A village craftsman, for example, said, 'If tha' didn't get kiddy baptized by t'parson, it would have to be put in a box and stuck in t'ground like some sort o'animal.' Other characteristic remarks in this context were 'It wouldn't be right, like a proper babby', 't'would be just like burying a dog or a sheep', and 'Tha's got to get a babby baptized, because if it died, it would be too late then'. It was said that at least once in recent years an unbaptized child was

---

40 *Kilvert's Diary*, ii 442-3: cf S.O. Addy, *Folk Tales and Superstitions* (ed J.D.A. Widdowson, Wakefield 1973), 120: 'A child which dies before it is christened will not go to heaven.'

41 W. Henderson, *Notes on the Folk Lore of the Northern Counties of England and the Borders* (reprinted Wakefield 1973), 6.

42 Obelkevich, *Religion and Rural Society*, 272.

43 E.g. the Sarum Rite, E.C. Whitaker, *Documents*, 233: cf K. Thomas, *Religion and the Decline of Magic* (Harmondsworth 1973), 40-1.

buried by its father in a box somewhere on the fells, but in the vast majority of cases children who have died before baptism have been buried without any ceremony in the graveyard of the church, as close to the wall as possible.[44]

That extended but vivid quotation was cited by most sociologists who wrote on this subject before 1980, probably because, until David Clark's book on Staithes in North Yorkshire was published in 1982, it was virtually all that could be found in print. But the beliefs of Gosforth could hardly be normative for Britain! Nevertheless, there is some continuity with the kind of beliefs recorded by Kilvert except that the worry over restless spirits flitting about has become a more down-to-earth worry that without baptism there was little distinction between a baby and an animal. However, it is rather odd that Professor Williams should have commented in his footnote that 'the north is, of course, traditionally associated with Hell and the lairs of fiends and giants', since that was precisely the kind of thing *not* mentioned by the villagers of Gosforth.[45]

Once more the fear of infant mortality stands out, and it is striking that after his first failure to get the terms of the Registration Bill amended in 1836, Henry Goulburn should have turned to this point as a second argument about the dangers of relaxing the requirement for baptism:

> Let the House remember, that upon the due performance of the rite of baptism depended the performance of some of the most solemn ceremonies of the Church,—the rite of confirmation—the visitation of the sick—and, still more, the burial of the dead. And let them reflect for a moment upon the responsibility they would incur, by giving parliamentary sanction to the omission of the rite of baptism, if, without having been baptised, a child afterwards brought to the burial ground for interment according to the ceremonies of the Church of England, and the incumbent acting conscientiously, according to the directions of his Church, and the requirement of the law, should upon ascertaining that circumstance be compelled to harrow up all the feelings of the weeping relatives and assembled friends by declining to read the burial service, so instructive to the hearers—so consoling to the relatives.[46]

A more practical reason than the law of the Church was the fact that most burial clubs made it a rule not to pay the burial money for those who had not been baptized, and thus, wrote J.H. Blunt in his *Directorium Pastorale*, 'the rule of the Church as to the absence of religious ceremony in the burial of the unbaptized has come to be more generally known'.[47] Because of the importance attached to a decent funeral, and especially the

---

44 W.M. Williams, *Gosforth: The Sociology of an English Village* (London 1956), 59-60.
45 Ibid, 228.
46 *Parliamentary Debates*, xxxiv 1013-14.
47 J.H. Blunt, *Directorium Pastorale* (new ed, London 1875), 163.

desire to avoid a pauper funeral, burial clubs were one of the commonest forms of insurance among the poor. Michael Anderson estimated that in Lancashire in the 1870s half the population were insured in burial or friendly societies, which was possibly the highest proportion in England.[48]

Some of the 'conscientious incumbents' that Goulburn described turned out to be increasingly unwilling to read the burial service over dissenters, which was a particular problem in those places where the parish churchyard was the only available place of burial. Three legal cases were necessary to determine the law; Kemp v Wickes in 1809, Martin v Escott in 1841, and Tichmarsh v Chapman in 1844. In each case an Anglican clergyman declined to bury a child baptized by a nonconformist minister, and in each case it was ruled in the Court of Arches that this was unlawful. As Sir Herbert Jenner Fust said in Tichmarsh v Chapman, 'Both lay and heretical baptism are irregular and contrary to the order of the Church; but both are valid for the purpose of burial'.[49] Nevertheless, the bitterness of feelings raised by these, and countless other examples, cannot be exaggerated; and they show the ignorance and mean-mindedness of some Anglican clergy at their worst. While the last case was proceeding, the clergyman concerned, William Chapman, Vicar of Bassingbourn in Cambridgeshire, also refused to bury a second child, Esther Fisher, whose body lay in the chimney of her aunt's house for two years before a *mandamus* was secured, compelling the burial to take place. The bishops generally advised the clergy that nonconformist baptisms were valid, but they were not able to control or discipline those who took a different view. It seems likely that the increase in such cases from the end of the eighteenth century not only reflects the growth of dissent, but also an increasing fear on the part of keen defenders of the Establishment that this growth was a threat to political stability comparable to the French Revolution.[50]

Wesleyan Methodists were particularly sensitive about the question of the legality of their baptisms, and clearly practice varied considerably from one part of the country to another. In January 1828 the Revd Joshua Marsden, a Wesleyan minister in Worcester, wrote to Jabez Bunting asking for advice on the legality or illegality of Wesleyan baptisms, whether such baptism was a legal disqualification to any office under Government, and whether a Methodist register was inadmissible in court. (This was before the repeal of the Test and Corporation Acts, which took place later in the year, and after the Protestant Dissenting Deputies had

---

48 M. Anderson, *Family Structure in Nineteenth Century Lancashire* (Cambridge 1971), 138.
49 Jagger, *Clouded Witness*, 68.
50 Manning, *The Protestant Dissenting Deputies*, 286-302; Jagger, *Clouded Witness*, 67-71.

already begun to consider asking for the introduction of civil registration of births.) Marsden wrote that 'the illegality of our baptisms prevails here to such an extent that though I have now been nearly six months on the Circuit, I have never been applied too (*sic*) to baptise a single child'.[51] Bunting replied that the current legal position was complex and referred him to the pamphlet sold by the Wesleyan Book Room on the Kemp v Wickes Judgment. But he concluded by saying that until a change in the law had been secured it was probably better to say as little as possible to the people. His reason indicated a clear awareness of the different motives that people had for bringing their children to be baptized:

> Those who consider Infant Baptism chiefly as a *secular* thing, and look mainly at the worldly considerations connected with it, may as well take their children to Church as Chapel, for any [good] that an Ordinance engaged in with such motives can do. And as to those who look at the *religious* advantages of that holy sacrament, *they* will usually be little mindful of the mere appendage of a more or less valid register, and consult their own consciences, rather than their children's secular interests, in making their choice of the administrator.[52]

It could be argued that this remark came from someone in a tradition which was already encountering problems with baptismal regeneration and therefore drifting in a secular direction as to the significance of the sacrament. On the whole, however, it is more plausible to argue the opposite point, namely that baptism was a significant religious event but that this was more likely to be appreciated by committed Christians.

J.H. Blunt included in his Directory samples of baptismal certificates which might be provided by nonconformists so that Anglican clergy might recognise them,[53] but controversy about nonconformist burials persisted until the Burials Act of 1881 confirmed the right of all parishioners to be buried in the parish churchyard according to the rite of their choice. In January 1882 the vicar of South Kilworth in Leicestershire reported that he had buried a seven-month old girl, whose parents were dissenters but whose grandparents were church people and communicants. The child had died unbaptized.

> Her baptism had been postponed owing to the mother's state of health and other causes. The grandparents and relatives here have been much distressed and very thankfully accepted my proposal that there should be a religious service at the graveside.[54]

---

51 W.R. Ward (ed), *The Early Correspondence of Jabez Bunting, 1820-29* (London 1972), 170.
52 Ibid, 171 (italics original).
53 Blunt, *Directorium*, 166-9.
54 Peterborough Visitation Returns 1882, South Kilworth.

Significantly, however, the vicar regarded that as a burial under the Burials Act. Not all clergy were prepared to take such a soft line, even after the Burials Act, but the effects of that attitude were mainly confined to the countryside. In the towns the development of municipal cemeteries with a clear division between consecrated and unconsecrated ground meant that the burials problem became less oppressive.

The one group of nonconformists, apart from the Quakers, who were not helped by the Anglican treatment of their baptism as 'lay baptism' were the Baptists. It has already been noted in chapter 1 that sometimes the children of Baptists were baptized. William Holland at Over Stowey had an interesting exchange with one of his Baptist parishioners, Mr Hurley, in January 1801. His child had been very ill:

> I told them that I would privately Baptise the child on condition that they would bring him to Church afterwards. We had a great deal of argument about it but I left them to their own feelings. At last they consented and they intimated that they would bring their other children to Church. I said I thought that was safer and without making any observations on the state they may be in if they died unbaptised yet certainly Baptism could be no injury to them, whereas the neglecting of it might be of infinite consequences. They seemed to be struck with this line of reasoning.[55]

Matters were not always so simple for the conscientious Anglican clergyman, as is illustrated not by a burial case but by a marriage case, perhaps the best known of the century. On 1 July 1834 Newman declined to marry Miss Jubber, the daughter of one of his Baptist parishioners. The memorandum Newman wrote of his conversation with her father reveals why the case became a *cause celèbre*:

> Is it one of your daughters who is going to be married?
> Yes.
> Had she been baptized?
> No.
> Indeed! (in a lower tone of voice) really, I cannot marry her.
> Well, that *is* superstition—that is superstition indeed.
> Why, how can I, (give Christian marriage,) to one who is still an outcast?
> That *is* superstition.
> Mr. Jubber, I did not come here that you might teach me, but to tell you my feelings of duty.[56]

The case was more complicated than might appear from that exchange, since Newman had previously had some inconclusive discussion with the family about the daughter's baptism, and felt that a fast one was being

---

55 Ayres, *Paupers and Pig Killers*, 58 (31 January 1801).
56 Ker and Gornall, *Letters and Diaries*, iv, 288-9 (italics original).

pulled when he was summoned to marry her at one and a half hours notice. Moreover, as this happened before 1837 the opportunity for civil marriage in such circumstances did not exist. The couple found another clergyman to marry them.[57] As Newman perceived, part of the problem was that the effect of the law in such cases was to encourage the belief that baptism was simply a form. But from another point of view, the case may be taken as a foreshadowing of the problems which were to arise when the Church began to require a commitment to the implications of the sacraments that were alien or mysterious to the mass of the population.

As well as these two main motives for baptism, naming and burial, there were a number of other beliefs which seem to be related either to folklore, or surviving pre-Reformation beliefs. There is much more evidence for belief in ghosts, witchcraft or possession by the devil than for beliefs about baptism. Colin Haydon has noted the problems of assessing such beliefs, particularly because so many were collected by folk-lorists in the nineteenth century, and concluded that they performed 'highly useful functions in a poorly educated rural society' and it is therefore plausible to suppose that they were widely believed.[58] Michael Snape takes a rather more critical view than Haydon, suggesting that the clergy in Lancashire were more concerned about these beliefs.[59] The simplest of the beliefs associated with baptism was that it was lucky, and the equally common belief that it was lucky for a child to cry—which seems suspiciously like making the best of a bad job. The latter belief is complicated by the fact that in parts of Yorkshire it was believed that it was unlucky for children to cry, which may be linked to the belief that a child's screams showed it was resisting Satan. That is certainly different from the case of a private baptism recorded by Armstrong where the explanation for the crying was that a rat was chewing the child's arm.[60] Also very common was the belief that baptism would help a child to thrive[61] — a concern found in the Sarum Rite which prescribes the reading of Mark 9:17-29 (the story of the epileptic child) as the Gospel 'because according to doctors it is a good protection against falling sickness'.[62] J.H. Blunt remarked that it was not very uncommon 'to find old women (nurses and midwives)

---

57 Ibid, 288-9, 292, 295, 297-301, 305-7, 310, 312-3, 322, 326-7, 328.

58 C. Haydon, 'The Church in the Kineton Deanery of the diocese of Worcester, c.1660-c.1800', in Gregory and Chamberlain, *National Church in Local Perspective*, 170-2; the quotation is from p. 172.

59 M.F. Snape, *The Church of England in Industrialising Society: The Lancashire Parish of Whalley in the Eighteenth Century* (Woodbridge 2003), 42-6.

60 Addy, *Folk Tales*, 120; H.B.J. Armstrong, *A Norfolk Diary* (London 1949), 245; Henderson, *Notes on Folk Lore*, 8; Porter, *Folklore*, 23.

61 R. Hoggart, *The Uses of Literacy* (Harmondsworth 1958), 29-30; Williams, *Gosforth*, 60; Thomas, *Decline of Magic*, 41.

62 Whitaker, *Documents*, 248.

confuse Baptism and vaccination', although such a confusion must have been of relatively recent origin given when vaccination began. He added that 'it is very rarely that uneducated people understand Baptism and Christening to be synonymous': in County Durham a distinction was made between baptism which anyone could do, and christening when the priest made the sign of the cross on the baby's forehead and godparents took obligations upon them. This, of course, reflects the Prayer Book requirement that any child privately baptized should be brought to the Church subsequently (discussed in chapter 1), and it may explain Atkinson's story at the beginning of the chapter.[63] The influence of nurses and midwives over baptismal practice could still be significant in certain cases, though it is not likely nowadays to be confused with vaccination. But it may be that the later twentieth-century policy against home confinements has done more than anything else to reduce the influence of this particular pressure towards speedy baptism.

Another curious incident was recorded by Kilvert. On 6 April 1870 he wrote,

> Mary Smith thought it would not be right to bring her baby to be baptized on Easter Day, because it was the highest Sunday in the year, seeming to consider that the day would be desecrated, profaned or at all events dishonoured by the baptism of her child. What a curious idea.[64]

This is certainly a turnabout from the time when Easter and Pentecost were the only baptismal seasons. Presumably the reason was some kind of confusion between baptism and churching, and the sense that it would be wrong for the unclean mother to take part in an Easter Day service. This is the opposite experience from William Holland, who preached at Asholt on the Fast Day on Wednesday 11 March 1800 commanded because of the War. He found that he had a child to christen and a woman to church and wrote, 'I thought a Fast day not very proper for a Christening and observed as much, it being to them I supposed a Feast Day.'[65]

Nevertheless, we should hesitate before assuming that there was no popular sense of the beliefs which lay behind certain actions related to baptism. Albert Pell, sometime MP for South Leicestershire, spent a period farming in the Fens near Wilburton in Cambridgeshire, which had a strong Baptist congregation, before moving to the Midlands. In his *Reminiscences* he referred to the time of year when people were baptized in the river, and continued

---

63 Blunt, *Directorium*, 165; W. Brockie, *Legends and Superstitions of the County of Durham*, ed R. Wood (Wakefield 1974), 180-1.
64 *Kilvert's Diary*, i, 82.
65 Ayres, *Paupers and Pig Killers*, 29 (12 March 1800).

That was an important event of which due notice was given. On one occasion the engineer of a large fen pumping-engine lower down stream was observed to be carrying a supply of water indoors. On being asked the meaning of this very singular operation, he said with a serious face, 'There's to be a "dipping" tomorrow, and my missis don't intend to drink all their sins as may drift down here.'[66]

One might cavil as to whether all Baptists believed that baptism was for the remission of sins, but there was certainly a literal understanding of the rite there.

Atkinson's story also indicated that private baptism was still common in the early nineteenth century. Chapter 1 has shown that this goes back at least as far as the Civil War. Dr Obelkevich interpreted this shift in terms of class consciousness:

> Farmers, gentry, and clergy, for whom membership in the local community was secondary to their class and family loyalties, preferred private baptism, withdrawn from the village congregation; baptism in these classes was more likely to be, as Bishop Jackson complained, 'a family festival with very few religious associations indeed'.[67]

However, the work done on the earlier period since his book was published means that, even if this were true, it was not a nineteenth-century novelty. The eighteenth-century evidence certainly showed the importance of the family festival element—and it would actually be a very odd doctrine of baptism that did not imply some element of festival. It is true that for the lower classes private baptism did not require sponsors, and it had always been difficult for clergy to resist a claim that there was danger of imminent death.[68] This probably explains the significance of the point made in the argument over baptismal regeneration that an affirmation of faith by sponsors was not required in the service for private baptism. Nevertheless, there remained local, and probably regional, variations. Mark Smith found that public baptism was the rule in Oldham and Saddleworth, and any private baptisms were almost invariably followed by public reception of the child in church.[69] There is not so much evidence for the extent of private baptism in nonconformity, but a Report of the Committee on Public Worship to the Synod of the Presbyterian Church of England in 1887 indicated that in 63% of the congregations where a figure was returned 'fully half of the

---

66 T. Mackay (ed), *The Reminiscences of Albert Pell* (London 1908), 121.
67 Obelkevich, *Religion and Rural Society*, 129, quoting J. Jackson, *A Charge delivered to the clergy of the diocese of Lincoln at his primary visitation, 1855* (London 1855), 24.
68 Blunt, *Directorium*, 162-3.
69 Smith, *Religion in Industrial Society*, 51.

baptisms were in private houses' — though the Committee added that, particularly in country areas, it formed part of what was 'to all intents and purposes a public Service'.[70]

The bishops tried hard in the middle of the nineteenth century to make public baptism once more the rule. The kind of problem they faced may be illustrated by the following letter in the *British Magazine* where a correspondent in June 1837 complained of the practice of

> allowing the nurse, or any other person, to bring the child to the church to be *named*, without any appearance or thought of sponsors, and without anything more than one or two collects used in the vestry-room; after which the infant is *named* and *registered*, and the whole business is finished and done.

After considering and dismissing various objections, including the length of time taken by public baptisms in a large parish, the writer concluded,

> Really, Mr Editor, is it so much more difficult to baptize twenty or thirty children on the Sunday afternoon, after the second lesson, than to sit to hear a long voluntary from a conceited organist, or two or three unauthorized psalms, hymns or anthems, thrown into the service at the discretion of the clerk, or chief singer?[71]

Evidence from dioceses suggests that by the 1880s they had achieved considerable success.[72] In some ways, however, this success was more apparent than real. Baptism was certainly brought back into the church, and it was usually celebrated on Sundays rather than weekdays: but the usual time came to be not after the second lesson at Morning or Evening Prayer, as the Prayer Book rubric required, but at a special Sunday afternoon service, perhaps linked with catechising or Sunday School. In such circumstances usually only the family of the child to be baptized was present. The transformation of this custom into the public baptisms of the twentieth century was the result of the more recent baptismal reform movement, and was assisted by a decline in the sheer volume of baptisms conducted.

Dr. Obelkevich suggested that as the outlook of the labourers shifted from community to class, they too demanded private celebrations. The eighteenth-century evidence shows this was not new. However, it might also have been as much a result of a new emphasis on family as on class. Studies made of several Welsh rural communities would support this view.

---

70 S.W. Carruthers, *Fifty Years 1876-1926: A brief survey of work and progress since the union* (London 1926), 19; Report of the Committee on Public Worship, *Minutes of the Synod of the Presbyterian Church of England, together with reports and other papers* iv, 1886-88 (London 1888), 508. This figure was based on returns from 122 out of 195 congregations.

71 *British Magazine*, xi (1837), 637, 639 (italics original).

72 Jagger, *Clouded Witness*, 88-90; Obelkevich, *Religion and Rural Society*, 129-30.

Welsh parishes were often scattered, and Welsh nonconformity often established its first chapels in outlying hamlets. Professor Rees in his study of Llanfihangel yng Ngwynfa, Montgomeryshire, pointed out that no nonconformist chapel had ever been built in the hamlet where the parish church lay, whilst seven other hamlets had one chapel each. He argued that nonconformity destroyed the religious unity of the parish:

> By dividing the community into a number of religious sects, and by re-emphasising family devotions, it dispersed religious observance through the countryside, thus bringing it into harmony with other aspects of social life.[73]

Within each hamlet, however, family tradition and loyalty to the local chapel sustained religious observance, though characteristically christening, marriage and burial retained only the barest elements of ritual.[74] In effect, therefore, the parish as such was not a social community, and this may well have been true in similar dispersed parishes in the hilly areas of England, and elsewhere. The parish cannot be assumed to be a social unity, in view of its very varied history in different regions.

These findings have been supported by other studies in rural Wales. In Tregaron, Cardiganshire, the link between home and family was embodied in the practice of home baptisms. In 1945 69% of baptisms from Bwlch-Gwynt Calvinistic Methodist Chapel were at home: the percentage had been 70% in 1816-22; and dropped to its lowest point, 33%, in the years 1860-66 just after the 1859 revival. Emrys Jones commented as follows:

> In the past illegitimacy has accounted for some of this, and to-day the illness of the mother, or of a member of the family who wishes to see the christening, accounts for some cases, but many parents are merely repeating custom. 'All the others were baptized at home, and I want this one to be baptized in the same way.' The hearth is the starting point.[75]

Nevertheless, Snape noted that illegitimate children were baptized in the parish church of Whalley between 1765 and 1784 without being drawn to the attention of the church courts, and we have already seen in chapter 1 that there was no sense in which clergy refused to baptize illegitimate children.[76] Indeed, they sometimes had no notice. William Holland described being confronted with a wedding of which he had not been warned by the parish clerk: 'It seems that the persons were but lately come to live into the Parish and they had lived together before and they

---

73 A.D. Rees, *Life in a Welsh Countryside* (Cardiff 1950), 104.
74 Ibid, 114-5, 125.
75 E. Davies and A.D. Rees (eds), *Welsh Rural Communities* (Cardiff 1960), 93.
76 Snape, *The Church of England in Industrialising Society*, 126.

brought a bouncing child to be Christened the very day of their Wedding.'[77]

The link between family and religious allegiance was also noted in Aberdaron and Glan-Llyn, with marriage being the only point at which religious allegiance might change.[78] In Glan-Llyn, where virtually every inhabitant was associated with one of the chapels, Trefor Owen noted that ironically the religious function of the family had changed:

> It no longer served as the basic unit of common worship underlying the wider community of the chapel congregation but became instead the controlling factor in deciding religious affiliation by accident of birth or marriage instead of by any act of volition performed by an individual on the dictates of his conscience.[79]

Intriguingly in the 1950s, baptism in Glan-Llyn was increasingly taking place in the chapels and not in the homes.[80] Whether this was a post-war phenomenon, or whether it is to be seen as a contrast to Tregaron is not clear. It is sufficient to make the point that the significance of baptism has to be set in the context of the relationship between the family and the religious and/or wider community.

However, it should not be assumed that the primary relationship is between the church or chapel and the particular community. Denominational allegiance could be important. Mark Smith noted that both Wesleyan Methodists and Congregationalists in Saddleworth drew on a scatter of surrounding settlements as well as the villages in which their chapels were situated. He found that significant minorities of both Wesleyans and Congregationalists lived nearer to a chapel of the other denomination than the one they attended—they certainly did not attend their nearest nonconformist chapel.[81]

The importance of family tradition in this matter is not dependent on Welsh evidence alone. Margaret Stacey in her study of Banbury and Peter Willmott and Michael Young in their study of Bethnal Green both stressed this point. In Bethnal Green in the 1950s Young and Willmott found that the various rites of passage were all family gatherings, but not always for the same families. At christenings, husbands and wives invited only parents and siblings. The pressure for churching, though not exactly parallel, was discovered to descend from mother to daughter.[82] David

---

77 Ayres, *Paupers and Pig Killers*, 49 (19 October 1800). The note to this entry says that wedding is recorded in the parish register but not the baptism.
78 Davies and Rees, *Welsh Rural Communities*, 166, 195.
79 Ibid, 200-1.
80 Ibid, 224.
81 Smith, *Religion in Industrial Society*, 195.
82 M. Young and P. Willmott, *Family and Kinship in East London* (London 1957), 39-40, 64; M. Stacey, *Tradition and Change* (Oxford 1960), 73, 137.

Clark in his study of Staithes in Yorkshire provided a much fuller discussion of the changes which have taken place in these customs in the twentieth century, emphasizing that baptism was but one part of a set of beliefs and rituals related to the change in status for mother and child. Although the parish church was not in Staithes itself most people in the nineteenth century had their children baptized there, even if they were members of the Wesleyan chapel. Baptisms in the chapel were rare before the 1930s, being confined to 'the better sort of folk'. In other cases the minister visited the home about a week after the birth and conducted the baptism with the minimum of ritual. But baptism remained important, as did churching, even among Methodists: and after the Methodist Church officially dropped its churching service in 1975, Clark discovered the mother in one active Methodist family had actually been into the chapel the day after she got home from hospital. Her husband's father would not have her in the house until she had been in: 'just to go in and out, that's enough'. Some families in the village would not even have the new-born child inside their house until it had been baptized, which was a long-standing tradition.[83]

The Staithes evidence seems to suggest that although folk religion may be integrated into formal religion (as perhaps was the case in the Welsh evidence), that integration will not necessarily be sustained if the folk-religious elements are forced out, or not provided for. But that conclusion can only be provisional: it would be quite reasonable to suppose that the social system of a North Yorkshire fishing village is significantly different from that of a Welsh upland village; and it would be plausible to suggest, as Professor Rees did, that in Wales the new religious synthesis was prophetic rather than priestly, giving it a significantly different balance from Yorkshire.[84] Staithes was certainly not the only place, or type of place, where it was customary for nonconformists to be baptized at the parish church. The vicar of Lockington, Leicestershire, said in 1872 that all were baptized, married and buried at the parish church, even though there was a Methodist chapel there: whilst Benjamin Armstrong in 1862 noted a comment made by the dissenting father of twins whom he had privately baptized a few days before: 'I ollus say *begin and end* with the Church whatever you do between-whiles.'[85]

Jeffrey Cox in his study of Lambeth compared baptisms at four churches between 1890 and 1910 and concluded that 'working-class mothers resolutely insisted upon Anglican rites of passage':

---

83 D. Clark, *Between Pulpit and Pew* (Cambridge 1982), 118-24.
84 Rees, *Welsh Countryside*, 164.
85 Peterborough Visitation Returns 1872: Lockington; Armstrong, *Armstrong's Norfolk Diary*, 96 (italics original).

In the middle-class parish of Christ Church, Gipsy Hill, the one poverty-stricken street supplied 10 percent of the infants christened in 1895-96... Congregational and Wesleyan chapels attracted a few parents who wished to have their children baptized (the Baptists, of course, did not), but even so it was the Church of England which drew the unskilled and semi-skilled—labourers, carmen, porters and gardeners.[86]

His explanation of this was a concern for respectability. In Scotland, where the Kirk Session would usually rebuke the parents of an illegitimate child, there is conflicting evidence for the nineteenth century. In some places mothers, and indeed fathers, of illegitimate children were prepared to face the rebuke of the Kirk Session in order to have their children baptized. But in Galloway and Aberdeenshire it was reported that such parents would leave their children unbaptized rather than face the Session, and it was alleged that they would go to the Roman Catholic or Episcopal Churches, where such a rebuke was not forthcoming.[87]

Though illegitimacy might seem a good test of 'respectability' in asking for baptism, it would be dangerous to generalise. Joseph Ashby's mother insisted on having him baptized at the parish church of Tysoe, thereby breaking more than a century of Quaker tradition: yet this seems to have been the result of religious principle rather than a desire to rescue some status for a bastard.[88] But who can decide on motives with confidence? Francis Kilvert wrote of Mrs Smith at Hill Corner who wanted her baby baptized: her husband had been talking to the Baptist minister who advised against it 'but she is determined to have it christened on Whitsunday'.[89] Of course, Kilvert was pleased, but how would the story read if the husband had kept a diary? Perhaps one conclusion can be offered with some confidence: those who decided to break with the practice of infant baptism, whether by becoming Baptists at one end, or by neglecting baptism altogether at the other, either needed the support of their peer group to do so, or they had to have remarkably strong personal convictions. Elizabeth Ashby's family Quakerism was in decay. Baptists often found it difficult to mix easily with others, and in Wales believer's baptism was the one significant obstacle to a change of denominational allegiance at marriage.[90]

However, Dr Obelkevich's emphasis upon class and more recent sociological work upon the family both seek to explain belief in terms of social structure; they make it epiphenomenal rather than allowing it an

---

86 J. Cox, *The English Churches in a Secular Society* (New York 1982), 98-9.
87 K.M. Boyd, *Scottish Church Attitudes to Sex, Marriage and the Family, 1850-1914* (Edinburgh 1980), 58, 104, 113, 122, 156.
88 M. Ashby, *Joseph Ashby of Tysoe* (Cambridge 1961), 5-6.
89 *Kilvert's Diary*, iii, 323.
90 Davies and Rees, *Welsh Rural Communities*, 229.

integrity in its own terms. To put the point crudely, they are still essentially under the spell of Karl Marx's view of ideology. Here the work of Sarah Williams on Southwark has given us a thoroughly worked out alternative view, based essentially upon the accounts of religious belief from the participants themselves. The implications of this lead to a critical re-evaluation of the theory of secularization, which has tended to dominate modern studies of religion, particularly in Western Europe.[91] In relation to baptism the significance of Dr Williams's work lies in her demonstration of a symbolic system of meaning, particularly around the rites of passage, which helped to constitute an urban community; thus it is wrong to suppose that such beliefs were abandoned in the process of migration from countryside to town in the nineteenth century. Hence she emphasises that the interpretation of symbolic meaning should not be confused with the interpretation of social structures.[92] Her interviews, which significantly were mainly with women, provided some characteristically vivid testimonies to the significance of both baptism and churching. Mrs Cotton, the daughter of a compositor from Peckham, said that her mother ensured that her daughters were all churched, her children and grandchildren were baptized, and members of her family were married in church: 'When you had a child, oh before you went out to have that baby christened you had to go to church, oh yes and she wouldn't let you in her house if you hadn't been churched'.[93] She also recalled how she and her sister were prohibited from entering her mother's house until they had been to church, even though this meant walking for miles through the fog in November to find a church which would conduct the ceremonies of baptism and churching at the same time. They ended up at St. George's Church where there was a light on:

> I had her other little girl with me, up the steps we went. They used to have a kind of nurse there. I spoke to her, she said, 'Oh yes straight away, Come in where is she?' I stood for that babe as well 'cos in them days you had to get another witness and anyway...I could hear this little kid and I could hear the mother speaking so I said 'Excuse me' (you couldn't see a hand before y'.) 'What's the matter love?' the woman said, 'don't be offended by what I am going to ask but could you come in the church and stand by my sister? the baby's being christened and we've got to get someone else where we've been.' 'Oh yeah', but whoever that woman was I don't

---

91 S.C. Williams, *Religious Belief and Popular Culture in Southwark, c.1880-1939* (Oxford 1999), v.

92 Ibid, 13.

93 Ibid, 89. Much of the oral material used in chapter 4 of Dr Williams's book also appeared in her essay, 'Urban Popular Religion and the Rites of Passage', in H. McLeod (ed), *European Religion in the Age of Great Cities* (London 1995), 216-36. However, the reader should note that in the earlier essay the interviewees are referred to by their maiden names rather than their married names, as in her later book.

know... My mum once you'd had a baby if you hadn't been to be churched she wouldn't have y' in her house and we knew it...[94]

Another woman, Molly Layton who was born in Walworth and whose parents and grandparents knew everyone in the street, emphasised that baptism and church were acts of thanksgiving: 'You had to be christened and to thank God for getting you over your confinement in those days, you know'.[95] But as well as the associated beliefs that baptism was lucky, there was an understanding that baptism made a child a Christian. Furthermore, participation in the rituals of the Church was understood as 'an indication of genuine religious belief'. Thus Miriam Moore, who went to the Primitive Methodist Surrey Chapel in Blackfriars Road, answered the question about her mother's church attendance by saying that she did not attend regularly, but 'she believed and I mean when any of us children were born she'd go to the church before she went out anywhere to be blessed and she'd make sure we was all christened'.[96] Mrs Cotton was critical of the vicar who succeeded the Revd W.J.J. Cornelius at All Saints, Dulwich, precisely because he would not accept that having children baptized and being churched was sufficient proof of belief in God and commitment to the Church. Furthermore, the pearly christenings and weddings characteristic of costermongers in Southwark should not be interpreted as evidence that folk superstition and rituals were more important than orthodox Christianity. Dr Williams concludes:

> Apparently incompatible narratives of religious belief formed one rationale for action, in which many dimensions of belief were present. The eclectic character of popular attitudes tends to be overlooked when the actions of participants are interpreted with reference to factors external to the meaning and interpretations which the actors themselves brought to bear upon their practices.[97]

This analysis helps us to understand the blurring of denominational allegiances at a popular level, something which was particularly reflected in the importance attached to Sunday School attendance alongside relative indifference as to which Sunday School was attended. It may also illuminate the apparent oddity of Miriam Moore's comment earlier in relation to a Primitive Methodist chapel, where there was a single prayer for Maternal Thanksgiving after Child-birth to be said (after written notice) immediately before the closing prayer in public worship.[98] Dr Williams suggests that this 'undenominationalism' may explain the

---

94 Ibid, 90.
95 Ibid, 96.
96 Ibid, 101.
97 Ibid, 104.
98 *Order of Administration of Baptism and other services for the use of the Primitive Methodists* (London n.d.), 24.

relative lack of interest in confirmation. This was a rite that involved a much more explicit commitment to a particular church tradition or congregation than the majority of people felt necessary.[99] And although Dr Williams's study explicitly related to working-class people in Southwark, one might add that even the middle classes have tended to float much more easily from one denomination to another than most ministers and most church historians have been prepared to recognise.

Clearly there is a risk that the attitudes in Southwark might be taken as normative for a new generation in the same way in which those in Gosforth were treated from the 1950s. Obviously the detailed picture will vary from place to place. What is beyond doubt, however, is that the understanding of the relationship between theology and popular religion needs to change, both for theologians as well as social historians. Although her study ended in 1939, Dr Williams emphasises the adaptation and continuity which characterized popular beliefs; thus she is sceptical of an over-simple talk of religious decline. Her conclusion is that 'we need to understand how successive generations continued to construct, communicate, and adapt religious language if we are to appreciate popular religion as a distinctive system of belief in its own right'.[100]

The twentieth century context subtly changed in a different way. The proportion of the population brought to baptism declined steadily. From 1885 to 1927 the proportion of infant baptisms to live births in the Church of England rose from 62.3% to 71.7%: in the period from 1928 to 1956 it dropped back to 60.2% despite a rise in 1950. In 1970 the number of baptisms at 347,167 was the lowest recorded. The pattern in the Church of Scotland was broadly similar. As might be expected there were significant regional variations in this trend. In 1956 the dioceses with the lowest percentage of baptisms (in relation to live births) were London and Liverpool at 46.4% and 47.7% respectively: Bradford, Southwark, Manchester and Bristol were next in ascending order. The diocese with the highest percentage was Hereford at 80.1% (Hereford also had the highest proportion of Anglican church attendance in 1851), followed by Carlisle at 75.5%: Rochester and Worcester were next with 71.8% each.[101] Whilst this revealed a rough correlation between low-practice urban dioceses and high-practice rural ones, the rank order of dioceses for the percentage of Easter Day communicants was not the same, though Hereford was still top. Dr Gay estimated that only 13% of baptized people aged thirteen and over were registered on parochial

---

99 Williams, *Religious Belief and Popular Culture*, 140-2.
100 Ibid, 176.
101 *Facts and Figures about the Church of England* (London 1959), 24-8; R. Currie, A. Gilbert and L. Horsley, *Churches and Churchgoers* (Oxford 1977), 167-70.

electoral rolls.[102] The relationship between baptism and active participation in the worshipping life of the Church of England was still a complex one. By 2001 the proportion of baptisms had dropped sharply. Carlisle was top with 43.7% (lower than the lowest diocese in 1956), followed by Hereford (38.2%) and Lincoln (35.9%); the dioceses with the lowest percentages were London (7.2%), Southwark (9.3%) and Birmingham (11.3%). However, London and Southwark also had the highest number of baptisms of children aged between one and twelve; just as Carlisle, Hereford and Lincoln also had very low numbers of infant thanksgivings (which were now recorded for the first time).[103] A comparative table for 1990-2001 also showed that the proportion of infants among those baptized had dropped from 80% in 1990 to 70% in 2001.

Nevertheless, even though the residual pressures towards infant baptism may be diminishing in contemporary so-called secular society, they can still manifest themselves with surprising strength. This is why the problems which arise when baptism is refused can be so intractable. John Habgood touched on this point in a fascinating discussion of folk religion as it affected an Established Church in his book, *Church and Nation in a Secular Age*. He quoted a letter written to him from a mother who had ceased to attend church and had her request for her son to be baptized refused:

> Mr K. has not changed his mind and feels it would be hypocritical of him to baptise my son. I feel that his pompous and arrogant attitude towards me is not that of a minister of God. I could no more bare my soul to him than to the devil. This is what really appals and disgusts me, that a man who is a vicar can look at an innocent babe and say, 'No, I will not baptize you; go somewhere else'.

Archbishop Habgood noted the emotion, both of the mother and the priest. 'When anyone doesn't get their own way, it is not uncommon for them to resort to vitriolic attack', the priest had written.[104]

Nor is this any longer a purely Anglican problem: Free Church ministers are now finding themselves asked to baptize children whom the vicar has refused, and thus they discover a tension between what can look like a pastoral opportunity and their understanding of the nature of the Church. Also involved, of course, is their understanding of the ministry—because what is being sought in these circumstances is more the services of a minister than an opportunity to participate in the life of the Church. Congregations without ministers, temporarily or permanently,

---

102 J.D. Gay, *The Geography of Religion in England* (London 1971), 26.

103 www.cofe.anglican.org (Diocesan and Parochial Statistics, 2002), Table 5 Parochial Baptisms etc. 2001.

104 J. Habgood, *Church and Nation in a Secular Age* (London 1983), 80.

do not normally get these requests. The difficulty the contemporary Church experiences here (where it is felt to be a difficulty) is partly due to a poverty of imagination over the alternatives to baptism which can conscientiously be offered in such circumstances, and partly due to an unwillingness seriously to engage with the folk religion which says that only baptism will do. That unwillingness stems in large part from a steady refusal by theologians to admit that the strength of feeling about baptismal practice depends on more than the strength of the particular theological reasons advanced to justify it. The underlying theological issue here is the relationship between the Church and the world, which assumes particular importance when the Church is tempted for whatever reason to retreat into a religious ghetto. Thus the ecumenical discussions, which are the subject of the final chapter, not only reflect the problem of bringing different theological traditions together, but also illustrate a deeper problem of relating majority and minority Christian traditions.

CHAPTER 8

The Sacrament of Unity

In the *International Review of Mission* for 1984 Bishop Basil Meeking, who was then serving the Secretariat (now Pontifical Council) for Promoting Christian Unity in Rome, remarked that 'it is in the Second Vatican Council's Decree on the Missionary Activity of the Church that one finds some of the strongest ecumenical affirmations'.[1] That decree insisted that the ecumenical spirit should be nurtured in new Christians, who 'should have a due appreciation that their sisters and brothers who believe in Christ are Christ's disciples, reborn in baptism and sharing in very many of the blessings of God's people'.[2] It built on the words in the Decree on Ecumenism of November 1964, which sketched out the basis for the Roman Catholic Church's participation in the modern ecumenical movement. Section 3 of the Decree made two important points, which always need to be held together. The first was that those who were born into those communities which had become separated from full communion with the Catholic Church should not be treated as being guilty of the sin of separation but rather as brothers and sisters. The second point explained why:

> Those who believe in Christ and have been truly baptized are in some kind of communion with the catholic church, even though this communion is imperfect.... All who have been justified by faith through baptism are members of Christ's body, and have a right to be called Christians, and so are deservedly recognised as sisters and brothers in the Lord by the children of the catholic church.[3]

Hitherto very little has been said about the Roman Catholic Church, mainly because for most of the period under consideration there was little discussion within that Church on baptism and even less exchange of views between Roman Catholics and other Christians about it. The ecumenical

---

1 B. Meeking, 'After Vatican II', *International Review of Mission*, lxxiii (1984), 57. For a more detailed appraisal of the teaching of Vatican II on baptism, see K.J. Becker, SJ, 'The Teaching of Vatican II on Baptism: A Stimulus for Theology', in R. Latourelle (ed), *Vatican II: Assessment and Perspectives*, ii (New York 1989), 47-99.

2 Decree on the Missionary Activity of the Church, § 15, in N.P. Tanner SJ (ed), *Decrees of the Ecumenical Councils* (London 1990), ii, 1024.

3 Decree on Ecumenism, §3 in Tanner, *Decrees*, 910.

movement made Roman Catholics more sensitive to the Christians who live around them, and the significant feature of the Second Vatican Council for the purpose of this book is that it made the common baptism shared by Christians the basis for further exploration into that which unites all Christians. Roman Catholic ecumenists have constantly referred to baptism in this context since then, and in a particular sense, therefore, baptism has become 'the sacrament of unity'—a point which is highlighted by the fact that the eucharist has remained the sacrament which most sharply focuses the division of Christians. The purpose of this final chapter is to examine the extent to which the ecumenical movement has helped to resolve some of the problems about baptism which have been discussed previously.

Baptism did not play this decisive role in the early years of the ecumenical movement. It is true that the second paragraph of the 'Appeal to all Christian People' from the Lambeth Conference of 1920 began with these words:

> We acknowledge all those who believe in our Lord Jesus Christ, and have been baptized into the name of the Holy Trinity, as sharing with us membership in the universal Church of Christ which is His Body.[4]

But Anglicans have always regarded the Anglican Communion as constituting only part of the universal Church of Christ; and sensitivity to the fact that their own ministry and sacraments were not recognized by Rome has always made at least some Anglicans cautious about similar statements of non-recognition in relation to other Churches. Though the Lambeth Appeal deliberately avoided calling other groups of Christians 'Churches' (just as the documents of the Second Vatican Council did, though then it was out of deference to the self-definition of some of the ecumenical observers themselves), it looked for a set of marks of the Church—the well-known Chicago-Lambeth Quadrilateral of scripture, creeds, sacraments and ministry—of which baptism was just one. An approach to ecumenism based on a set of marks of the Church is more rounded but can also become more exclusive, whereas one based on the single criterion of baptism is more open-ended but ecclesiologically more vague.

As is well-known, the conversations between the Church of England and the English Free Churches following the Lambeth Appeal concentrated mainly on the ministry, and to a lesser extent on holy communion, as the defining characteristic of the Church, or at least as the one most in dispute. The statement on baptism approved by the Joint Conference of 1922 was plain in the extreme: 'Baptism is by the ordinance of Christ and of His Apostles the outward and visible sign of

---

4 *Conference of the Bishops of the Anglican Communion, 1920* (London 1920), 133.

admission into membership of the Church.'⁵ The Baptist Union's response to these conversations was the first time the Union as such had had to present any kind of doctrinal statement to other churches about what it believed positively about the church, baptism and communion. This is the significance of the order of the following sentence:

> Because we hold the Church to be a community of Christian believers, the ordinance of baptism is administered among us to those only who make a personal confession of repentance and faith.⁶

The primary emphasis on the Church as a community of those who have declared their faith was to remain constant for the rest of the century. The 1926 Leeds Assembly of the Baptist Union which adopted the response also heard a series of addresses on the significance of baptism, representing an impressive consensus in the denomination.⁷ But the relatively negative response to the goal of reunion as such was also to prove a dominating factor, which meant that the believer baptist voice in ecumenical discussion was to remain muted.

Baptism did not loom large at the First World Faith and Order Conference at Lausanne in 1927 either. Bishop Brent's opening sermon did not mention it, nor did Archbishop Germanos make any reference to it in his opening statement for the Orthodox. Bishop Azariah of Dornakal pointed out sharply that the Churches had no united answer to the questions:

> Should a man join the Church, and if so, what Church?
> Should he be baptized, and if so, by what baptism?⁸

But his questions were not taken up in that form. There was, of course, a discussion and a statement on the sacraments. Dr Vernon Bartlet, as an English Congregationalist representative, spoke of the need to see the sacraments in relation to prophetic Hebraism (an idea which had also been developed by the Baptist scholar, Henry Wheeler Robinson).⁹ He argued that originally baptism was essentially baptism with the Spirit, and explained the development of infant baptism as a consequence of primitive notions of family solidarity. But as most Churches regarded Church membership as incomplete without personal confession of faith,

---

5 G.K.A. Bell (ed), *Documents on Christian Unity, 1920-24* (London 1924), 137, 147.

6 G.K.A. Bell (d), *Documents on Christian Unity, Second Series* (London 1930), 104-5; the complete text is 102-7.

7 Cross, *Baptism and the Baptists*, 62-7.

8 H.N. Bate (ed), *Faith and Order: Proceedings of the World Conference, Lausanne, August 3-21, 1927* (New York 1928), 103.

9 See chapter 6.

there was no reason why Baptists should not regard infant baptism as 'the first stage of the full rite'.[10] Oliver Quick also contributed to this discussion, arguing in brief the essential points of his book on the sacraments, which was published that year. The Statement finally approved by the Conference said either a lot or a little, depending on one's point of view:

> We believe that in Baptism administered with water in the name of the Father, the Son and the Holy Spirit, for the remission of sins, we are baptized by one Spirit into one body. By this statement it is not meant to ignore the differences in conception, interpretation and mode which exist among us.[11]

But although to modern minds the second sentence may seem to take away anything said in the first, the significance of this initial agreement should not be belittled.

In the responses to the Lausanne Conference, edited by Leonard Hodgson, the only British Churches to make more than a passing reference to the statement on baptism were the Congregational Union and the Churches of Christ. (The Baptist Union had not been officially represented at Lausanne, although Dr W.T. Whitley and Dr J.E. Roberts had attended in a personal capacity.[12]) The Churches of Christ submitted a three-page statement, clearly drafted by William Robinson, setting out their justification for believer's baptism and stating that the baptismal controversy was fundamental.[13] The Congregational Union, after noting that there were considerable divergences of view among themselves on the sacraments, defined baptism as

> a symbol of the consecration of the recipient to God's special possession and the fellowship of His Church. In regard to infants it becomes a dedication by the parents of the child to God in the Church of Christ. It involves an acceptance by the Church of its responsibility for the spiritual nurture of the child.[14]

Forsyth's sacramental theology had obviously made little impact yet upon his fellow-Congregationalists.

The Continuation Committee appointed at Lausanne set up a Theological Commission to work on the doctrine of the Ministry and the Sacraments, which produced a substantial report for the Edinburgh Faith and Order Conference in 1937. A significant proportion of the members of this Commission were from Britain. Papers were contributed from theologians of different Churches, including one from A.C. Underwood

---

10 Bate (ed), *Faith and Order*, 293-6.
11 Ibid, 473.
12 Cross, *Baptism and the Baptists*, 84.
13 L. Hodgson (ed), *Convictions* (London 1934), 71-4.
14 Ibid, 52.

for the Baptists, and one from William Robinson for Disciples or Churches of Christ. Underwood's paper was deliberately intended as an addition to that prepared by Professor I.G. Matthews of Crozer Seminary, Pennsylvania, U.S.A., whom he regarded as virtually reducing the sacraments to *nuda signa*. 'Baptists are sacramentalists though they reject sacredotalism', wrote Underwood; 'but their sacramentalism is ethical through and through.' Furthermore they regarded regeneration, conversion and the new-birth as one and the same experience: 'It is called regeneration when it is regarded from the side of God, and conversion when looked at from the side of man.' So baptism was not 'merely declaratory': 'in every baptism of a believer there is a bestowal of the Holy Spirit'.[15] William Robinson made a similar point when he wrote that 'in a true *personal* relationship there must be sacramental *action*, and further, that in sacramental *action* emphasis is to be placed not only on what is of our response (what is subjective), but on what is *given* (what is objective)'.[16]

The Commission's report suggested a definite movement in this direction among the English Free Churches, citing the Methodist statement of 1936 that baptism is 'not only an outward symbol but also a channel of inward Grace'.[17] The reunion of Methodism in 1933 almost inevitably led to the dominance of Wesleyan views on the sacraments, which were the only ones cited in the report. The report on the doctrine of baptism dealt with three points: the necessity of baptism, baptismal regeneration and the question of infant baptism.[18] The Conference itself adopted a general statement on baptism which went a little further than Lausanne in agreeing on its necessity: but the questions of baptismal regeneration, the admission of unbaptized persons to Holy Communion and the relation of confirmation to baptism were left undiscussed. Baptists, supported by a representative of the Disciples of Christ, added a note to the effect that they accepted the statement in reference to believer's baptism only.[19] This highlighted an interesting little change between the Theological Commission's report and the position taken by the Conference. The Theological Commission, in discussing the validity

---

15 R. Dunkerley (ed), *The Ministry and the Sacraments* (London 1937), 226-7; cf Cross, *Baptism and the Baptists*, 87-90; Fowler, *More Than a Symbol*, 98-100.

16 Dunkerley (ed), *Ministry and Sacraments*, 262 (italics original).

17 Ibid, 21-2, cf 235. The complete text of the 'Memorandum on Infant Baptism' (*Minutes of the Methodist Conference 1936,* pp. 400-1), is reproduced in *Statements and Reports of the Methodist Church on Faith and Order, i, 1933-1983* (London 1984), 31-2. Intriguingly the phrase quoted in the report comes from the section on adult baptism.

18 Ibid, 38-40.

19 L. Hodgson (ed), *The Second World Conference on Faith and Order* (London 1938), 243-4, cf 321-2. Oddly the report adopted by the Conference omitted references to faith and grace, and the nature of the Church referred to in the section.

of the sacraments, had observed that there was 'universal agreement among Christian theologians that a Sacrament cannot be efficacious as a means of Grace unless there is faith in the recipient', to which they had added the following footnote, 'The application of this principle to the baptism of infants requires special consideration which cannot be given to it here.'[20] The Conference, however, decided to cut the gordian knot by omitting the reference to the recipient, and in their statement on the nature of the sacraments simply stated that 'Faith is therefore a necessary condition for the effectual reception of grace': the Baptists added a note to say that they would wish the statement to read 'Faith on the part of the recipient...'.[21]

In England, the Joint Conference between the Church of England and the Free Churches published the now virtually forgotten *Outline of a Reunion Scheme* in 1938. This provided that membership in the proposed united Church should be confined to those who had been baptized and also that both infant baptism plus confirmation and believer's baptism should be available within the united Church.[22] The Free Church Federal Council's response to this in 1941 indicated the continuing resistance among Congregationalists to the imposition of a rule about baptism, despite the strong line taken by John Whale in his contribution to *Ministry and the Sacraments*. (Whale was one of several Congregationalists, including Nathaniel Micklem and Daniel Jenkins, who argued for a stronger sacramental emphasis in the 1930s and 1940s.) The Congregational Union Assembly had asked that a place be found in the visible Church for those 'who conscientiously refrain from the use of sacraments', and the report expressed concern that the requirement that members should be baptized seemed to conflict with the definition of the Church accepted in 1922 which had been modified to include all believers whether baptized or not. The Baptists had also indicated that they did not regard baptism as the rite of admission to the Church anyway.[23] So it might be said of the developments between 1920 and 1941, not only that baptism was not a central issue, but also that some deft footwork was put in to ensure that it did not become so.

Nothing more was done about the Anglican–Free Church proposals after the war. Archbishop Fisher's experience of the South India proposals had led him to seek an alternative to reunion schemes, and so he suggested in a Cambridge University sermon in 1946 that the Free Churches might take episcopacy into their system. After some five years

---

20 Dunkerley, *Ministry and Sacraments*, 27.
21 Hodgson, *Second World Conference*, 240.
22 'Outline of a Reunion Scheme', II.2 and IV.3, G.K.A. Bell (ed), *Documents on Christian Unity, Third Series, 1930-1948* (London 1948), 75. 77-8.
23 'Reply of the Free Church Federal Council', IV.1, V.2, Bell, *Documents, Third Series*, 108-9, 116.

of discussion only the Methodist Church accepted the invitation but to Fisher's intense annoyance the Anglican–Methodist Conversations produced a proposal for exactly the kind of scheme he had hoped to avoid. The report of 1963 produced a succinct statement of what Christian baptism meant in the New Testament, concluding with the strong statement that 'baptism is received by faith which is a response to the gospel that is proclaimed and involves a confession of Christ as Saviour and Lord'.[24] Noting that, as both Churches regarded infant baptism as a legitimate development, it was not necessary to deal with issues raised by believer baptists, the report took the usual line of saying that in infant baptism the faith exercised was that of the Church, not of the child, and added,

> Further, the confession of faith in infant baptism is not to be discounted because it is made by the Church, unless we are to yield to an intransigent individualism which ignores the inseparable relation between the individual and the fellowship of believers in the Church.[25]

In the report of the Anglican–Methodist Unity Commission of 1968 there was also a chapter on 'Baptism and Confirmation', which attempted first to allay fears over the doctrine of baptismal regeneration, and secondly to expound the necessity of confirmation and reception into full membership as the opportunity for individual conscious response in faith to Christ's saving work, which needed to be regarded as integral to baptism.[26]

Involvement in the ecumenical movement acted as the main spur for Baptists to clarify their views of baptism, though with mixed results. Ernest Payne, who became General Secretary of the Baptist Union in 1951, was also very much involved in the World Council of Churches after attending the Continuation Committee meeting at Clarens in 1947. He had translated Karl Barth's lecture on baptism of 1943, and published *The Fellowship of Believers* in 1944 to challenge the individualism in Baptist thought represented in Arthur Dakin's *The Baptist View of Church and Ministry* (1944). R.C. Walton also criticised Dakin in *The Gathered Community* (1946), which offered a high view of the church as a channel of grace and denied the necessity of rebaptizing those baptized in infancy; but this was too much for most Baptists at that time.[27] Payne chaired a Commission on the Doctrine of Baptism for the Baptist World

---

24 *Conversations between the Church of England and the Methodist Church* (London 1963), 30.
25 Ibid, 31.
26 *Anglican–Methodist Unity, Part 2, The Scheme* (London 1968), 74-82, especially 78-9.
27 Fowler, *More Than a Symbol*, 100-5; Cross, *Baptism and the Baptists*, 186-7.

Alliance in 1950, and presented its report in an address on 'Baptism in Present-Day Theology' at Cleveland. In this, he warned that despite the challenges to infant baptism presented by Brunner, Barth and Dix, Baptists should not think that their case was universally conceded; and he regretted that on many matters connected with baptism Baptists were either unclear or divided.[28] A group of Baptist ministers began work in 1955, which resulted in the publication of *Christian Baptism* in 1959. The editor, Alec Gilmore, had summarised some of the difficulties for Baptists in three articles in 1954-55.[29] Neville Clark had published *An Approach to the Theology of the Sacraments* in 1956. *Christian Baptism* contained contributions from both of them, as well as discussions of baptism in the New Testament from R.E.O. White and G.R. Beasley-Murray.[30] White published his own book, *The Biblical Doctrine of Initiation*, in 1960, and Beasley-Murray published *Baptism in the New Testament* in 1962. Although, as its title suggests, White's book was primarily concerned with the biblical doctrine, his final chapter dealt with baptism in the modern Church, including a detailed response to paedobaptist apologetic. Beasley-Murray concentrated on a narrower field, but did so exhaustively in a way that almost left his work beyond challenge as exegesis. His conclusion was careful but devastating:

> In the light of the foregoing exposition of the New Testament representations of baptism, the idea that baptism is a purely symbolic rite must be pronounced not alone unsatisfactory but out of harmony with the New Testament itself. Admittedly, such a judgment runs counter to the popular tradition of the Denomination to which the writer belongs, as it does to some of the significant contributions to the study of baptism that have appeared from theologians of other Churches in recent years. But the New Testament belongs to us all and we all stand judged by it.[31]

Nevertheless, as Anthony R. Cross has shown, despite the increasing number of Baptist scholars in the later twentieth century who have endorsed a sacramental view of baptism, it has not proved any easier to secure general assent to that among the ordinary members of Baptist congregations. Indeed, the more faith was emphasised as the primary requisite for entry into the Church, the less relevant a sacramental understanding of baptism seemed to become.

The other issue which was posed for Baptists with increasing pressure in an ecumenical context was their attitude to infant baptism. Neville Clark had stated starkly at the end of his essay in 'The Theology of

---

28 Cross, *Baptism and the Baptists*, 187-9.
29 A. Gilmore, 'Some Recent Trends in the Theology of Baptism', *Baptist Quarterly* xv, 7 (July 1954), xv, 8 (October 1954) and xvi, 1 (January 1955).
30 See Fowler, *More Than a Symbol*, 107-33.
31 G.R. Beasley-Murray, *Baptism in the New Testament* (London 1962), 263.

Baptism' in *Christian Baptism* that 'the rebaptism as believers of those who have received baptism in infancy constitutes a blow at the heart of the Christian faith... The whole meaning of the rite hinges on its once-for-allness, its unrepeatability.'[32] This conclusion was no more welcome than when Walton had mentioned it some fifteen years earlier. Yet it proved to be the direction in which even Beasley-Murray was slowly moving. In his *Baptism in the New Testament*, he had asked whether Baptists could 'not refrain from requesting the baptism of those baptized in infancy who wish to join our churches and administer baptism to such only where there is a strong plea for it from the applicant?'[33] At the Baptist World Alliance Commission Conference on Doctrine in 1965 he went a litle further:

> We have two baptisms, one for infants and the other for confessors of faith. If it be asked wherein the unity of the church does lie, if not in one baptism, the answer surely must be: *in the common confession of that to which biblical baptism points*, namely the redemption of God in Christ and participation in it through the Holy Spirit by faith.[34]

He suggested that where people had been baptized as infants and had professed their faith subsequently, they should be received by Baptist churches by transfer; where they had not made a confession of faith, they should be baptized as believers.[35] Alec Gilmore was prepared to go further and to recognise infant baptism as baptism in his book, *Baptism and Christian Unity*, in 1966.[36] But this remained a minority view.

The discussions on baptism so far described were all before the Second Vatican Council had completed its work. Roman Catholics were generally not involved in them, although Dr Marianus Johannes Vetter of Berlin contributed a statement on the Roman Catholic position for the work of the Theological Commission which prepared *Ministry and the Sacraments* in 1937. The Second Vatican Council, therefore, came at a time when certain issues concerning baptism had been clarified, but little progress had been made towards their resolution. Baptism had occupied a subordinate place in ecumenical discussions after 1920, when the dominating issues were always the ministry, and to a lesser extent the eucharist. Despite a sacramental revival amongst the Free Churches, a

---

32 A. Gilmore (ed), *Christian Baptism* (London 1959), 325.
33 Beasley-Murray, *Baptism in the New Testament*, 392.
34 G.R. Beasley-Murray, 'Baptists and the Baptism of Other Churches', in J. Nordenhaug (ed), *The Truth That Makes Men Free: Official Report of the Eleventh Congress, Baptist World Alliance* (Nashville 1966), 268 (italics original), quoted in Cross, *Baptism and the Baptists*, 169.
35 Ibid, 270-2, see Cross, *Baptism and the Baptists*, 170.
36 Cross, *Baptism and the Baptists*, 171; Fowler, *More Than a Symbol*, 145-50.

strong tradition survived which was suspicious of any insistence on baptism, or the sacraments generally. Not all the developments since 1965 have been due to Roman Catholic participation, but the fact of Roman Catholic participation has given them wider significance. For ease of exposition these developments will be considered under four headings: movement towards the mutual recognition of baptism and church union schemes which cross the baptismal divide; the continuing discussion of infant baptism; the relation of baptism and faith; and the relation of baptism and church.

In Britain there has been both a movement towards mutual recognition of baptism, with the Common Baptismal Certificate approved in 1971, and a church union scheme which crosses the baptismal divide exemplified by the United Reformed Church. The Faith and Order Department of the British Council of Churches was first spurred into study of the baptismal question by a request from the Council to draw up a statement

> regarding the problem created in inter-Church relations when parents, seeking the baptism of their infants, do not accept the obligations required by one Church and therefore request baptism in another.[37]

It is interesting that attempts in various Churches practising infant baptism to develop a more rigorous baptismal discipline should have had this result. The resolution prompted some reflection on the underlying pattern and understanding of Christian initiation, as well as a direct answer to the pastoral question. The Nottingham Faith and Order Conference of 1964 noted both a convergence on the nature of initiation and also a number of outstanding problems. It, therefore, unanimously resolved to ask the British Council of Churches to initiate consultations among the member churches about these problems with a view to action.[38] The Faith and Order Department was not at first enthusiastic, but by the spring of 1967 it had changed its mind, largely because both in reunion discussions and in informal contacts with Roman Catholic representatives the importance of establishing an agreement about procedure and records in relation to baptism had become apparent. The result was an Enquiry into Baptismal Practice, which was largely carried out by Fr F.C. Fenn, SJ, Study Secretary of the Department.

The Report was essentially a description of existing practice, but it provided the basis for the agreement to adopt a Common Baptismal Certificate in 1971, a suggestion made by the Joint Working Group between the British Council of Churches and the Roman Catholic Church.

---

37 *Report of the Inter-Church Enquiry into Baptismal Practice* (London 1970), 3.
38 R.E. Davies and D.L. Edwards (eds), *Unity begins at home* (London 1964), 64-7, 77.

All those Churches in Britain which practised infant baptism, including the Roman hierarchy for England and Wales but excluding that for Scotland (which agreed subsequently), agreed to accept a certificate in the proposed form as evidence of Christian baptism. It was not accepted by the Baptists or by Churches of Christ because it made no reference to profession of faith; but they were prepared to issue a certificate in the same form for baptisms conducted among them. The Common Baptismal Certificate was a step forward, and was prompted by Roman Catholic initiative. Some of its limitations were revealed in 1983 when the Board of the Division of Ecumenical Affairs of the BCC began discussion on a possible 'Part II' of the Certificate which would refer to profession of faith, confirmation and first communion. This immediately revealed a diversity of view not only on the sequence of subsequent stages in Christian initiation, which was not surprising, but also on the more fundamental question of whether anything further was necessary to initiation at all. In view of the range of understandings of baptism which clearly still existed, a Working Party was established, which eventually reported in 1988. Special attention was paid to Inter-Church families and to Local Ecumenical Projects (established as Areas of Ecumenical Experiment following the Nottingham Faith and Order Conference), because in different ways these raised the question of joint confirmations involving two or more Churches. A further section teased out the various meanings of terms like initiation, formation, church membership, belonging and incorporation. The final section was not so much a set of conclusions as a set of questions to the Churches, asking them how far they could move in the direction of joint preparation for baptism and confirmation, joint celebrations of baptism and the renewal of baptismal vows, and formal recognition of multiple church membership.[39]

The pattern for church union schemes which crossed the baptismal divide was laid down in the 1938 'Outline of a Reunion Scheme', which envisaged a dual practice of infant baptism plus confirmation and believer's baptism. The explication of the underlying theology and the working out of some of the practical problems of this were not quite so simple. Although the United Reformed Church is the only example of such a union in Britain, the negotiations for the Church of North India and the abortive proposals for an English Covenant are also relevant. The Indian negotiations, which began in 1929, involved Anglicans, Methodists, Presbyterians, Congregationalists, Baptists, Churches of Christ and Brethren, so the question of baptism was raised in a way in which it had not been in South India. It proved relatively straightforward to devise a statement of the doctrine of baptism which was acceptable to both

---

[39] *Christian Initiation and Church Membership* (British Council of Churches: London 1988). The author was a member of this Working Party.

paedobaptists and believer baptists, and also to set out the parallel routes to communicant membership of the Church. But the problem of whether someone baptized as an infant could receive baptism as a believer upon a change of conviction on the matter, and the way in which alternative views could be held together, caused much difficulty. An appendix in the Third Edition of the Plan of Union (1957) which required difficult cases to be referred to the Bishop of the Diocese proved very divisive among Baptist churches. In the Fourth Edition of the Plan (1965) the troublesome appendix was simply dropped and no direction was given at all. In this form the Plan was approved and the Church of North India inaugurated in 1970.

At about the same time as the breakthrough was achieved in North India, Churches of Christ in Great Britain and Ireland accepted the open invitation given by the Joint Committee for Conversations between the Congregational Union of England and Wales and the Presbyterian Church of England to other Churches to join them in their discussions. Recognising that it would be wrong to hold up progress between the two major parties on the baptismal question which was not an issue between them, Churches of Christ sought only observer status. But they did persuade the Joint Committee to draft the section of the Basis of Union on baptism in such a way that nothing would have to be deleted and very little amended at a subsequent point if Churches of Christ were to unite. Thus the Basis of Union as agreed in 1972 began with a statement of the doctrine of baptism which was applicable to infant baptism or believer's baptism: and the second part of it made explicit provision for baptism at an age of responsibility as well as for infant baptism, even though infant baptism was the prevailing practice. The main achievement at that stage was to secure baptism as a necessary condition of church membership, since a large number of Congregational Churches still wished it to be optional. When in 1972 formal negotiations began between Churches of Christ and the United Reformed Church, the main addition required in the section on baptism was a clause to deal with the holding together of different convictions in the same Church. Some wording for this was taken from the North India Scheme, but the provisions made were much more explicit. The conscientious convictions of ministers and church members were to be respected: both forms of baptism were to be made available in the worshipping life of each local congregation: and hard cases of conscience were to be pastorally reconciled according to the Basis of Union (which forbade rebaptism) by the Elders Meeting. This revised Basis was approved and the majority of Churches of Christ united with the United Reformed Church in 1981. The main lesson learned from this experience was that an appropriate way of recognizing and honouring different convictions about baptism required much more thought than the setting out of alternative practices of baptism.

This point is particularly relevant in considering the abortive Proposals for a Covenant in England, and the reaction of Baptists to them. The Churches' Unity Commission (which produced the 'Ten Propositions' in 1976 as the basis for a covenant) had proposed a mutual recognition of membership and had assumed the equivalence of a dual practice of baptism. The fact that a covenant, rather than a union scheme, was being proposed meant that it was not necessary to consider how conflicting convictions should be reconciled. Churches of Christ had less difficulty with this proposal than the Baptists for two reasons: the first was that, unlike many Baptists, they were prepared to regard infant baptism as baptism, albeit incomplete without subsequent personal profession of faith; the second was that their negotiations with the United Reformed Church ensured that the problem of conflicting convictions would be handled there, so it was less important for the Covenant Proposals to deal with it.

For the Baptist Union Council, on the other hand, this issue was a sticking point:

> We could not commend to our churches any covenant which involved a bar to the administration of believers' baptism in the case of a paedobaptist whose conscience might lead him or her to the conclusion that fidelity to Scripture and the Gospel required such baptism. *We are clear that the exercise of responsible pastoral freedom must be preserved at this point and possibly others precisely because the covenant is not based on real theological agreement on the baptismal issue.*[40]

So the Baptists did not join the Churches' Council for Covenanting when it was set up in 1978. In fact, it was not so much that there was no real theological agreement on the baptismal issue, as that there was not sufficient agreement.

Moreover, despite the position taken up by some Baptist theologians, it was far from clear that the Baptist Union could participate in any covenant which involved acknowledging infant baptism as baptism because of its own Declaration of Principle. The best that Baptist churches could offer was a recognition of membership based on profession of faith, but not baptism. Even if the particular legal problems surrounding the Baptist Union's Declaration of Principle were left on one side, a Baptist theologian like Dr Morris West was worried by the possibility that the sentences on baptism in the World Council of Churches Faith and Order Commission's draft Statement might mean different things to different people.[41] Some differences might be inevitable, but how many were tolerable in an agreed statement? Nevertheless, by 1994 Beasley-Murray was prepared to see infant baptism as attesting 'the

---

40 *Visible Unity in Life and Mission* (London 1977), 3 (emphasis original).
41 *Louisville: Consultation on Baptism* (1980), 14.

commencement of the work of grace within the baptized', especially if accompanied by a recovery of the catechumenate. Therefore, he suggested that 'churches which practise believer's baptism should consider acknowledging the legitimacy of infant baptism, and allow members in Paedobaptist churches the right to interpret it according to their consciences'. In effect this would mean refraining from 'rebaptism'.[42] More pointedly, he said, 'In reality there is no such thing as a Baptist theology of baptism accepted by all Baptists: what they do not themselves possess they should not demand of others.'[43] Morris West welcomed Beasley-Murray's conclusion.[44] But it needs to be understood that this movement reflected the intense ecumenical involvement over many years of those concerned at national or international level. By 1994 Local Ecumenical Partnerships, as they were now called in England, had been in existence for nearly thirty years; when Beasley-Murray first wrote, they did not exist. Those who lacked the personal experience of such encounters, however, remained for the most part completely unmoved by such arguments. In fact, the Baptists were probably more divided by ecumenical developments than any other mainstream Church. As will have become clear, several of their leading theologians were deeply involved in Faith and Order discussions; other ministers took a leading role in the development of the British Council of Churches in the 1970s and 1980s—Hugh Cross, John Nicholson and Roger Nunn, for example. Yet the broadening of that Council to include Roman Catholics in 1990 raised other hackles among some Baptists which had nothing to do with baptism; and several ministers and members quietly transferred to the United Reformed Church, now that it was committed to honouring different convictions about baptism.

Although some progress was made on mutual recognition of baptism and the holding together of different convictions about baptism within one Church, therefore, the question of infant baptism remained. Hence, there was still much hesitation about accepting the equivalence of two patterns of Christian initiation. The Baptist reservations have been mentioned, namely that the faith, rather than the baptism, of those baptized as infants is what really counts in recognition. With this, of course, there was associated a residual scepticism about the sacramental nature of baptism, though this is rarer in Britain than it once was. There was also something of a movement in precisely the opposite direction

---

42 G.R. Beasley-Murray, 'The Problem of Infant Baptism: An Exercise in Possibilities', *Festschrift Günther Wagner*, ed. Faculty of Baptist Theological Seminary, Rüschlikon (Berne 1994), 9, 13-14, quoted in Cross, *Baptism and the Baptists*, 339-40. He cited Oliver Quick's *The Christian Sacraments* in support, which he had previously examined critically in 1962.
43 Ibid, 7, quoted in Cross, *Baptism and the Baptists*, 463.
44 Cross, *Baptism and the Baptists*, 340.

among Anglicans. In 1969 the Archbishops of Canterbury and York appointed a Commission, under the chairmanship of Bishop Roberts of Ely, to consider Christian initiation; and its report was published in 1971. Although its main recommendations were rejected by the General Synod, a number of the things it hoped for have come to pass. Theologically, it reversed the thinking of the Joint Committees of the 1940s and 1950s, which had stressed that baptism and confirmation belonged together as separated parts of a single act. Instead, the Ely Commission took the view that baptism did not need to be 'completed':

> It is the one and complete sacrament of Christian initiation, and the whole course of Christian life up to and beyond death should be a progressive realisation of what Baptism effectively declares in a single sacramental moment... It is initiation, not a sacrament of progress in Christian faith and life, still less a reward for any kind of spiritual achievement... The individual who enters [the] group should progressively appropriate its faith, hope, and love, so as to make these his own as he comes to share more fully and consciously in the life of the Church. This is as true of the person baptised as a believer as it is of the person baptised in infancy.[45]

So the condition for entrance was a sincere desire to join; and it was wrong to interpret this desire in intellectual, ecclesiastical or liturgical terms. The Commission also recommended that confirmation be seen as a service of commissioning for responsible membership in the Church rather than a prerequisite for communion. Thus, although the Commission's report was entitled *Christian Initiation* they did not use the term to denote a total process in the way in which it had been used in 1944, and continued to be used, for example, in the documents of the Churches' Unity Commission. Theologically, the Commission was described by one of its members as 'Geoffrey Lampe's Commission', and the similarity of its recommendations to the argument of *The Seal of the Spirit* will be apparent.

Whilst believer baptists had difficulty in accepting the Commission's argument in relation to infant baptism because no role was given to faith, the trend of Anglican practice in the 1970s was in the direction of believer's baptism. In 1976 the Church of England baptized 7,993 'persons of riper years', and the number of baptisms in the Baptist Union was 5,138. In 1978, when the basis of Anglican returns had been changed the Church of England baptized 35,843 persons over the age of one as compared with 216,650 under one (though the majority of those were still under twelve): in 1977 the Baptist Union baptized 4,989. In 2001 the Church of England baptized 8,430 people over twelve; in other words, that number was tending to rise in absolute terms. When the *Alternative Service Book* was published in 1980 a combined service of believer's

---

45 *Christian Initiation* (London 1971), 27.

baptism and confirmation was printed as the normative service, and according to the bishops, it was rare in the 1980s for a confirmation involving a number of candidates not to include at least one adult baptism.

The Roman Catholic Church shared some of the same experiences. The Constitution on the Sacred Liturgy of 1963 laid down that the catechumenate should be restored and that the rites of baptism for adults and infants should be revised. In particular, it was required that the rite for the baptism of infants should be 'adapted to the reality of the situation with babies',[46] and the roles and duties of parents and godparents were to become clearer in the rite itself. The new rite for adults was similarly designed to bring out its distinctive features. So it was explained that adults

> hear the preaching of the mystery of Christ, the Holy Spirit opens their hearts, and they freely and knowingly seek the living God and enter the path of faith and conversion. By God's help they will be strengthened in their preparation and at the proper time they will receive the sacrament fruitfully.[47]

The significance of baptism in this process was described as follows:

> The renunciation of Satan and the profession of faith form one rite which reaches its full strength in the baptism of adults. Since baptism is a sacrament of faith by which the catechumens adhere to God, and at the same time are given new life by him, it is fitting that the washing with water is preceded by each person's actions.[48]

This was strong language, which did not hesitate to place the adherence of the catechumens to God before their being given new life by him. The same document, in dealing with adults baptized in infancy who have not received further catechetical instruction, made it clear that their circumstances differ from those of catechumens:

> They have already become members of the Church and children of God by baptism. Hence their conversion is based on the baptism they have already received and they must unfold its power.[49]

Furthermore, the catechist was instructed to remember their special situation when teaching them, though without any indication of how to do this.

---

46 Constitution on the Sacred Liturgy, §67, Tanner, *Decrees*, 833.
47 *Rite of Christian Initiation of Adults*, §1 (London 1976), 1.
48 Ibid, §211, 64.
49 Ibid, §295, 99.

There is, of course, nothing new about the contrast outlined here, and those who have never found it a problem before will probably not find this juxtaposition problematic either. But the attempt to do justice to the difference between infant and adult baptism may have sharpened the question of whether, or more precisely in what sense, one baptism is being talked about. Perhaps the very strength of language in the new rite for adults was one factor in producing some of the hesitations which prompted the Holy Office to issue its 'Instruction on Infant Baptism' in October 1980. It was concerned to meet the hesitations of those who wished for a catechumenate of shorter or longer duration before baptizing, or who wished baptism to be delayed until the time when a personal commitment could be made. The Instruction summarized the development of infant baptism and the Church's teaching about it and then dealt with five major objections. On the question of baptism and faith, it was declared that baptism was never administered without faith, except that in the case of infants it was the faith of the Church. Conscious appropriation of grace was declared unnecessary because a child is a person long before it can show it by acts of consciousness and freedom. The view that baptizing children was a restriction of their freedom was said to be simply an illusion, because there was no such thing as pure human freedom and every creature was bound by indefeasible duties to God. The Instruction rejected any proposal that infant baptism should be avoided in a pluralistic society as subverting the basis of the Church's mission: and finally, the idea that infant baptism reflected a concern for numbers at the expense of stirring up a lively faith was also rejected as ignoring the urgency of ensuring that every child should receive the infinite blessing of eternal life.[50] It is interesting that the argument about parents taking decisions for their children was also cited as a justification for infant baptism by the Church of England Doctrine Commission in a report of 1971.[51]

Whatever may be thought about the validity of these various arguments, it is clear that the issue is whether it is right for parents to delay baptism for their children. In particular, it needs to be recognised that both the decision to request baptism and the decision not to are decisions taken on behalf of the child. The position was put admirably in a Joint Report on Baptism from the Reformed, Roman Catholic and Old Catholic Churches in Switzerland, published in 1973, which affirmed the right of parents to defer the baptism of their children until they could themselves give their assent, and continued,

---

50 Instruction on Infant Baptism, §§16-26, A. Flannery (ed), *Vatican Council II: More Post-Conciliar Documents* (Leominster 1982), 107-11.

51 *Baptism, Thanksgiving and Blessing* (London 1971), 7.

> What must be decisive here is that the parents, in either case, are aware of the seriousness of baptism. To baptize children but also *not* to baptize them, implies a decision. In the same way that parents and sponsors who have their children baptized assume a great responsibility before God and man, so too those parents who wish to leave the baptism to a child itself at a later time, assume a definite responsibility. They expose the child in any case to a later situation which still is uncommon and thus requires a high degree of personal independence.[52]

This rightly pricks the rhetoric sometimes used in defence of believer's baptism about leaving children free to decide for themselves. It is also a reminder of the fundamental difference between the situation of children brought up in a Christian home, and people coming freshly to faith in missionary contexts. At the beginning of the twenty-first century it is less clear than thirty years ago that 'the later situation...is still uncommon'.

A third area of continuing discussion is the relationship between baptism and faith. It has already been noted that the Edinburgh Faith and Order Conference modified its general statement that the faith of the recipient was necessary to the effectual reception of sacramental grace in order to take account of infant baptism. Reference was made in chapter 6 to Oliver Quick's distinction between the symbolic and instrumental understanding of the sacraments, and his view that the move towards infant baptism involved a shift in emphasis from the instrumental to the symbolic. Yet Quick was obviously not prepared to regard infant baptism as a wholly symbolic rite, and Dr Beasley-Murray drew attention to some of the difficulties involved in his position generally in 1962.[53] The most obvious of these is whether a rite can ever be partly instrumental, and if, as seems likely, the answer to this is No, then what does talk about shifts in emphasis mean?

The standard answer to the objection that an infant has no personal faith is that infant baptism takes place on the basis of the Church's faith, as stated more recently, for example, in the Instruction of the Holy Office. But if in infant baptism the need for faith is adequately discharged by the exercise of the Church's faith, why is the same not true in believer's baptism? What does the profession of faith by a believer add to a service of believer's baptism? Clearly the consent of the candidate is necessary, but that is implicit in the baptism happening at all, or could be met by asking a simple liturgical question, 'Do you wish to be baptized?' As has already been seen, however, the new Roman rite for adult baptism emphasises that baptism is a sacrament of faith and uses strong language about the faith of the candidate, and in this most paedobaptist Churches would agree, except perhaps the Church of Scotland which has come near

---

[52] Quoted in N. Ehrenstrom, *Mutual Recognition of Baptism in Interchurch Agreements* (Geneva 1978), 33 (italics original).
[53] Beasley-Murray, *Baptism in the New Testament*, 382-6.

to making infant baptism theologically normative. If, however, a declaration of faith by a candidate baptized as a believer is necessary, then what is the force of saying that the rite of baptism at an age of responsibility is normative? Or, more precisely, what does it mean to say that it is normative when most baptisms are infant baptisms?

It may be too harsh to describe infant baptism as 'a practice in search of a theology', as Neville Clark has done.[54] But it is necessary to take care to describe the theology of it in such a way that the integrity of believer's baptism is not undermined. So whilst it is right that the liturgy for infant baptism should take account of the fact that the recipients are infants, nothing should be asserted in the theology of baptism that derives special force from this fact. For example, a diocesan bishop was quoted in the Ely Report as saying, 'Theologically, infant baptism brings home to us that our Lord does something that we cannot do for ourselves—we are as helpless as the helpless child'.[55] Assertions about the centrality of the prevenient grace of God in baptism are not strengthened by confusing them with statements about the inability of infants to make any response at all, otherwise the whole argument is liable to a *reductio ad absurdam*. Is it, then, equally inappropriate to demand any profession of faith in the service, since this can only be asked of a believer? Edmund Schlink argued that 'the more certainly baptism is recognized as God's saving deed, the more certainly it is recognized that the baptized is simply the receiver'. On this Beasley-Murray commented that

> We do no service to theology or the Church by playing down the significance of faith in association with baptism, on the ground that faith is in any case the gift of God, and that baptism is primarily the act of God rather than the act of man.[56]

If pressed, this would make baptism the only sacrament (with the possible exception of extreme unction if one counts seven rather than two) in which the active participation of the receiver is not judged essential. What effect does this have on the general coherence of sacramental theology?

The Ely Report stressed that baptism was a beginning, the start of a process of growing into faith; and pointed out rightly that this was as true of a believer as an infant. This approach was also followed by the Faith and Order Commission of the World Council of Churches. The report on baptism presented at Louvain in 1971 said that 'the baptism of infants looks forward to...personal confession of faith and commitment'.[57] In *Baptism, Eucharist and Ministry*, the point was expressed in this way:

---

54 N. Clark, 'The Theology of Baptism', in Gilmore, *Christian Baptism*, 320.
55 *Christian Initiation*, 95.
56 Schlink, quoted Beasley-Murray, *Louisville Consultation*, 166.
57 *Faith and Order, Louvain 1971* (Geneva 1971), 47.

Baptism is both God's gift and our human response to that gift. It looks towards a growth into the measure of the stature of the fullness of Christ (Eph. 4:13). The necessity of faith for the reception of the salvation embodied and set forth in baptism is acknowledged by all churches. Personal commitment is necessary for responsible membership in the body of Christ.[58]

The paragraph is a masterpiece of compression. The question is whether it can be expounded without falling apart. It is right to emphasize that baptism looks forward to a growth in faith: but to stand on the starting line with eyes fixed only on the finishing line may mean that one does not notice some others are starting a little way ahead. Does this matter? One risk in the emphasis on the diverse elements in baptism which has properly been prominent since the Montreal Faith and Order Conference of 1963, is that it may be concluded that the sequence of elements in the process of initiation is of no theological significance. That cannot be assumed: it needs to be argued. And it needs to be recognized, as Dr Beasley-Murray did, that ecumenical discussion of baptism is peculiarly fraught with suspicion and defensiveness.

Although the Churches' responses to the baptism section of *Baptism, Eucharist and Ministry* were generally the most positive of all, it was clear that there were difficulties in securing wider agreement for a convergence statement drafted by a group of people who had grown to trust one another over several years. The criticism of the use of 'baptism' as the subject of so many active verbs in the statement was found not only in the Baptist Union's response, but also in that of the Church of Scotland.[59] However, the Baptist Union found the statement that 'any practice which might be interpreted as "rebaptism" must be avoided' wholly unacceptable in its present form. On the other hand, in looking to 'a total process of Christian initiation' as the most promising way forward to mutual recognition, it pointed out that statements which might be defensible where 'baptism' was a shorthand term for total initiation became suspect if applied to infant baptism alone.[60] The United Reformed Church also drew attention to the danger of possible ambiguities in language in the text, as did the Methodist Church.[61] The Society of Friends acknowledged 'that the grace of God is experienced by many through the outward rite of baptism', but went on to affirm that 'no ritual, however carefully prepared for, can be guaranteed to lead to growth in the Spirit... Our understanding of baptism is that it is not a single act of initiation but a continuing growth in the Holy Spirit and a

---

58 *Baptism, Eucharist and Ministry*, Baptism §8 (Geneva 1982), 3.
59 M. Thurian (ed), *Churches respond to BEM*, i (Geneva 1986), 70, 95.
60 Ibid, 71.
61 Ibid, 103-4; M. Thurian, *Churches Respond to BEM*, ii (Geneva 1986), 220. The author was the primary drafter of the United Reformed Church response.

commitment which must be continually renewed.' Nor could they see that 'this rite should be used as the only way of becoming a member of the body of Christ'.[62] The Church of England, while offering a general welcome to the baptism section, was concerned about the text's warning of the dangers of indiscriminate baptism, fearing that those requesting baptism might be 'required to produce unreasonable evidence of the authenticity of their faith'. 'So-called "indiscriminate baptism" reflects a view of the Church as a "mixed community"; a more rigorous policy emphasises the "gathered" nature of the Church.'[63] Relatively few of the responses, even those which generally welcomed the statement, indicated any readiness to change current practice to embrace the wider insights in the Churches as a whole; the United Reformed Church was one of the few exceptions.

The Anglican response to *BEM* was a long way away from the concern of Brunner and Barth about the credibility of the Church in the modern world, and even from the rather apologetic tone of Sumner about the baptized who did not live up to their calling. But it is an appropriate introduction to the final set of issues concerning the relation of baptism to the Church. It has often been noticed in ecumenical discussions that the real problem for Baptists is not baptism but the doctrine of the Church. Morris West at the Louisville Consultation suggested that paedobaptists and believer baptists started from different models of the Church:

> Those practising infant baptism see the Church as an ontologically given community into which a child is incorporated, whereas Baptists view the Church as a community which is constituted by the activity of God on the individual, who responds and believes and becomes a participating member of the community.[64]

This does not quite catch the distinction, since presumably for Baptists also the Church has been constituted by the prior action of God in history before God acts on a particular individual. It might be better to distinguish between a situation in which an individual's response to God's action is marked by joining the Church through baptism, and one in which an individual, already made part of the Church by baptism, appropriates that reality by personal response later. The role of baptism in the two situations is clearly different. It is also interesting to reflect on what difference, if any, would be made to West's statement if the last part was in the plural, i.e. 'by the activity of God on individuals, who respond and believe and become participating members of the community'.

---

62 M. Thurian (ed), *Churches respond to BEM*, iv (Geneva 1987), 219-20.
63 M. Thurian (ed), *Churches respond to BEM*, iii (Geneva 1987), 37.
64 *Louisville Consultation*, 15.

This highlights the fact that the believer baptist position is often criticised because it is said to be too individualistic. In fact, some Reformed and even Roman Catholic views of baptism are open to the same criticism. *Lumen Gentium*, the Second Vatican Council's Constitution on the Church, stated that the Roman Catholic Church recognized that it was 'joined to those who, though baptized and so honoured with the christian name, do not profess the faith in its entirety or do not preserve the unity of communion under the successor of Peter'.[65] At one level this stated nothing new, since the baptism of lay people and even of heretics had been recognized since Augustine's time. The basis for the recognition of Protestants did not lie in anything that they might be, but rather in the act of God. This is splendidly objective, though it does run the risk of being cold to the point of condescension. But the Decree on Ecumenism set its remarks on baptismal unity in the context of a reference to the 'large communities' of Christians separated from Rome, and there was a clear though cautious movement towards probing the ecclesial significance of these communities. The same point was raised by the significant use of the phrase *'subsistit in'* in the statement, also in *Lumen Gentium*, that the unique Church of Christ 'subsists in the catholic church, governed by the successor of Peter and the bishops in communion with him'.[66] The Decree on Ecumenism stated that baptism

> is oriented towards the complete profession of faith, complete incorporation into the institution of salvation such as Christ willed it to be, and finally towards the completeness of unity which eucharistic communion gives. Though the ecclesial communities which are separated from us lack that fullness of unity with us which flows from baptism, and though we believe they have not retained the authentic and full reality of the eucharistic mystery, especially because the sacrament of orders is lacking, nevertheless when they commemorate his death and resurrection in the Lord's supper, they profess that it signifies life in communion with Christ and look forward to his coming in glory.[67]

Baptism is thus a beginning in a slightly different sense from the way discussed in the previous paragraph, yet the point is linked because baptism leads to full incorporation into the Body of Christ which is his Church.

---

65 Constitution on the Church, §15, Tanner, *Decrees*, 860.

66 Ibid, §8, Tanner, *Decrees*, 854. This was a change made between the first and final drafts of the text from 'est'. See F.A. Sullivan, SJ, 'The Significance of the Vatican II Declaration That the Church of Christ "Subsists in" the Roman Catholic Church', in Latourelle, *Vatican II*, 272-87. The Congregation of the Doctrine of the Faith has recently claimed that there is no difference between the two words, which makes the arguments in the Council about which should be preferred seem rather strange.

67 Decree on Ecumenism, §22, Tanner, *Decrees*, 919-20.

Although the Ecumenical Directory asked that 'the whole question of the theology and practice of Baptism should be brought up in dialogue between the Catholic Church and other separated churches or communities',[68] this has not always been prominent. The Anglican–Roman Catholic International Commission, for example, did not consider this topic, and their *Final Report* contained only a single passing reference in the Preface when it was stated that 'in the New Testament it is clear that the community is established by a baptism inseparable from faith and conversion'.[69] But the purpose of this reference was to say something about the *koinonia* of the Church. The message of the English and Welsh Bishops after the Roman Catholic Church's Pastoral Congress at Liverpool in 1980, *The Easter People*, emphasised the way in which baptism was an impulse to Christian unity.[70] What still needs more attention is the balance between the 'church-forming' characteristics of baptism and the 'church-forming' characteristics of the ministry. If all the baptized are incorporated into the Body of Christ, then all must in some sense be part of the Church—one Church. Baptism can only be recognized without pressing the corresponding question of recognition of churchmanship, if it is understood in an individualistic way which would be unacceptable in most quarters today. So Jean Tillard, one of the leading Roman Catholic theologians in the ecumenical movement in the later twentieth century, wrote,

> The mutual recognition of baptism constitutes an ecumenical decision whose ecclesiological bearing has been underestimated. It means that where there is *true* baptism there is *truly* incorporation into Christ, and also entry into the Church of God. It follows from this that in every baptized person and in the entire Christian community as it celebrates baptism the Spirit of the Lord is at work.... Since the Schisms of the sixteenth century the ecclesial communities, still indwelled by the Spirit, evolved parallel and unconnected. They slowly took on distinctive features which gave them their own physiognomy. Stable and consistent traditions came to birth, the Lutheran, Anglican, Calvinist, Methodist etc. Now it would be to cast doubt on the presence of the Spirit in those communities which make baptism their central reality to deny the enrichment which many of their emphases bestow on the ecclesial life of the West, though there are often corresponding imbalances in them. They remain a challenge for the Roman Catholic Church.[71]

---

68 Quoted in Ehrenstrom, *Mutual Recognition*, 8.

69 Anglican–Roman Catholic International Commission, *The Final Report* (London 1982), 8. Nor has it been a topic for discussion in the second round of the Commission's discussions.

70 *The Easter People* (London 1980), §§195-200, 67-68.

71 J.M.R. Tillard, 'The Roman Catholic Church and Bilateral Dialogues', *One in Christ*, xix 4 (1983), 368-9 (italics original).

Such a statement emphasises how far things have changed since the tracts of Richard Mant.

Despite some of the difficulties discussed in this chapter, therefore, it seems as though the Churches are being brought into a new sense of their relationship to one another through a rediscovery of the significance of baptism. The questions which provide the agenda for further theological reflection could perhaps be summarised as follows: not whether there should be a dual practice of infant and believer's baptism in the Church, but how two convictions may be held together; not whether believer's baptism is right, but whether parents may rightly delay baptism for their children and what understanding of the relation between children and the Church this implies; not whether infant baptism is justifiable, but whether it properly preserves the emphasis on personal faith necessary to the theological truth that God deals with us as persons; and not whether baptism unites us in one Church, the Body of Christ, but what kind of Church it unites us in. But it is also impossible to escape from two other questions: how far does this theological agenda reflect the concerns of those who continue to seek baptism for themselves and their children at the beginning of the twenty-first century? and how can the Churches respond faithfully to them, as well as to their theologians? The inadequacies of the secularization thesis are increasingly recognized by sociologists and historians, but how does the kind of religious belonging represented by much popular religion especially, but not only, in baptism relate to the Church's teaching and expectations? As yet, there is little sign that these issues are being seriously addressed by theologians. Yet systematic theology cannot escape from history.

This book began with a discussion of the consequences of the Restoration Settlement and the Evangelical Revival, one of which was that the old normative patterns of baptism were broken. In the early nineteenth century Robert Hall's strong insistence that division was *within* the Church provided a ray of hope. His solution, which verged on making baptism a matter of private conviction, was not satisfactory, but his instinct was right: a way through which respected different convictions had to be found. In the twentieth century the Church's evangelical task became greater, as did its concern for unity. It is important that baptism should not become any more divisive than it has been: the many and varied insights into its meaning should be drawn together, so that, through a deeper understanding, the unity of the Church may be built up. Luther derived great comfort in moments of deepest doubt from being able to say, 'I am baptized': Christians in Britain and elsewhere today need to be able to draw similar strength from being able to say, '*We* are baptized'.

Bibliography of Works Referred to in the Text

(This list is simply in alphabetical order of author, or title where a specific author is not named, since there is no easy way of categorising the sources used.)

S.O. Addy, *Folk Tales and Superstitions* (ed J.D.A. Widdowson, Wakefield 1973)
W.L. Alexander, *Memoirs of the Life and Writings of Ralph Wardlaw, D.D.* (Edinburgh 1856)
M. Anderson, *Family Structure in Nineteenth Century Lancashire* (Cambridge 1971)
O. Anderson, 'The Incidence of Civil Marriage in Victorian England and Wales', *Past and Present* 69 (1975)
—, 'Rejoinder', *Past and Present* 84 (1979)
Anglican-Methodist Unity, Part 2, The Scheme (London 1968)
Anglican-Roman Catholic International Commission, *The Final Report* (London 1982)
C. Annesley and P. Hoskin, *Archbishop Drummond's Visitation Returns 1764* i-iii (Borthwick Texts and Calendars: York 1997, 1998, 2001)
H.B.J. Armstrong, *A Norfolk Diary* (London 1949)
—, (ed), *Armstrong's Norfolk Diary* (London 1963)
M. Ashby, *Joseph Ashby of Tysoe* (Cambridge 1961)
J.C. Atkinson, *Forty Years in a Moorland Parish* (3 ed, London 1907)
Augustine, *On Baptism, against the Donatists*, P. Schaff (ed), *Select Library of the Nicene and Post-Nicene Fathers*, iv (1887; reprinted Grand Rapids 1979)
—, *Tractate 80 on the Gospel of St John*, P. Schaff (ed), *Select Library of the Nicene and Post-Nicene Fathers*, vii (1888, reprinted Grand Rapids 1983)
J. Ayres (ed), *Paupers and Pig Killers: The Diary of William Holland, a Somerset Parson, 1799-1818* (Harmondsworth 1986)
D.M. Baillie, *The Theology of the Sacraments and other papers* (London 1957)
J. Baillie, *What is Christian Civilization?* (2 ed, London 1947)
Baptism, Eucharist and Ministry (Geneva 1982)
Baptism, Thanksgiving and Blessing (London 1971)
A. Barrett, *Catholic and Evangelical Principles viewed in their present application to the Church of God in a series of letters to a friend* (London 1843)
K. Barth, *The Teaching of the Church regarding Baptism* (London 1948)
—, *Church Dogmatics, iv, The Doctrine of Reconciliation, Part 4* (Edinburgh 1969)
M. Barth, *Die Taufe—ein Sakrament?* (Zürich 1951)
J.H. Barton and W.F. Swift 'The Sunday Service of the Methodists', *Proceedings of the Wesley Historical Society*, xxxii, 5 (March 1960)
H.N. Bate (ed), *Faith and Order: Proceedings of the World Conference, Lausanne, August 3-21, 1927* (New York 1928)
G.R. Beasley-Murray, *Baptism in the New Testament* (London 1962)

—, 'Baptists and the Baptism of Other Churches', in J. Nordenhaug (ed), *The Truth That Makes Men Free: Official Report of the Eleventh Congress, Baptist World Alliance* (Nashville 1966)
—, 'The Problem of Infant Baptism: An Exercise in Possibilities', *Festschrift Günther Wagner*, ed. Faculty of Baptist Theological Seminary, Rüschlikon (Berne 1994)
D.W. Bebbington (ed), *The Baptists in Scotland* (Glasgow 1988)
—, *William Ewart Gladstone: Faith and Politics in Victorian Britain* (Grand Rapids 1993)
G.K.A. Bell (ed), *Documents on Christian Unity, 1920-24* (London 1924)
—, (ed), *Documents on Christian Unity, Second Series* (London 1930)
—, (ed), *Documents on Christian Unity, Third Series, 1930-1948* (London 1948)
P. Bell (ed), *Episcopal Visitations in Bedfordshire, 1706-1720* (Bedfordshire Historical Record Society, vol 81, 2002)
E. Berens, *A Memoir of the Life of Bishop Mant* (London 1849)
J. Beresford (ed), *Woodforde: Passages from the Five Volumes of the Diary of a Country Parson 1758-18* (London 1935)
C. Bethell, *A General View of the Doctrine of Regeneration in Baptism* (4 ed, London 1845)
T. Biddulph, *Baptism: a seal of the Christian Covenant* (London 1816)
R. Blakeborough, *Wit, Character, Folklore and Customs of the North Riding of Yorkshire* (reprinted Wakefield 1973)
J.H. Blunt, *Directorium Pastorale* (new ed, London 1875)
J. Bossy, 'Blood and Baptism: Kinship, Community and Christianity in Western Europe from the Fourteenth to the Seventeenth Centuries', D. Baker (ed), *Sanctity and Secularity; Studies in Church History* x (Oxford 1973)
—, 'Godparenthood: the Fortunes of a Social Institution in Early Modern Christianity', K. von Greyerz (ed), *Religion and Society in Early Modern Europe, 1500-1800* (London 1984)
K.M. Boyd, *Scottish Church Attitudes to Sex, Marriage and the Family, 1850-1914* (Edinburgh 1980)
G.R. Bray, *The Anglican Canons 1529-1947* (Church of England Record Society: Woodbridge 1998)
J.H.Y. Briggs, *The English Baptists of the Nineteenth Century* (Baptist Historical Society: Didcot 1994)
British Critic
British Magazine
W. Brockie, *Legends and Superstitions of the County of Durham* (ed R. Wood, Wakefield 1974)
G.W. Bromiley, *Baptism and the Anglican Reformers* (London 1953)
P. Brooke, 'Controversies in Ulster Presbyterianism, 1790-1836', unpublished Cambridge Ph.D. thesis 1980
S.A. Brooke, *Life and Letters of Frederick W. Robertson* (new ed, London 1883)

O. Brose, *Frederick Denison Maurice: Rebellious Conformist, 1805-1872* (Athens, OH, 1971)
E. Brunner, *The Divine-Human Encounter* (London 1944)
C. Burrage, *The Church Covenant Idea* (Philadelphia 1904)
—, *The Early English Dissenters in the light of recent research (1550-1641)* (Cambridge 1912)
J. Calvin, *Commentary on the Epistle to the Ephesians* (ed D.W. Torrance and T.F. Torrance, Edinburgh 1965)
A. Carson, *Baptism in its Mode and Subjects considered* (Edinburgh 1831)
—, *Reasons for Separating from the General Synod of Ulster* in *Works*, iv (Dublin 1856)
S.W. Carruthers, *Fifty Years 1876-1926: A brief survey of work and progress since the union* (London 1926)
W. Carus, *Memoirs of the Life of the Rev. Charles Simeon, M.A.* (London 1847)
W.O. Chadwick, *The Mind of the Oxford Movement* (London 1960)
L. Châtellier, *The Religion of the Poor* (ET Cambridge 1997)
Christian Initiation (London 1971)
Christian Initiation and Church Membership (London 1988)
Christian Observer
Christian Remembrancer
Church of Scotland: Interim Report of the Special Commission on Baptism, May 1955 (Edinburgh 1955)
Church Quarterly Review
R.W. Church, *The Oxford Movement: Twelve Years, 1833-1845* (3 ed, London 1892)
D. Clark, *Between Pulpit and Pew* (Cambridge 1982)
H. Cnattingius, *Bishops and Societies* (London 1952)
J.T. Coleridge, *Memoir of the Revd John Keble* (3 ed, London 1870)
Conference of the Bishops of the Anglican Communion, 1920 (London 1920)
Conversations between the Church of England and the Methodist Church (London 1963)
F.A. Cox, *On Baptism* (London 1824)
J. Cox, *The English Churches in a Secular Society* (New York 1982)
D. Cressy, *Birth, Marriage and Death: Ritual, Religion, and the Life-Cycle in Tudor and Stuart England* (Oxford 1997)
A.R. Cross, *Baptism and the Baptists: Theology and Practice in Twentieth-Century Britain* (Carlisle 2000)
N. Curnock, *The Journal of John Wesley* (London 1909-16)
R. Currie, A. Gilbert and L. Horsley, *Churches and Churchgoers* (Oxford 1977)
A.W.W. Dale, *Life of R.W. Dale* (London 1905)
R.W. Dale, *A Manual of Congregational Principles* (London 1884)
—, *History of English Congregationalism* (London 1907)
E. Davies and A.D. Rees (eds), *Welsh Rural Communities* (Cardiff 1960)
E.T. Davies, *Religion in the Industrial Revolution in South Wales* (Cardiff 1965)

G.C.B. Davies, *Henry Phillpotts, Bishop of Exeter, 1778-1869* (London 1954)
H. Davies, *The Worship of the American Puritans, 1629-1730* (New York 1990)
—, *The Worship of the English Puritans* (London 1948)
—, *Worship and Theology in England: From Watts and Wesley to Maurice, 1690-1850* (Princeton, NJ, 1961)
R.E. Davies and D.L. Edwards (eds), *Unity begins at home* (London 1964)
R.E. Davies, 'Our Doctrines', R.E. Davies and G. Rupp (eds), *A History of the Methodist Church in Great Britain*, i (London 1965)
W. Merlin Davies, *An Introduction to F.D. Maurice's Theology* (London 1964)
F. Deconinck-Brossard, '"We live so far North": the Church in the North-East of England', J. Gregory and J.S. Chamberlain (eds), *The National Church in Local Perspective: The Church of England and the Regions, 1660-1800* (Woodbridge 2003)
C.S. Dessain (ed), *The Letters and Diaries of John Henry Newman, xvii, 1855-57* (London 1967)
G. Dix, *The Theology of Confirmation in Relation to Baptism* (London 1946)
The Works of the Rev. P. Doddridge, D.D., v (Leeds 1804)
G. Donaldson, *The Scottish Reformation* (Cambridge 1960)
Doctrine in the Church of England (London 1938)
A.L. Drummond and J. Bulloch, *The Scottish Church, 1688-1843* (Edinburgh 1973)
R. Dunkerley (ed), *The Ministry and the Sacraments* (London 1937)
A.I. Dunlop, 'Baptism in Scotland after the Reformation' in D. Shaw (ed), *Reformation and Revolution* (Edinburgh 1967)
G. Dyer, *History of the University and colleges of Cambridge* (London 1814)
The Easter People (London 1980)
Eclectic Review
J. Edwards, *Freedom of the Will* (ed P. Ramsay, New Haven, CT, 1957)
N. Ehrenstrom, *Mutual Recognition of Baptism in Interchurch Agreements* (Geneva 1978)
L. Ellsworth, 'Charles Lowder and the Ritualist Movement', unpublished Cambridge Ph.D. thesis 1974
T. Erskine, *The Brazen Serpent* (Edinburgh 1831)
—, *The Brazen Serpent* (3 ed, Edinburgh 1879)
W.J.C. Ervine, 'Doctrine and Diplomacy: Some Aspects of the Life and Thought of the Anglican Evangelical Clergy, 1797-1837', unpublished Cambridge Ph.D. thesis, 1979
H. Escott, *A History of Scottish Congregationalism* (Glasgow 1960)
G. Ewing, *An Essay on Baptism* (2 ed, Glasgow 1824)
Facts and Figures about the Church of England (London 1959)
Faith and Order, Louvain 1971 (Geneva 1971)
D. Fergusson (ed.), *Christ, Church and Society: Essays on John Baillie and Donald Baillie* (Edinburgh 1993)
K. Fincham, *Visitation Articles and Injunctions of the Early Stuart Church* i (Church of England Record Society, Woodbridge 1994)

—, *Visitation Articles and Injunctions of the Early Stuart Church* ii (Church of England Record Society, Woodbridge 1998)
J.D.C. Fisher, *Christian Initiation: Baptism in the Medieval West* (London 1965)
H. Fishwick (ed), *Extracts from the Church Book of Altham and Wymondhouses, AD 1649-1725* (Chetham Society vol 33, Manchester 1894)
W.F. Flemington, *The New Testament Doctrine of Baptism* (London 1948)
R. Floud and P. Thane, 'The Incidence of Civil Marriage in Victorian England and Wales', *Past and Present* 84 (1979)
M.R.D. Foot (ed), *The Gladstone Diaries, i, 1825-1832* (Oxford 1968)
C. Forster (ed), *Thirty Years Correspondence between John Jebb and Alexander Knox* (London 1834)
P.T. Forsyth, *The Work of Christ* (London 1959)
—, *Lectures on the Church and the Sacraments* (London 1917)
—, *Lectures on the Church and the Sacraments*, (ed J.K. Mozley, London 1947)
S.K. Fowler, *More Than a Symbol: The British Baptist Recovery of Baptismal Sacramentalism* (Carlisle 2002)
L.P. Fox, 'The Work of the Revd Thomas Tregenna Biddulph, with special reference to his influence on the evangelical movement in the West of England', unpublished Cambridge Ph.D. thesis 1953
B.J.N. Galliers, 'Baptism in the Writings of John Wesley', *Proceedings of the Wesley Historical Society*, xxxii, 6 (June 1960)
J.D. Gay, *The Geography of Religion in England* (London 1971)
Gentleman's Magazine
A.R. George, 'The Means of Grace', in R.E. Davies and G. Rupp (eds), *A History of the Methodist Church in Great Britain*, i (London 1965)
S. Gilley, *Newman and his Age* (London 1990)
A. Gilmore, 'Some Recent Trends in the Theology of Baptism', *Baptist Quarterly* xv, 7 (July 1954), xv, 8 (October 1954) and xvi, 1 (January 1955)
—, (ed), *Christian Baptism* (London 1959)
T.R. Glover, *The Conflict of Religions in the Early Roman Empire* (London 1909)
—, *Jesus in the Experience of Men* (London 1921)
C. Gore (ed), *Lux Mundi* (15 ed, London 1904)
G.C. Gorham, *Examination before Admission to a Benefice by the Bishop of Exeter* (London 1848)
Susanna's Apology against the Elders (1659), in E. Graham, H. Hinds, E. Hobby and H. Wilcox (eds), *Her Own Life* (London 1989)
J. Gregory, *Restoration, Reformation and Reform, 1660-1828: Archbishops of Canterbury and their Diocese* (Oxford 2000)
O. Gregory, *A brief Memoir of the Rev. Robert Hall, A.M.*, in *The Works of Robert Hall, A.M.*, vi (London 1833)
J. Habgood, *Church and Nation in a Secular Age* (London 1983)
A. Haldane, *The Lives of Robert Haldane and James Alexander Haldane* (5 ed, Edinburgh 1855)
P. Hall (ed), *Reliquiae Liturgicae*, iii (Bath 1847)

R. Halley, *The Sacraments: An Inquiry into the nature of the Symbolic Institutions of the Christian Religion usually called the Sacraments. Part 1, Baptism* (London 1844)

—, *A Short Biography of the Rev. Robert Halley, together with a Selection of his Sermons* (London 1879)

A. Tindal Hart, *The Man in the Pew* (London 1966)

R. Hayden, 'Still at the Crossroads: Revd J.H. Shakespeare and Ecumenism', K.W. Clements (ed), *Baptists in the Twentieth Century* (London 1983)

C. Haydon, 'The Church in the Kineton Deanery of the diocese of Worcester, c.1660-c.1800', J. Gregory and J.S. Chamberlain (eds), *The National Church in Local Perspective: The Church of England and the Regions, 1660-1800* (Woodbridge 2003)

W. Henderson, *Notes on the Folk Lore of the Northern Counties of England and the Borders* (reprinted Wakefield 1973)

L. Hodgson (ed), *Convictions* (London 1934)

—, (ed), *The Second World Conference on Faith and Order* (London 1938)

R. Hoggart, *The Uses of Literacy* (Harmondsworth 1958)

C. Hole, *A Manual of English Church History* (London 1910)

B.G. Holland, *Baptism in Early Methodism* (London 1970)

H.E. Hopkins, *Charles Simeon of Cambridge* (London 1977)

A.F. Hort, *Life and Letters of Fenton John Anthony Hort* (London 1896)

R.A. Houlbrooke, *Death, Religion and the Family in England, 1480-1750* (Oxford 1998)

—, *The English Family, 1450-1700* (London 1984)

—, (ed), *English Family Life, 1576-1716* (Oxford 1988)

F. von Hügel, *Essays and Addresses, First Series* (London 1921)

Instruction on Infant Baptism, in A. Flannery (ed), *Vatican Council II: More Post-Conciliar Documents* (Leominster 1982)

E. Isichei, *Victorian Quakers* (Oxford 1970)

W.M. Jacob, *Lay People and Religion in the Early Eighteenth Century* (Cambridge 1996)

P.J. Jagger, *Clouded Witness* (Allison Park, Pa 1982)

J. Jackson, *A Charge delivered to the clergy of the diocese of Lincoln at his primary visitation, 1855* (London 1855)

T. Jackson, 'A defence of Mr Wesley and of his doctrines', *Wesleyan Methodist Magazine*, xlvii (1824)

J. Jewel, *Treatise of the Sacraments*, J. Ayre (ed), *The Works of John Jewel, Bishop of Salisbury*, ii (Cambridge 1847)

J.M. Jones, 'The Church Covenant in Independency', *Transactions of the Congregational Historical Society*, xvi 2 (December 1949)

R.T. Jones, *Congregationalism in England, 1662-1962* (London 1962)

W. Jones (ed), *The Works of Mr Archibald M'Lean with a Memoir of his Life and Writings*, vi (London 1823)

I. Ker, *John Henry Newman: A Biography* (Oxford 1988)

I. Ker and T. Gornall, *The Letters and Diaries of John Henry Newman, i, 1801-26* (Oxford 1978), *iii, 1832-1833* (Oxford 1979), *iv, 1833-1834* (Oxford 1980)
J. Kinghorn, *Arguments against the practice of mixed Communion and in support of Communion on the plan of the Apostolic Church* (London 1827)
C. Kingsley, *Alton Locke* (with a prefatory memoir by T. Hughes, London 1887)
Charles Kingsley: His Letters and Memories of his Life, edited by his wife (London 1878)
F. Knight, *The Nineteenth-Century Church and English Society* (Cambridge 1995)
G.W.H. Lampe, *The Seal of the Spirit* (2 ed, London 1967)
R. Latourelle (ed), *Vatican II: Assessment and Perspectives*, ii (New York 1989)
Liberal Evangelicalism, by Members of the Church of England (London n.d.)
H.P. Liddon, *Life of Edward Bouverie Pusey* (ed J.O. Johnston and R.J. Wilson, London 1893-4)
Louisville: Consultation on Baptism (1980)
D.W. Lovegrove, *Established Church, Sectarian People: Itinerancy and the transformation of English Dissent, 1780-1830* (Cambridge 1988)
F.M. McClain, *Maurice: Man and Moralist* (London 1972)
T. Mackay (ed), *The Reminiscences of Albert Pell* (London 1908)
A. Mackennal, *Sketches in the Evolution of English Congregationalism* (London 1901)
J. McManners, *Church and Society in Eighteenth-Century France, ii, The Religion of the People and the Politics of Religion* (Oxford 1998)
B.L. Manning, *The People's Faith in the Time of Wyclif* (Cambridge 1919)
—, *The Protestant Dissenting Deputies* (ed O. Greenwood, Cambridge 1952)
R. Mant, *Two Dialogues on Baptism between a Minister of the Church of England and one of his Parishioners* (London 1810)
—, *An Appeal to the Gospel* (5 ed, Oxford 1813)
—, *Two Tracts intended to convey correct notions of Regeneration and Conversion according to the sense of Holy Scripture and of the Church of England* (London 1815)
W.M. Marshall, 'The Dioceses of Hereford and Oxford, 1660-1760', J. Gregory and J.S. Chamberlain (eds), *The National Church in Local Perspective: The Church of England and the Regions, 1660-1800* (Woodbridge 2003)
A.J. Mason, *The Faith of the Gospel* (London 1888)
—, *The Relation of Confirmation to Baptism* (2 ed, London 1893)
J.J. Matheson, *Memoir of Greville Ewing* (London 1843)
F. Maurice, *Life of Frederick Denison Maurice* (London 1884)
[F.D. Maurice] A Clergyman of the Church of England, *The Kingdom of Christ, or Hints on the Principles, Ordinances, and Constitution of the Catholic Church in letters to a Member of the Society of Friends* (London 1838)
F.D. Maurice, *The Prophets and Kings of the Old Testament* (Cambridge 1853)
—, *The Doctrine of Sacrifice* (London 1893)
—, *The Prayer Book and the Lord's Prayer* (London 1902)
—, *The Kingdom of Christ* (Everyman ed, London 1906)

J. Medway, *Memoirs of the Life and Writings of John Pye Smith* (London 1853)
B. Meeking, 'After Vatican II', *International Review of Mission*, lxxiii (1984)
Methodist Magazine
Grignion de Montfort, *Cantiques des Missions* (Poitiers 1759)
G.C. Moore, *Life of Dr Carson* (New York 1851)
R. Moore, *Pit-men, Preachers and Politics* (Cambridge 1974)
J. Morris, *F.D. Maurice and the Crisis of Christian Authority* (Oxford 2005)
A. Mozley, *Letters of the Rev. J.B. Mozley, D.D.* (London 1885)
—, *Letters and Correspondence of John Henry Newman* (London 1891)
J.B. Mozley, *The Primitive Doctrine of Baptismal Regeneration* (London 1856)
—, *Review of the Baptismal Controversy* (London 1862)
I. Murray (ed), *George Whitefield's Journals* (London 1960)
N.R. Needham, *Thomas Erskine of Linlathen: his Life and Theology, 1788-1837* (Edinburgh 1990)
F.W. Newman, *Phases of Faith* (6 ed, London 1860: reprinted, ed. U.C. Knoepflmacher, Leicester 1970)
J.H. Newman, *Lectures on Justification* (3 ed, London 1874)
—, *Parochial and Plain Sermons* (new ed, London 1881)
—, *Apologia pro Vita Sua* (London 1959)
J.C.S. Nias, *Gorham and the Bishop of Exeter* (London 1957)
P. Nockles, *The Oxford Movement in Context* (Cambridge 1994)
B.W. Noel, *Essay on the Union of Church and State* (2 ed, London 1849)
G.F. Nuttall, *Visible Saints: the Congregational Way, 1640-1660* (Oxford 1957)
J. Obelkevich, *Religion and Rural Society: South Lindsey 1825-1875* (Oxford 1976)
S.P. Ollard and P.C. Walker, *Archbishop Herring's Visitation Returns 1743*, i-v (Yorkshire Archaeological Society Record Series, lxxxi 1928, lxxii, 1929, lxxv, 1929, lxxvii, 1930, lxxix 1931)
Order of Administration of Baptism and other services for the use of the Primitive Methodists (London, n.d.)
A.C. Outler (ed), *The Works of John Wesley*, i (Nashville 1984); ii (Nashville 1985)
J.H. Overton, *The English Church in the Nineteenth Century* (London 1894)
Parliamentary Debates
E.A. Payne, *The Baptist Union: A Short History* (London 1959)
A. Peel, *These Hundred Years* (London 1931)
Peterborough Episcopal Visitation Returns, 1872 (Northamptonshire County Record Office)
Peterborough Episcopal Visitation Returns, 1882 (Northamptonshire County Record Office)
W. Plomer (ed), *Kilvert's Diary* (London 1939)
A. Pollard, *Let Wisdom Judge: University Addresses and Sermon Outlines by Charles Simeon* (London 1959)
E. Porter, *The Folklore of East Anglia* (London 1974)

F.J. Powicke, 'Frederick Denison Maurice (1805-1872): A Personal Reminiscence', *Congregational Quarterly*, viii (1930)
W.H.B. Proby, *Letters on Christian Religion* (London 1884)
—, *Annals of the 'Low-Church' Party in England* (London 1888)
E.B. Pusey, *Scriptural Views of Holy Baptism* (London 1836)
O.C. Quick, *The Christian Sacraments* (4 ed, London 1948)
H. Rack, *Reasonable Enthusiast* (London 1989)
A.M. Ramsey, *F.D. Maurice and the Conflicts of Modern Theology* (Cambridge 1951)
J. Randolph, *Charge delivered to the Clergy of the Diocese of Bangor at his Primary Visitation* (Bangor 1808)
A.D. Rees, *Life in a Welsh Countryside* (Cardiff 1950)
J.S. Reid, *A History of the Presbyterian Church in Ireland* (Belfast 1867)
Remains of Alexander Knox, Esq. (London 1834)
Report of the Committee on Public Worship, *Minutes of the Synod of the Presbyterian Church of England, together with reports and other papers* iv, 1886-88 (London 1888)
Report of the Inter-Church Enquiry into Baptismal Practice (London 1970)
Report of Select Committee of the House of Lords on the Deficiency of Means of Spiritual Instruction and Places of Divine Worship in the Metropolis, H.C. 387 (1858-59)
J.H. Rigg, *Modern Anglican Theology* (3 ed, London 1880)
—, *The Churchmanship of John Wesley* (London n.d. [1887])
—, *The Living Wesley* (2 ed, London 1891)
Rite of Christian Initiation of Adults (London 1976)
W. Robbins, *The Newman Brothers* (London 1966)
F.W. Robertson, *Sermons: Second Series* (new ed, London 1884)
D. Robinson (ed), *Visitations of the Archdeaconry of Stafford, 1829-1841* (London 1980)
H. Wheeler Robinson, 'The Place of Baptism in Baptist Churches To-day', *Baptist Quarterly*, i 5 (January 1923)
—, *Baptist Principles* (3 ed, London 1938)
—, 'Believers' Baptism and the Holy Spirit', *Baptist Quarterly*, ix, 7 (July 1939)
—, *The Life and Faith of the Baptists* (2 ed, London 1946)
W. Robinson, *Essays on Christian Unity* (London 1922)
H.H. Rowdon, 'Secession from the Established Church in the early nineteenth century', *Vox Evangelica*, iii (1964)
E. Royle, *Queen Street Chapel and Mission, Huddersfield* (Huddersfield Local History Society, Huddersfield 1994)
E.G. Rupp, *Religion in England, 1688-1791* (Oxford 1986)
J. Ryland, *A Candid Statement of the Reasons which induce the Baptists to differ in opinion and practice from their Christian brethren* (2 ed, London 1827)
M.J. Shaen, *Memorials of Two Sisters* (London 1908)

L.E. Schmidt, *Holy Fairs: Scotland and the Making of American Revivalism* (2 ed, Grand Rapids 2001)

R. Schofield, '"Monday's child is fair of face": favoured days for baptism, marriage and burial in pre-industrial England', *Continuity and Change*, xx (2005)

N. Scotland, *John Bird Sumner, Evangelical Archbishop* (Leominster 1995)

T.L. Sheridan, *Newman on Justification* (Staten Island, NY, 1967)

M. Smith, *Religion in Industrial Society: Oldham and Saddleworth, 1740-1865* (Oxford 1994)

C. Smyth, *Simeon and Church Order* (Cambridge 1940)

M.F. Snape, *The Church of England in Industrialising Society: The Lancashire Parish of Whalley in the Eighteenth Century* (Woodbridge 2003)

—, 'The Church in a Lancashire Parish: Whalley, 1689-1800', J. Gregory and J.S. Chamberlain (eds), *The National Church in Local Perspective: The Church of England and the Regions, 1660-1800* (Woodbridge 2003)

D.A. Spaeth, *The Church in an Age of Danger: Parsons and Parishioners 1660-1740* (Cambridge 2000)

—, 'The Failure of Reform in the Diocese of Salisbury', J. Gregory and J.S. Chamberlain (eds), *The National Church in Local Perspective: The Church of England and the Regions, 1660-1800* (Woodbridge 2003)

J. Spurr *The Restoration Church of England, 1646-1689* (New Haven, CT, 1991)

M. Stacey, *Tradition and Change* (Oxford 1960)

B. Stanley, *The History of the Baptist Missionary Society* (Edinburgh 1992)

Statements and Reports of the Methodist Church on Faith and Order, i, 1933-1983 (London 1984)

C. Stell, *An Inventory of Nonconformist Chapels and Meeting-Houses in Eastern England* (English Heritage: Swindon 2002)

W.R.W. Stephens, *Life and Letters of Walter Farquhar Hook* (7 ed, London 1885)

D. Stewart, *The Seceders in Ireland* (Belfast 1950)

F.G. Stokes (ed), *The Blecheley Diary of the Rev. William Cole* (London 1931)

W. Stone, *The Religion and Art of W. Hale White* (Stanford 1954)

M. Storey, *Two East Anglian Diaries, 1641-1729* (Suffolk Records Society vol xxxvi, Woodbridge 1994)

J. Stoughton, *History of Religion in England* (2 ed, London 1901)

C. Stovel, *The Baptismal Regeneration Controversy* (London 1843)

E.H. Sugden (ed), *Wesley's Standard Sermons* (London 1921)

[J.B. Sumner], *Apostolical Preaching considered in an Examination of St Paul's Epistles* (London 1815)

J.B. Sumner, *Apostolical Preaching considered in an Examination of St Paul's Epistles* (9 ed. London 1850)

D.E. Swift, *Joseph John Gurney* (Middletown, CT, 1962)

W.F. Swift, 'The Sunday Service of the Methodists', *Proceedings of the Wesley Historical Society*, xxix, 1 (March 1953)

N. Sykes, *Edmund Gibson, Bishop of London* (Oxford 1926)

N.P. Tanner, SJ (ed), *Decrees of the Ecumenical Councils* (London 1990)

J. Telford (ed), *The Letters of the Rev. John Wesley* (London 1931)
K. Thomas, *Religion and the Decline of Magic* (Harmondsworth 1973)
D.M. Thompson, *Denominationalism and Dissent, 1795-1835: a question of identity* (Dr Williams's Library: London 1985)
—, (ed), *Stating the Gospel: Formulations and Declarations of Faith from the Heritage of the United Reformed Church* (Edinburgh 1990)
M. Thurian (ed), *Churches respond to BEM*, i-iv (Geneva 1986-7)
J.M.R. Tillard, 'The Roman Catholic Church and Bilateral Dialogues', *One in Christ*, xix 4 (1983)
P. Toon, *Evangelical Theology, 1833-1856* (London 1979)
G. Tracey (ed), *The Letters and Diaries of John Henry Newman, vi, 1837-38* (Oxford 1984)
H. Tristram, *John Henry Newman: Autobiographical Writings* (New York 1957)
J. Tulloch, *Movements of Religious Thought in Britain during the Nineteenth Century* (London 1885: reprinted, ed. A.C. Cheyne, Leicester 1971)
J.M. Turner, *Conflict and Reconciliation* (London 1985)
L. Tyerman, *The Life and Times of the Rev. John Wesley* (London 1870)
—, *The Life of the Rev. George Whitefield* (London 1876)
A.C. Underwood, *A History of the English Baptists* (London 1947)
A.M. Urdank, *Religion and Society in a Cotswold Vale: Nailsworth, Gloucestershire 1760-1865* (Berkeley, CA, 1990)
A.R. Vidler, *F.D. Maurice and Company* (London 1966)
Visible Unity in Life and Mission (London 1977)
M.J. Walker, *Baptists at the Table* (Baptist Historical Society: Didcot 1992)
J.N. Wall, Jr (ed), *George Herbert, The Country Parson, The Temple* (London 1981)
W. Wall, *The History of Infant Baptism* (ed H. Cotton, Oxford 1836)
W.R. Ward (ed), *The Early Correspondence of Jabez Bunting, 1820-29* (London 1972)
—, (ed), *Early Victorian Methodism: the Correspondence of Jabez Bunting, 1830-1858* (Oxford 1976)
—, *Parson and Parish in Eighteenth-Century Hampshire* (Hampshire Record Series, vol 13, Winchester 1995)
—, (ed), *Parson and Parish in Eighteenth-Century Surrey* (Surrey Record Society, vol 34, Guildford 1994)
R. Wardlaw, *A Dissertation on the Scriptural Authority, Nature and Uses of Infant Baptism* (2 ed, Glasgow 1826)
D. Waterland, *Regeneration Stated and Explained according to Scripture and Antiquity* (1739), W. van Mildert (ed), *The Works of the Revd Daniel Waterland*, vi (Oxford 1823)
C.C.J. Webb, *Religious Thought in the Oxford Movement* (London 1928)
A.B. Webster, *Joshua Watson* (London 1954)
D. Webster, 'Simeon's Pastoral Theology', A. Pollard and M. Hennell (eds), *Charles Simeon* (London 1959)

J. Wedgwood, *John Wesley and the Evangelical Reaction of the Eighteenth Century* (London 1870)
E.C. Whitaker, *Documents of the Baptismal Liturgy* (London 1970)
B.R. White, *The English Baptists of the Seventeenth Century* (London 1983)
E. White, 'Broad Church Doctrine and Independency', *Congregational Union Jubilee Lectures* (London 1882)
W. Hale White, *The Early Life of Mark Rutherford* (London 1913)
G. Whitefield, *The Christian's Companion* (London 1739)
—, *Sermons on Important Subjects* (London 1832)
—, *Sermons on Various Subjects* (London 1739)
—, *Sermons on Various Subjects* (London 1739) [a different collection from the preceding one]
R. Whittingham (ed), *Works of the Rev John Berridge* (London 1838)
R. Wilberforce, *The Doctrine of Holy Baptism* (2 ed, London 1849)
S.C. Williams, *Religious Belief and Popular Culture in Southwark, c.1880-1939* (Oxford 1999)
—, 'Urban Popular Religion and the Rites of Passage', H. McLeod (ed), *European Religion in the Age of Great Cities* (London 1995)
W.M. Williams, *Gosforth: The Sociology of an English Village* (London 1956)
R.L. Winstanley (ed), *The Diary of James Woodforde*, vol x 1782-84 (The Parson Woodforde Society, 1998)
T. Witherow, *Historical and Literary Memorials of Presbyterianism in Ireland, Second Series (1731-1800)* (London 1880)
H.G. Wood, *Frederick Denison Maurice* (Cambridge 1950)
—, *Terrot Reaveley Glover* (Cambridge 1953)
www.cofe.anglican.org (Diocesan and Parochial Statistics, 2002)
D. Young, *F.D. Maurice and Unitarianism* (Oxford 1992)
M. Young and P. Willmott, *Family and Kinship in East London* (London 1957)
G. Yuille (ed), History of the Baptists in Scotland (Glasgow 1926)

General Index

Archer, Isaac 1, 7
Armstrong, H.B.J. 140, 152, 158
Atkinson, J.C. 138, 141, 153, 154

Baillie, Donald 137
Baillie, John 132-3
baptism,
    covenant of 5, 25, 57, 85
    fees for 11, 15, 16, 142,
    legal significance of 15,
    142, 144-5, 146, 148, 149,
    150
    private 1-2, 3, 4, 5, 16-17,
    18, 19
    use of the cross in 3, 4, 5,
    7, 8, 17, 18-19
Baptism, Eucharist and Ministry xii, 183, 184, 185
Baptist Union 60, 65, 127, 128, 167, 168, 171, 177, 179, 184
Baptists,
    General 47, 49-50
    Particular 47, 49, 50, 52
    Scotch 50, 51, 52, 53, 54
Barrett, A. 82-83, 84, 85
Barth, Karl 116, 130, 131-2, 133-4, 171, 185
Beasley-Murray, G.R. 172, 173, 177-8, 182, 183, 184
Bedfordshire 8, 9, 10-11, 15, 22
Berridge, John 22-3, 25, 26, 32-3
Bethell, Bishop Christopher 42, 67, 68, 70-2
Biddulph, T.T. 41, 80
Brethren 42, 73, 99, 175
British Council of Churches 174, 175
Brunner, E. 130-1, 132, 133, 172, 185
Budd, Henry 101, 102
Bunting, Jabez 81, 82, 85, 149, 150

Calvin, John xiii, 2, 45, 77, 78, 83, 85, 131
Calvinism 67, 70, 104-5, 109, 115
Calvinistic Methodists 72
Calvinists 44, 47, 50, 94
Carmichael, Robert 50
Carson, Alexander 54, 63-4, 65
Church of England 3, 6, 7, 8, 25, 26, 32, 35, 39, 43, 44, 59, 65, 66, 69, 70, 81, 82, 87, 94, 104, 115, 116, 119, 122, 124, 128, 135-6, 140, 142, 143, 144, 148, 149, 150, 159, 162, 163, 166, 170, 171, 175, 179, 181, 183, 185, 187
Church of Scotland 4, 23, 51, 59, 133, 135, 136, 159, 162, 182, 184
Churches of Christ 127, 168, 169, 175, 176, 177
Clark, Neville 172-3, 183
Communion xii, 1, 49, 115, 166, 169, 173
Congregationalists 5, 9, 10, 11, 25, 46, 47, 48, 49, 51, 54, 59, 65, 94, 109, 110, 113, 114, 115, 124, 129, 157, 159, 167, 168, 170, 176
Cox, F.A. 55-6, 57-8
Cubitt, George 82

Dale, R.W. xv, 59, 65, 111-2, 124, 126, 135
Doddridge, Philip 15, 19, 20, 39
Drummond, Archbishop Robert 8-9, 10, 13, 20

Erskine, Thomas 95-6, 103
Eucharist (see Communion)
Evangelical Revival xii, xiv, 11, 45, chapter 3 *passim*, 72
Ewing, Greville 51-2, 55-6, 59, 63, 65, 109

Fisher, Archbishop Geoffrey 170-1
Flemington, W.F. 134-5
fonts 3, 6, 8, 141, 144, 146
Forsyth, P.T. 116, 124-7, 135, 137, 168
France 12, 15, 24
Friends, Society of xiv, 5, 6, 8, 9, 10, 11, 13, 28, 33, 46, 97, 98-100, 101, 102, 128, 151, 159, 184
Fuller, Andrew 47, 52, 61

Gibson, Bishop Edmund 30
Gilmore, Alec 172, 173
Glas, John 50, 52
Glover, T.R. 128, 129
godparents 2, 3, 4, 7, 18, 20, 22, 141, 142-3, 144, 145, 154, 155, 160
Goode, William 84
Gore, Bishop Charles 93
Gorham, G.C. 85-87, 107
Gorham Judgement xii-xiii, 42, 68, 84, 88, 90, 104, 106, 115
Gosforth 147-8, 162
gossips (see godparents)
Gurney, J.J. 99, 100

Haldane, James 51, 52, 59, 60, 65, 73
Haldane, Robert 51, 52, 53, 59-60, 73
Hall, Robert 60-3, 64, 65, 188
Halley, Robert 109-10, 112
Halliday, W.F. 127
Hampshire 9, 10
Hapgood, Archbishop John 163
Herefordshire 17
Herring, Archbishop Thomas 8
Holland, H. Scott 93
Hort, F.J.A. xi, 93, 107, 112, 117
Huddersfield 10, 13, 14

Independents (see Congregationalists)
infant mortality 1, 2, 74-5, 79, 82, 84, 91, 148, 154

Jackson, Thomas 43-4
James, John Angell 58, 59

Kilvert, Francis 140-1, 147, 148, 153, 159
Kinghorn, Joseph 60, 62, 63, 65, 110
Kingsley, Charles 104, 105-6, 107
Knox, Alexander 67, 68-70, 71

Lampe, G.W.H. 118, 136, 179
Luther, Martin xiii, 131, 188

Mackennal, Alexander 108
M'Lean, Archibald 50, 52, 53
Mant, Bishop Richard 33-7, 40, 41, 42, 67, 68, 80, 188
Mason, A.J. 117-8, 119, 122, 124
Maurice, F.D. xv, 91, chapter 5 *passim*, 117
Methodist Church 169, 171, 184
Methodists,
    Primitive 161
    Wesleyan 9, 11, 34, 36, 42, 43, 49, 149, 157, 158, 159
midwives 2, 3, 4, 8, 152-3
Mozley, J.B. 68, 87, 89-91, 113
Mozley, J.K. 122, 125, 127

Newman, Francis 73-4
Newman, John Henry xiv, 40, chapter 4 *passim*, 144, 151, 152
Noel, B.W.H. 112
Northumberland 13, 14
Nottinghamshire 14, 15, 18

Oman, John 127, 137
Oxford Movement xiv, 65, chapter 4 *passim*, 92

Paget, Francis 116
parish registers 8, 15, 19
Phillpotts, Bishop Henry 85-6, 87, 115
Prayer Book 6, 15, 18, 35, 39, 66, 69, 70, 75, 81, 84, 87, 139, 143, 146, 153, 155
Presbyterians 4, 9, 10, 11, 25, 47, 48, 49, 54, 175, 176
Pusey, Edward Bouverie chapter 4 *passim*, 67, 92, 93, 97, 98, 103

General Index

Quakers (see Friends, Society of)
Quick, Oliver 120-3, 125, 168, 182

Ramsey, Archbishop Michael 93-4
Randolph, Bishop John 36
regeneration, baptismal xii, xiv, chapter 2 *passim*, 49, 50, 64, 65, 66, 67, 68, 69, 70, 72-80, 83, 84, 86, 87, 89, 90, 93, 101-2, 103, 109, 115, 125, 129, 139, 142, 150, 154, 169, 171
Rigg, J.H. 93
Robertson, F.W. 104-5, 111
Robinson, H. Wheeler 124, 128-30, 167
Robinson, William 127, 168, 169
Roman Catholics xi, 2, 23, 41, 82, 84, 87, 104, 105, 106, 118, 147, 165, 175, 178. 181, 182, 187
    Second Vatican Council 165, 166, 173-4, 180, 186

Scott, John 41, 45
Shakespeare, J.H. 127-8
Shropshire 7, 34, 35
Simeon, Charles 33, 37-8, 51
sponsors (see godparents)
Spurgeon, Charles 66
Staithes North Yorkshire 148, 158
Stephenson, J.H. 97
Stovel, Charles 65-6, 80, 129, 142
Southwark 160-2
Suffolk 1

Sumner, Archbishop J.B. 38-41, 72, 87, 185
Surrey 9, 10, 17, 18

Underwood, A.C. 168-9
United Reformed Church 174, 175, 176, 177, 178, 184, 185

Van Mildert, Bishop William 27, 30, 42-3, 44
visitations 3, 8, 9, 10-14, 15, 20, 139

Wake, Archbishop William 8, 10
Wall, William 6-7, 82, 90
Wardlaw, Ralph 51-3, 55, 57, 58, 59, 63, 65, 100, 109, 110
Waterland, Daniel 27, 29-30, 31, 35, 37, 42, 72
Watson, Richard 81
Wesley, John xi, xiv, 22, 26-9, 31, 32, 42, 43, 44, 45, 49, 81, 82, 84
West, Morris 177, 185
Westcott, Bishop B.F. 93, 115, 117
Whitefield, George 23, 30-1, 32, 36, 42, 43, 44
Wiltshire 7
Woodforde, James 16-17, 18

York, diocese of 8, 9-10, 13-14

Zwingli, U. 64, 77, 78, 117, 124

Studies in Christian History and Thought
(All titles uniform with this volume)
Dates in bold are of projected publication

David Bebbington
Holiness in Nineteenth-Century England
David Bebbington stresses the relationship of movements of spirituality to changes in their cultural setting, especially the legacies of the Enlightenment and Romanticism. He shows that these broad shifts in ideological mood had a profound effect on the ways in which piety was conceptualized and practised. Holiness was intimately bound up with the spirit of the age.
2000 / 0-85364-981-2 / viii + 98pp

J. William Black
Reformation Pastors
Richard Baxter and the Ideal of the Reformed Pastor
This work examines Richard Baxter's *Gildas Salvianus, The Reformed Pastor* (1656) and explores each aspect of his pastoral strategy in light of his own concern for 'reformation' and in the broader context of Edwardian, Elizabethan and early Stuart pastoral ideals and practice.
2003 / 1-84227-190-3 / xxii + 308pp

James Bruce
Prophecy, Miracles, Angels, *and* Heavenly Light?
The Eschatology, Pneumatology and Missiology of Adomnán's Life of Columba
This book surveys approaches to the marvellous in hagiography, providing the first critique of Plummer's hypothesis of Irish saga origin. It then analyses the uniquely systematized phenomena in the *Life of Columba* from Adomnán's seventh-century theological perspective, identifying the coming of the eschatological Kingdom as the key to understanding.
2004 / 1-84227-227-6 / xviii + 286pp

Colin J. Bulley
The Priesthood of Some Believers
Developments from the General to the Special Priesthood in the Christian Literature of the First Three Centuries
The first in-depth treatment of early Christian texts on the priesthood of all believers shows that the developing priesthood of the ordained related closely to the division between laity and clergy and had deleterious effects on the practice of the general priesthood.
2000 / 1-84227-034-6 / xii + 336pp

Anthony R. Cross (ed.)
Ecumenism and History
Studies in Honour of John H.Y. Briggs

This collection of essays examines the inter-relationships between the two fields in which Professor Briggs has contributed so much: history—particularly Baptist and Nonconformist—and the ecumenical movement. With contributions from colleagues and former research students from Britain, Europe and North America, *Ecumenism and History* provides wide-ranging studies in important aspects of Christian history, theology and ecumenical studies.

2002 / 1-84227-135-0 / xx + 362pp

Maggi Dawn
Confessions of an Inquiring Spirit
Form as Constitutive of Meaning in S.T. Coleridge's Theological Writing

This study of Coleridge's *Confessions* focuses on its confessional, epistolary and fragmentary form, suggesting that attention to these features significantly affects its interpretation. Bringing a close study of these three literary forms, the author suggests ways in which they nuance the text with particular understandings of the Trinity, and of a kenotic christology. Some parallels are drawn between Romantic and postmodern dilemmas concerning the authority of the biblical text.

2006 / 1-84227-255-1 / approx. 224 pp

Ruth Gouldbourne
The Flesh and the Feminine
Gender and Theology in the Writings of Caspar Schwenckfeld

Caspar Schwenckfeld and his movement exemplify one of the radical communities of the sixteenth century. Challenging theological and liturgical norms, they also found themselves challenging social and particularly gender assumptions. In this book, the issues of the relationship between radical theology and the understanding of gender are considered.

2005 / 1-84227-048-6 / approx. 304pp

Crawford Gribben
Puritan Millennialism
Literature and Theology, 1550–1682

Puritan Millennialism surveys the growth, impact and eventual decline of puritan millennialism throughout England, Scotland and Ireland, arguing that it was much more diverse than has frequently been suggested. This Paternoster edition is revised and extended from the original 2000 text.

2007 / 1-84227-372-8 / approx. 320pp

Galen K. Johnson
Prisoner of Conscience
John Bunyan on Self, Community and Christian Faith

This is an interdisciplinary study of John Bunyan's understanding of conscience across his autobiographical, theological and fictional writings, investigating whether conscience always deserves fidelity, and how Bunyan's view of conscience affects his relationship both to modern Western individualism and historic Christianity.

2003 / 1-84227-223-3 / xvi + 236pp

R.T. Kendall
Calvin and English Calvinism to 1649

The author's thesis is that those who formed the Westminster Confession of Faith, which is regarded as Calvinism, in fact departed from John Calvin on two points: (1) the extent of the atonement and (2) the ground of assurance of salvation.

1997 / 0-85364-827-1 / xii + 264pp

Timothy Larsen
Friends of Religious Equality
Nonconformist Politics in Mid-Victorian England

During the middle decades of the nineteenth century the English Nonconformist community developed a coherent political philosophy of its own, of which a central tenet was the principle of religious equality (in contrast to the stereotype of Evangelical Dissenters). The Dissenting community fought for the civil rights of Roman Catholics, non-Christians and even atheists on an issue of principle which had its flowering in the enthusiastic and undivided support which Nonconformity gave to the campaign for Jewish emancipation. This reissued study examines the political efforts and ideas of English Nonconformists during the period, covering the whole range of national issues raised, from state education to the Crimean War. It offers a case study of a theologically conservative group defending religious pluralism in the civic sphere, showing that the concept of religious equality was a grand vision at the centre of the political philosophy of the Dissenters.

2007 / 1-84227-402-3 / x + 360pp

Byung-Ho Moon
Christ the Mediator of the Law
Calvin's Christological Understanding of the Law as the Rule of Living and Life-Giving

This book explores the coherence between Christology and soteriology in Calvin's theology of the law, examining its intellectual origins and his position on the concept and extent of Christ's mediation of the law. A comparative study between Calvin and contemporary Reformers—Luther, Bucer, Melancthon and Bullinger—and his opponent Michael Servetus is made for the purpose of pointing out the unique feature of Calvin's Christological understanding of the law.

2005 / 1-84227-318-3 / approx. 370pp

John Eifion Morgan-Wynne
Holy Spirit and Religious Experience in Christian Writings, c.AD 90–200

This study examines how far Christians in the third to fifth generations (c.AD 90–200) attributed their sense of encounter with the divine presence, their sense of illumination in the truth or guidance in decision-making, and their sense of ethical empowerment to the activity of the Holy Spirit in their lives.

2005 / 1-84227-319-1 / approx. 350pp

James I. Packer
The Redemption and Restoration of Man in the Thought of Richard Baxter

James I. Packer provides a full and sympathetic exposition of Richard Baxter's doctrine of humanity, created and fallen; its redemption by Christ Jesus; and its restoration in the image of God through the obedience of faith by the power of the Holy Spirit.

2002 / 1-84227-147-4 / 432pp

Andrew Partington,
Church and State
The Contribution of the Church of England Bishops to the House of Lords during the Thatcher Years

In *Church and State*, Andrew Partington argues that the contribution of the Church of England bishops to the House of Lords during the Thatcher years was overwhelmingly critical of the government; failed to have a significant influence in the public realm; was inefficient, being undertaken by a minority of those eligible to sit on the Bench of Bishops; and was insufficiently moral and spiritual in its content to be distinctive. On the basis of this, and the likely reduction of the number of places available for Church of England bishops in a fully reformed Second Chamber, the author argues for an evolution in the Church of England's approach to the service of its bishops in the House of Lords. He proposes the Church of England works to overcome the genuine obstacles which hinder busy diocesan bishops from contributing to the debates of the House of Lords and to its life more informally.

2005 / 1-84227-334-5 / approx. 324pp

Michael Pasquarello III
God's Ploughman
Hugh Latimer: A 'Preaching Life' (1490–1555)

This construction of a 'preaching life' situates Hugh Latimer within the larger religious, political and intellectual world of late medieval England. Neither biography, intellectual history, nor analysis of discrete sermon texts, this book is a work of homiletic history which draws from the details of Latimer's milieu to construct an interpretive framework for the preaching performances that formed the core of his identity as a religious reformer. Its goal is to illumine the practical wisdom embodied in the content, form and style of Latimer's preaching, and to recapture a sense of its overarching purpose, movement, and transforming force during the reform of sixteenth-century England.

2006 / 1-84227-336-1 / approx. 250pp

Alan P.F. Sell
Enlightenment, Ecumenism, Evangel
Theological Themes and Thinkers 1550–2000

This book consists of papers in which such interlocking topics as the Enlightenment, the problem of authority, the development of doctrine, spirituality, ecumenism, theological method and the heart of the gospel are discussed. Issues of significance to the church at large are explored with special reference to writers from the Reformed and Dissenting traditions.

2005 / 1-84227-330-2 / xviii + 422pp

Alan P.F. Sell
Hinterland Theology
Some Reformed and Dissenting Adjustments

Many books have been written on theology's 'giants' and significant trends, but what of those lesser-known writers who adjusted to them? In this book some hinterland theologians of the British Reformed and Dissenting traditions, who followed in the wake of toleration, the Evangelical Revival, the rise of modern biblical criticism and Karl Barth, are allowed to have their say. They include Thomas Ridgley, Ralph Wardlaw, T.V. Tymms and N.H.G. Robinson.

2006 / 1-84227-331-0 / approx. 350pp

Alan P.F. Sell and Anthony R. Cross (eds)
Protestant Nonconformity in the Twentieth Century

In this collection of essays scholars representative of a number of Nonconformist traditions reflect thematically on Nonconformists' life and witness during the twentieth century. Among the subjects reviewed are biblical studies, theology, worship, evangelism and spirituality, and ecumenism. Over and above its immediate interest, this collection provides a marker to future scholars and others wishing to know how some of their forebears assessed Nonconformity's contribution to a variety of fields during the century leading up to Christianity's third millennium.

2003 / 1-84227-221-7 / x + 398pp

Mark Smith
Religion in Industrial Society
Oldham and Saddleworth 1740–1865

This book analyses the way British churches sought to meet the challenge of industrialization and urbanization during the period 1740–1865. Working from a case-study of Oldham and Saddleworth, Mark Smith challenges the received view that the Anglican Church in the eighteenth century was characterized by complacency and inertia, and reveals Anglicanism's vigorous and creative response to the new conditions. He reassesses the significance of the centrally directed church reforms of the mid-nineteenth century, and emphasizes the importance of local energy and enthusiasm. Charting the growth of denominational pluralism in Oldham and Saddleworth, Dr Smith compares the strengths and weaknesses of the various Anglican and Nonconformist approaches to promoting church growth. He also demonstrates the extent to which all the churches participated in a common culture shaped by the influence of evangelicalism, and shows that active co-operation between the churches rather than denominational conflict dominated. This revised and updated edition of Dr Smith's challenging and original study makes an important contribution both to the social history of religion and to urban studies.

2006 / 1-84227-335-3 / approx. 300pp

Martin Sutherland
Peace, Toleration and Decay
The Ecclesiology of Later Stuart Dissent
This fresh analysis brings to light the complexity and fragility of the later Stuart Nonconformist consensus. Recent findings on wider seventeenth-century thought are incorporated into a new picture of the dynamics of Dissent and the roots of evangelicalism.
2003 / 1-84227-152-0 / xxii + 216pp

G. Michael Thomas
The Extent of the Atonement
A Dilemma for Reformed Theology from Calvin to the Consensus
A study of the way Reformed theology addressed the question, 'Did Christ die for all, or for the elect only?', commencing with John Calvin, and including debates with Lutheranism, the Synod of Dort and the teaching of Moïse Amyraut.
1997 / 0-85364-828-X / x + 278pp

David M. Thompson
Baptism, Church and Society in Britain from the Evangelical Revival to *Baptism, Eucharist and Ministry*
The theology and practice of baptism have not received the attention they deserve. How important is faith? What does baptismal regeneration mean? Is baptism a bond of unity between Christians? This book discusses the theology of baptism and popular belief and practice in England and Wales from the Evangelical Revival to the publication of the World Council of Churches' consensus statement on *Baptism, Eucharist and Ministry* (1982).
2005 / 1-84227-393-0 / approx. 224pp

Mark D. Thompson
A Sure Ground on Which to Stand
The Relation of Authority and Interpretive Method of Luther's Approach to Scripture
The best interpreter of Luther is Luther himself. Unfortunately many modern studies have superimposed contemporary agendas upon this sixteenth-century Reformer's writings. This fresh study examines Luther's own words to find an explanation for his robust confidence in the Scriptures, a confidence that generated the famous 'stand' at Worms in 1521.
2004 / 1-84227-145-8 / xvi + 322pp

Carl R. Trueman and R.S. Clark (eds)
Protestant Scholasticism
Essays in Reassessment

Traditionally Protestant theology, between Luther's early reforming career and the dawn of the Enlightenment, has been seen in terms of decline and fall into the wastelands of rationalism and scholastic speculation. In this volume a number of scholars question such an interpretation. The editors argue that the development of post-Reformation Protestantism can only be understood when a proper historical model of doctrinal change is adopted. This historical concern underlies the subsequent studies of theologians such as Calvin, Beza, Olevian, Baxter, and the two Turrentini. The result is a significantly different reading of the development of Protestant Orthodoxy, one which both challenges the older scholarly interpretations and clichés about the relationship of Protestantism to, among other things, scholasticism and rationalism, and which demonstrates the fruitfulness of the new, historical approach.

1999 / 0-85364-853-0 / xx + 344pp

Shawn D. Wright
Our Sovereign Refuge
The Pastoral Theology of Theodore Beza

Our Sovereign Refuge is a study of the pastoral theology of the Protestant reformer who inherited the mantle of leadership in the Reformed church from John Calvin. Countering a common view of Beza as supremely a 'scholastic' theologian who deviated from Calvin's biblical focus, Wright uncovers a new portrait. He was not a cold and rigid academic theologian obsessed with probing the eternal decrees of God. Rather, by placing him in his pastoral context and by noting his concerns in his pastoral and biblical treatises, Wright shows that Beza was fundamentally a committed Christian who was troubled by the vicissitudes of life in the second half of the sixteenth century. He believed that the biblical truth of the supreme sovereignty of God alone could support Christians on their earthly pilgrimage to heaven. This pastoral and personal portrait forms the heart of Wright's argument.

2004 / 1-84227-252-7 / xviii + 308pp

Paternoster
9 Holdom Avenue,
Bletchley,
Milton Keynes MK1 1QR,
United Kingdom
Web: www.authenticmedia.co.uk/paternoster

www.ingramcontent.com/pod-product-compliance
Lightning Source LLC
Chambersburg PA
CBHW070313230426
43663CB00011B/2118